LIFELONG AND CONTINUING EDUCATION

Monitoring Change in Education
Series Editor: Cedric Cullingford

Also in the series:

Lifelong and Continuing Education

What is a Learning Society?

Edited by
PAUL OLIVER

Ashgate

ARENA

Aldershot • Burlington USA • Singapore • Sydney

Published by
Ashgate Publishing Ltd
Gower House
Croft Road
Aldershot
Hants GU11 3HR
England

Ashgate Publishing Company
131 Main Street
Burlington
Vermont 05401-5600
USA

Ashgate website: http://www.ashgate.com

Reprinted 2001

British Library Cataloguing in Publication Data
Lifelong and continuing education : what is a learning
society?. - (Monitoring change in education)
  1. Continuing education 2. Continuing education - Philosophy
  I. Oliver, Paul
  374

Library of Congress Catalog Card Number: 99-71887

ISBN 1 84014 905 1

Printed and bound in Great Britain by Biddles Limited,
Guildford and King's Lynn.

Contents

Notes on Contributors

Dr Paul Oliver is Deputy Dean of the School of Education and Professional Development at the University of Huddersfield.

Barbara Merrill is a senior researcher in the Department of Continuing Education, University of Warwick. Previously she worked in the field of secondary and community education. Her research interests include access issues, especially the access of non-traditional adult students to further and higher education and gender and lifelong learning. Her current research includes comparative European projects on access and APEL. She is coordinator of the ESREA Access Network.

Richard Edwards is Senior Lecturer in Education at the School of Education, Open University, UK. He contributes to distance education courses in post-school education and training. His research interests include: social theory and educational change; policy analysis; and guidance in learning. He has published extensively; his most recent book in *Changing Places? Flexibility, Lifelong Learning and a Learning Society* (1997, Routledge).

Dr Celia Deane-Drummond is currently Senior Lecturer in Theology at Chester College. She is Director of the MA in Adult Education with Theological Reflection. She was a visiting lecturer in theology for the Extra-Mural department of Manchester University before taking up her present post in 1994.

Robin Usher is Professor of Education and Director of Research and Consultancy in the Faculty of Education, Language and Community Services at RMIT University, Melbourne, Australia. He is co-author of *Postmodernism and Education* and *Adult Education and the Postmodern Challenge* (both published by Routledge). He has worked in the UK and Australia and has published extensively on education and contemporary culture, lifelong learning and performativity, the place of research in the 'postmodern' university, and developments in work-based learning.

Julia Preece is lecturer in Higher Education at the University of Surrey. She was formerly responsible for a community education research project at Lancaster University and has written extensively on issues concerning adult learners in community settings.

Katherine Hughes is a tutor at Ruskin College. She teaches in the area of Social Studies. She also runs the Ruskin Learning Project which consists of short-courses and activities for people with few qualifications.

Loraine Powell is a senior lecturer in the School of Education and Professional Development at the University of Huddersfield. As regional consultant for the Enterprise Awareness in Teacher Education Initiative, she focused particularly on staff development as a major change strategy. As a lecturer in education management her interests are in the continuing development of teachers, self assessment and the effectiveness of excellence approaches. Her doctoral research at the University of Lincolnshire is focused on adding value through the implementation of the Business Excellence model.

Anna Paczuska is the Access Links Coordinator at South Bank University. She has worked on a number of projects to develop the use of the assessment of prior experiential learning (APEL) for progression to higher education. She is currently researching how admissions tutors understand non-traditional qualifications in admissions to higher education.

Rosemary Moreland has been working in the field of adult education and community development since 1987. She has taught on a wide range of formal and non-formal adult education courses. She has carried out research into formal, non-formal and informal learning opportunities and in 1994 was awarded a Doctor of Philosophy in this field. More recently, she has carried out research into critical thinking skills and her special interests include lifelong learning and learning to learn.

Ian Martin is Senior Lecturer in the Department of Community Education University of Edinburgh. He has written extensively on adult and community-based education, and is co-editor with Jim Crowther and Mae Shaw of *Popular Education and Social Movements in Scotland Today* published by the National Institute of Adult Continuing Education in 1999 He is on the editorial board of the Scottish journal *Concept*, a founding member of the Popular Education Forum for Scotland and convenor of the Edinburgh Biennial Adult Education Conference.

Dr Gillian Trorey is Principal Lecturer in Post-Compulsory Education and Training in the School of Education and Professional Development at the University of Huddersfield. She has a particular interest in education for the land based sector and was the editor of 'Environmental Issues in Education', a previous volume in this series.

Cedric Cullingford is Professor of Education at the University of Huddersfield. Recent books include 'The Human Experience: the Early Years', 'Children's Literature and its Effects' and 'The Causes of Exclusion'.

Barrie Cooper is Regional Education Advisor for the Royal Society for the Protection of Birds, and a member of the Government of the Yorkshire and the Humber Education for Sustainable Development Forum. He was co-author of the book 'Ecosystems and Human Activity'.

Jill Mannion Brunt is Director of Teaching in ScHARR at the University of Sheffield. Previously Assistant Principal at the Northern College of Adult Residential Education. Worked for three years setting up Employee Development Schemes in the North of England. Have held several Dept of Employment/DfEE contracts for workplace learning, including setting up adult education guidance projects in District General Hospitals.

Mary Morrison is Senior Lecturer in the School of Education and Professional Development, at the University of Huddersfield.

Preface

Education is becoming more and more central to the purposes of nation: and yet there continues to be a multiplicity of views about the principl purposes of education. Nowhere is this more evident than in discussions (Lifelong Learning where the polarity between education for person: fulfilment and education to contribute to the state, is brought into shar focus. The chapters in this volume help to illuminate this debate, in som cases by exploring the concept of Lifelong Learning and in others b illustrating its application to specific situations. The first chapter examine some features of the concept, and the second by Barbara Merrill discusse aspects of lifelong learning within the European-wide contex Richard Edwards analyses some of the theoretical features of lifelon learning within current policy, while Celia Deane-Drummond explores th application of lifelong learning to the situation of an adult educatic postgraduate programme. Robin Usher analyses the evolving notions (adult education, and Julia Preece's chapter discusses connections betwee community education and higher education. Katherine Hughes provides a empirical study of the issues surrounding mental health in adult educatio and Loraine Powell's chapter examines the issues of self-development ar professional development within teaching. Anna Paczuska discusses way of recognising the learning of mature students within a lifelong learnir context, and Rosemary Moreland writes about the role of voluntary ar community organisations within lifelong learning. Ian Martin examine some of the social issues raised by lifelong learning, while Gillian Trore Cedric Cullingford and Barrie Cooper make links between environment education and lifelong learning. Jill Mannion Brunt explores th relationship between employers and the issue of lifelong learning, whi finally Cedric Cullingford and Mary Morrison discuss parentir programmes and lifelong learning. It is hoped that this wide range (papers on the subject of lifelong learning will further current debate on th topical issue.

Acknowledgements

A great deal of valued help has been received from the Series Editorial Board and from Professor Cedric Cullingford. In addition, this volume could not have come to fruition without the help and expertise of Susan Smith and Susan Ellis of the Academic Typing Services unit, at the University of Huddersfield.

1 The Concept of Lifelong Learning

PAUL OLIVER

Abstract

Lifelong learning is a concept which is found increasingly in current debate on education, particularly within the framework of discussion on widening participation and adapting to changes in patterns of employment. In the very wide use of the term, and also in its sometimes rather uncritical use, lie certain dangers. Its impact can be very much reduced, and there is a real risk that it will lose any sense of significance. The remedy is to explore the concept carefully and thence to be judicious in its employment, while at the same time seeking to specify carefully the conceptual boundaries of its use.

Introduction

Educational concepts which are in widespread use during any particular period are often of interest from a philosophical point of view because they can tend to be used rather uncritically, and without the precision of thought which may accompany the use of a more uncommon word. Such concepts are perhaps used in official publications, journal articles and the educational press, and are then replicated in a variety of internal documents in schools, colleges and universities. 'Lifelong learning' is perhaps a concept of this type at the moment.

When a notion such as lifelong learning is at the same time a term of significant approbation and commendation, then there is *a fortiori*, a justification for being cautious. If for example, one happened to read in the educational press that a college had developed a new range of courses with the specific intention of eschewing the possibility of lifelong learning, then one would scarcely believe ones eyes. Mission statements, post specifications and institutional aims seem increasingly to include the term lifelong learning. Yet this very frequency of use, combined with the sense that it must somehow be a good thing, tends to engender a feeling that one

1

does not really need to ask questions about the concept. It is as if, by ta
consent, the term has moved into a superior realm of concepts; a realm
which it would be at the very best bad taste, and at worst a sign of impli
ignorance, to challenge a concept.

The Concept

What tends to be happening when we apply an unconditional approval to
complex and often ill-defined concept such as lifelong learning, is that
may be thinking of a generic or perhaps very generally-contextualis
understanding of the idea. We perhaps loosely concede that the notion
people acquiring learning throughout their existence must *de facto* be
good thing. Within the parameters of such a relatively limited view, w
would argue? But learning of course, does not take place within
sociological or psychological vacuum where constraints such as lack
resources or lack of motivation fail to operate. There are for examp
innumerable economic constraints on the educational process. The wou
be lifelong learner may have to pay course fees, require access to
computer and printer, need to purchase books, and have the money to tra
to a place of study. We cannot reasonably discuss lifelong learning with
also considering aspects of the economics of access to knowledge.

Moreover, the aims and purposes of lifelong learning are certainly r
completely unproblematic. One person may argue that the princi
purpose is the general spiritual and intellectual uplifting of people in or
to become better and more-fulfilled citizens in a genuinely participati
democracy. Such lofty ideals may be countered by another who sugge
that lifelong learning has essentially utilitarian purposes in terms of helpi
to ensure a frequently retrained and re-educated workforce able to ad
easily to fresh economic imperatives and hence ensure the prosperity of
nation state.

No doubt others would suggest competing purposes. When we t
about the aims of lifelong education we must concede that there
competing imperatives, and that ones priorities may depend *inter alia*
whether one is providing an educational service or acting as a consum
The provision of lifelong learning is described by some writers as
apparently intrinsic good.

> The case for lifelong learning does not need to be strenuously argued to those who have a vision of a richer and more fulfilled future for individuals, for society and for humankind as a whole.   (Longworth and Davies, 1996: 8)

This is not a type of argument which seems particularly persuasive. Is there any reasonable individual who could fail to be in favour of a richer and more fulfilled future for the human race? Yet once we accede to this principle it is as if we are advised that we should uncritically accept the principle of lifelong learning. Rationality beckons however, and before we are too swayed by the rhetoric, a number of questions come to mind. It is not that one is suspicious that lifelong learning may not be a good thing after all, but rather that one simply wants to know with what one is getting involved. What will I learn in lifelong learning? Will it be substantially different to what I might have learned before I heard of the term? Who will transmit knowledge or skills to me? Perhaps I will be expected to teach myself? Will lifelong learning be free of any ideology, and hence will I be able (or indeed encouraged) to challenge both the content and means of transmission? Will lifelong learning be free to all those who wish to participate? May I have as many educational resources as I wish, or will they in fact be rationed? Is lifelong learning international, or just something for this country? If I live in Sub-Saharan Africa may I have as much life-long learning as if I happen to live say in Denmark? Who benefits from lifelong learning other than myself? Will my lifelong learning help me get a better job? If yes, and everyone else is doing this lifelong learning, will there be enough nice jobs to go round?

Naive questions some may say; but naive questions are often the simplest, most direct and indeed most difficult to answer. And of course I nearly forget, to whom should I go to receive an answer to the above questions? The essential difficulty is that if everyone treats lifelong learning as if it is a self-verifying good, then nobody will ask these kind of questions, and hence there will be no answers.

However, it is pleasing to note that for some, lifelong learning is a problematic concept.

> There is the struggle to give meaning to lifelong education as there have always been struggles in schooling: schooling or lifelong education for discovering creativity and developing the individual; schooling or lifelong education for domestication and manipulation?   (Gelpi, 1985: 8)

When governments put large amounts of money into lifelong learning it is not a subversive question to ask 'Why?' If a government invests rather more than might reasonably be expected in lifelong learning, it may be for the enhanced creativity of the individual citizen, or it may be to serve the interests of the state; or of course, it may be for a combination of both types of benefit.

If we are to take the concept of lifelong learning literally, and presumably we must, then it signifies not merely another, (perhaps rather trendier) version of adult education, but something rather different. It certainly occupies a longer timespan: from the cradle to the grave. Once this is acknowledged, then we can see that lifelong learning embraces the formal, compulsory state education system of children and young people, as well as the education of adults. It must include the entire range of educational opportunities regarded as an integrated whole. The term is not therefore prescriptive in the sense of specifying a range of administrative structures within which education can operate, but rather it appears to advocate a state of mind, a psychological approach to the process of learning. The 'lifelong' part of the term suggests a breaking down of the barriers between the different stages of education, resulting in a unified view of the learning process. It follows from this that there is an apparent advocacy of the individual stages of education interacting to support each other, so that the process of learning for older people creates a society in which the compulsory stage of education for younger people can flourish.

Hence it is difficult to separate the term from a view of society as a whole. Lifelong learning suggests something of the nature of the society in which it occurs. It would be difficult to envisage lifelong learning taking place on any large scale in a society which was antithetical to the educational endeavour. There is an assumption in the term that it exists within a society which is largely supportive of education and within which individual members of that society have a respect for the overall process of education. Lengrand (1975: 21) has encapsulated this concept of the 'lifelong' nature of learning and the way in which it suggests an integration of education at different stages of life:

> It will be seen that the concept of lifelong education is circular: there can only be lifelong education worthy of the name if people receive in childhood a fair and rational education, based on life's needs and enlightened by the findings and data of sociology, psychology and physical and mental hygiene; but an

education of this kind cannot be achieved unless adult education itself is firmly established in peoples' minds and way of life and unless it has a solid institutional basis.

Another important feature of lifelong learning is that it is not merely for a few individuals in society, but for all. The response to the Dearing Report into Higher Education (DfEE, 1998: 3) emphasises this:

> The Government sees higher education playing a key role in lifelong learning and wants to see it making an even bigger contribution in future by:
>
> increasing and widening participation, particularly from groups who are under-represented in higher education, including people with disabilities and young people from semi-skilled or unskilled family backgrounds and from disadvantaged localities.

However, the proclamation that lifelong learning encapsulates a notion of wider participation does not of itself result in wider participation. We must ask ourselves about the reasons for some groups being under-represented in education, and examine strategies to remedy the situation. It is unlikely however, that merely exhortations to participate on the one hand, or on the other, financial incentives to institutions which recruit a wider range of students, will of themselves radically change the situation. Education must often be pursued for its own sake, rather than for instrumental ends, otherwise disappointment and demotivation may result. While it may be argued that a greater interest in education may result in greater life chances, it is easy to understand that those with a computer linked to the Internet, with the money to buy books and travel to college or university, may be at a considerable advantage over those with more limited resources.

If lifelong learning is to be more than a utopian vision, then the question of motivation must be seriously addressed. People must have a reason to wish to engage with this philosophy or world-view. There are many other competing contemporary world views, some of which may be conceived as being rather more exciting than study. If lifelong learning is to be a success and to win ground in a world of competing ideologies, then it must be sufficiently attractive. As Hand et al. (1994: 2) argue:

For many people in the workforce, their current situation may not be totally desirable, but it is not so bad that they are motivated actively to seek ways out; and, even if they are so motivated, it does not inevitably follow that they will see learning as a relevant option, much less a preferred one. Together, these twin issues of inertia, and the saliency of learning define the scale of the task involved in creating an environment in which individuals are motivated to learn.

Lifelong learning will not occur entirely in standard educational institutions. If, as a concept, it carries implications of the involvement of the whole of society, then it is likely to incorporate all types of learning under a wide variety of different situations. It may involve work-based learning, distance learning, training, personal study, informal learning groups and formal institutionalised study. Linked with this is the notion that all human beings are both potentially interested in, but also capable of, extending their learning. Lifelong learning is thus intertwined with a vision of the potentiality of human beings. While a laudable vision, it should be tempered with the acknowledgement that potential must always require a practical realisation, and that is not unconnected with an economic context.

The consultation paper, The Learning Age (DfEE, 1998) contains a wide-ranging discussion of the United Kingdom government's vision of lifelong learning. One of many themes in this discussion is the argument that lifelong learning can help to build a united society.

> The development of a culture of learning will help to build a united society, assist in the creation of personal independence, and encourage our creativity and innovation. (p.10)

And again:

> Learning contributes to social cohesion and fosters a sense of belonging, responsibility and identity.

However, it is very difficult to appreciate an *a priori* argument for lifelong learning to lead to a united society or to social cohesion. The existence of the latter may depend on a variety of factors including a just and fair system of government, a relatively equal distribution of resources and life chances, and a successful economy. Indeed, relatively unsophisticated hunter-gatherer or agrarian societies may exhibit social cohesion without any of the advantages of the type of education or lifelong learning enunciated in the above document.

Indeed the spread of education throughout society can sometimes lead to dissatisfaction, and indeed rebellion against, the established order as individuals become better equipped to analyse and evaluate the structures within which they are asked to live. For similar reasons, learning does not necessarily engender 'a sense of belonging', but quite the contrary may result in individuals constructing a critique of those in society with power, status and influence.

Nothing in this brief analysis should be construed as suggesting that a society committed to lifelong learning is not a desirable end. It is not the broad purpose which is challenged, but rather the extent of the claims which are made for that end, and the lack of precision which sometimes accompanies the use of the concept. The chapters in this book provide a variety of contributions which help us to appreciate more precisely the current usage of this significant contemporary idea.

References

DfEE (1998) *Higher Education for the 21st Century. Responses to the Dearing Report*, London, DfEE.

DfEE (1998) *The Learning Age: a renaissance for a new Britain*, London, DfEE.

Gelpi, E. (1985) *Lifelong Education and International Relations*, London, Croom Helm.

Hand, A., Gambles, J. and Cooper, E. (1994) *Individual Commitment to Learning*, London, Employment Department.

Lengrand, P. (1975) *An Introduction to Lifelong Education*, London, Croom Helm and Paris, UNESCO.

Longworth, N. and Davies, W.K. (1996) *Lifelong Learning*, London, Kogan Page.

2 Degrees of Adult Participation: Lifelong Learning in European Universities

BARBARA MERRILL

Abstract

This chapter contextualises and examines the meaning of lifelong learning in European universities. European universities are undergoing changes but to what extent has this impacted upon issues of widening access to students, particularly adults who have traditionally been excluded from higher education? Different conceptual understandings and interpretations of lifelong learning are explored in relation to adult education. Lifelong learning in universities is discussed by using examples from three European countries.

Introduction

European universities are having to make changes in response to the demands of a post-industrial society. Elitism is giving way to en emerging mass-based higher education system (Trow, 1989). 'Higher education systems in all developed countries are being transformed by the same pressures and in similar ways' (Scott, 1995: ix). Economic, social and political changes have forced many universities to open up their doors and partially dissolve their ivory towers. Establishing partnerships at regional and national levels with industry and other organisations and agencies is symptomatic of such changes. This has initiated debate as to the purpose of the university. Implicit in this are questions about who universities are for and the nature of their role in relation to lifelong learning in a learning society. In the UK, expansion since the late 1980s has transformed the composition of undergraduate students, particularly in the 'new' universities. Universities, particularly 'new' universities, can no longer be seen as the education sector for 18-21 year olds particularly, as an increasing number of adults participate. The move towards and discussions about lifelong learning in universities is not confined to the UK: it is part of a European discourse.

Lifelong learning appeared on the European Commission's policy agenda in the early 1990s. In discussing higher education (The Memorandum on Higher Education in the European Community, 1991) the European Commission recognised that:

> an overall increase in demand for higher education would appear likely. This increase should reflect the circumstances of a new decade and show even more growth in the participation of males and females and a greater expansion in part-time and continuing education students.   (p. 7)

A growing interest in lifelong learning was highlighted in the European Commission's 1995 White Paper, 'Towards a Learning Society'. This was followed a year later with a more public promotion through designating 1996 as 'The European Year of Lifelong Learning'. In practice the event yielded an abundance of conferences and publications discussing the merits of lifelong learning. In policy terms at national and European levels the concept refers largely to adult education learning, policy and practice. Lifelong learning is, therefore, discussed in terms of the post compulsory sector rather than the education system as a whole.

This chapter examines the role of lifelong learning and adult education in relation to European universities, focusing particularly at the undergraduate level. My interests centre on access issues and the experiences of adults in higher education within a comparative European framework. This chapter draws on research work currently being undertaken with colleagues in other European countries. The present trend favours lifelong learning. To what extent is the rhetoric on lifelong learning being transformed into sustainable and worthwhile practice within higher education across Europe? Can similar patterns of responses in terms of policy and practice to lifelong learning be identified across the European Union? Are equality issues being addressed allowing all those who want to participate in education the opportunity to do so or do structures and policies ensure that those who have already benefited from education continue to do so? The idea of a learning society and lifelong learning has been around for a long time, initially promoted by the Organisation for Economic Co-operation and Development (OECD) and the United Nations Educational, Scientific and Cultural Organisation (UNESCO) during the early 1970s so this begs the question of why the renewed interest and emphasis during the 1990s?

Locating Lifelong Learning Discourse

Lifelong learning is generally perceived as a good thing by governments, policy-makers and educationalists. It is now embedded, uncritically, within political and academic discourses in Europe.

> In examining the nature of lifelong learning within Europe it is important to understand the ideological, political and cultural forces behind the current interest in and promotion of lifelong learning. (Merrill, 1997: 98)

Political support for lifelong learning by European governments and the European Commission rests on economic arguments: lifelong learning is essential if Europe is to survive economically within a globalised world. Social inclusion is perceived as necessary if social cohesion is to be achieved. Lifelong learning is, therefore, viewed as a means of social control to promote the integration of individuals into society. Knowledge, therefore, becomes an important commodity in an information society. The socially excluded are those who lack knowledge; they are the new underclass (Castells, 1996). In post-industrial society the front end model of education is insufficient. Initial schooling no longer equips people with all the educational knowledge and skills required throughout adult life:

> Central to a learning society is the proposition that the economic, social and cultural challenges confronting individuals and social formations in the late 20th century and into the 21st century make reliance on initial education as a preparation for the full extent of adult life unsustainable. The capacity to meet those challenges requires continuing learning and recurrent opportunities to learn. (Edwards, 1997: 174)

A study commissioned by the German Federal Ministry of Education, Science, Research and Technology to coincide with the EC's Year of

Lifelong Learning stresses that learning is essential to the survival of society:

> The international lifelong learning policies pursued by UNESCO, the European Commission, the Council of Europe, the OECD, the Club of Rome and a large number of national governments could provide the momentum necessary to mount a much-needed educational reform that would trigger a broader and more intensive development and mobilisation of human resources for dealing in an intelligent, creative way with the developing social crises that threaten our survival.   (Dohmen, 1996: 8)

Modernity has transformed the labour market and economy. Jobs are no longer for life. Instead employees can expect to have a series of jobs, possibly part-time or short-term contracts, which may be interspersed by periods of unemployment. Learning new or updating skills is necessary if workers are to be flexible and multiskilled. Within this discourse vocational education is given prominence. Such ideology can be clearly identified in various Government reports using the term 'lifetime learning' rather than lifelong learning. For example:

> Creating a culture of lifetime learning is crucial to sustaining and maintaining our international competitiveness ... The skill levels of the workforce are vital to our national competitiveness. Rapid technological and organisational change mean that, however good initial education is, it must be continuously reinforced by further learning throughout working life. This must happen if skills are to remain relevant, individuals employable, and firms able to adopt and compete.
> (Department of Education and Employment, 1995: 3, 4)

More recently the Government's Green Paper, 'The Learning Age' affirms the link between education and economic advancement: 'learning is essential to a strong economy and an inclusive society' (DfEE, 1998: 11).

On a wider European and global basis current UK policy interest echoes earlier political usage of the lifelong learning concept by OECD and UNESCO, *Learning to Be* (Faure et al., 1972), UNESCO's report stressed the importance of governments to provide lifelong learning opportunities as a human right while emphasising the economic benefits of such a policy. Concern with the social aspects of lifelong learning is also present in the

European Commission's (1995) White Paper, *Towards the learning Society*:

> There is a need to whet society's appetite for education and training throughout life ... Everyone must be able to seize their opportunities for improvement in society and for personal fulfilment, irrespective of their social origin and educational background.   (European Commission, 1995: 2, 3)

However, while appearing liberal the overriding purpose is economic. The policy serves the political and economic values and needs of a market economy:

> Policy makers such as the European Commission ... have spoken of a learning society as an ideal state, in which individuals and organisations acquire and apply new skills in order that they keep pace with the changing environment. Usually this view rests largely upon economic grounds, and the learning society is envisaged as a means of sustaining competivity in the future.
>   (Field, 1996: 2)

UK and European Commission's reports view the responsibility for learning within a learning society as resting firmly with the individual. The proposals for individual learning accounts and Education for Industry outlined in the Green Paper (1998) epitomise individualised approaches to learning. Advocating lifelong learning as being essential to Europe's economic competiveness and survival has, therefore, become a uniting rallying cry for a diverse range of organisations, agencies and groups:

> ... a consensual and dominant rhetoric has been propagated with evangelical fervour about the need for nothing short of a 'revolution' or 'quantum leap' to maintain competiveness and economic prosperity. This remarkable consensus is publicly celebrated by government and opposition spokesmen, leaders of business and of the trade unions, professional organisations, academic specialists and voluntary groups. Lifelong learning has been chosen by them, like some new wonder drug, as the solution to a wide range of economic, social and political problems ...   (Coffield, 1998: 10)

Concepts, Lifelong Learning and Adult Education

A multitude of organisations claim ownership, albeit from different perspectives, to the concepts lifelong learning and learning society. Defining lifelong learning, therefore, becomes problematic as 'the term is used in various ways by different writers' (Knapper and Cropley, 1985: 15). However, it is generally linked to earlier concepts such as recurrent education, continuing education and lifelong education. Discourse about lifelong learning is placed firmly within the domain of adult education. For Edwards:

> ... the emergence of an interest in and discourse of lifelong learning in the contemporary period both results in and reflects changes in the settings and practices in which adults learn and the forms of governmentality to which they are subject.   (Edwards, 1997: 187)

A paradigm locked into adult education ignores the role of initial education although the UNESCO report *Learning to Be* (Faure, 1972) advocated that, as a strategy, lifelong education should be used to reform the whole education system.

The following offers a flavour out of the many definitions on lifelong learning. Knapper and Cropley (1991) do not perceive it as anything new but simply the use of good existing educational practices:

> One way of looking at lifelong education is to regard it as a rationalisation of a number of existing trends in contemporary educational theory and practice. These emerged in a variety of settings without necessarily any reference to lifelong education. Prominent among the theoretical issues that have been stressed are democratisation of education, elimination of inequality in education and achievement of higher levels of self-actualisation ... lifelong education can also be thought of an encompassing a philosophy or model of education. In this sense, the term is used to refer to: a set of goals for education; a set of procedures for realising these goals; a set of values.
>   (Knapper and Cropley, 1991: 16, 17).

Longworth and Davies draw on the work of the European Lifelong Learning Initiative (ELLI):

Lifelong learning is the development of human potential through a continuously supportive process which stimulates and empowers individuals to acquire all the knowledge, values, skills and understanding they will require throughout their lifetimes and to apply them with confidence, creativity and enjoyment in all roles, circumstances, and environments.

(Longworth and Davies, 1996: 22)

Discussions on lifelong learning mostly refer to learning in formal contexts of further or higher education. Informal learning is ignored yet learning which takes place in the family, community and workplace is an important aspect of adult life. German adult educationalists (Alheit, 1996 and Dohmen, 1996) however, argue for the inclusion and recognition of a variety of learning situations:

Walter and Stauber (1998) take the idea further by linking lifelong learning - including informal learning - to a person's biography and subjectivity:

... the notion of lifelong learning points to the learning individuals in the shaping of their biography ... A main criterion for 'new learning' therefore is connectivity: how far do new knowledge and competencies fit into the previous learning biography ...? Subjective decisions therefore are in the centre of any strategies of lifelong learning ...   (Walther and Stauber, 1988: 13)

Past failure in the education system can be turned into a positive act:

'The pressure towards individual responsibility always contains the possibilities of individual shaping as well ... Lifelong learning thus includes the competence to redefine the personalisation of failure and transform it into positive learning motivation.   (Walther and Stauber, 1988: 13)

Walther and Stauber (1998), like Schuller (1996) critique the traditional notion of education whereby learning is divided into life stages:

Lifelong learning as a new educational concept accords to a new understanding of life courses that doesn't presume any longer a clear cut sequence of life phases but conceives transitions as accompanying and structuring elements of the whole life course ... on the terminological level lifelong learning implies the de-structurisation - or better: destandardisation - of life courses in which traditionally 'youth' represented the phase of learning.

(Walther and Stauber, 1998: 16)

The availability of lifelong learning is a prerequisite for a learning society. The two concepts are intertwined. Lifelong learning can only become a reality in a society whose educational values and structure facilitates people to return to learn throughout their lives and where to do this is regarded as the norm. It necessitates conceiving of education in a different way. Boundaries between initial and adult education have to be deconstructed. Through socialisation education becomes a 'normal' activity throughout one's life from the cradle to the grave:

> The learning society is, by definition, a society which takes learning seriously. Its members come to understand that learning is not fully accomplished by any age or biographical point but is a responsibility to be fulfilled more or less continually through the lifespan.   (Barnett, 1996: 14)

Changing attitudes to learning is not enough; organisational cultures and structures also need to transform if a learning society is to occur. Although primarily associated with business organisations the concept 'learning organisation' is increasingly being discussed in relation to educational institutions and higher education institutions in particular (Duke, 1992; Barnett, 1996). In industry the concept relates to the empowerment of the workforce. Understanding of learning organisations has, therefore, been more fully developed by organisational theorists such as Handy (1990). For Duke (1992), a key question is 'how far universities may, as key teaching and learning institutions, practically speaking adopt the new paradigm of lifelong learning?' (1992: xii).

Universities as Lifelong Learning Institutions

An examination of lifelong learning raises important questions about the nature of education in society. Antikainen et al., for example, situate a learning society within a political framework as a new programme of education reform following the 'new liberal or right project of the 1980s' (1996: 99).

If universities are to become learning organisations they need to adapt and change. Elitism needs to be replaced with a more community oriented mission. This is not an easy task as Knapper and Cropley point out:

Attempts to implement the principles of lifelong education in institutions of higher education are confronted by formidable difficulties. These include the fact that organisations are inherently passive, that they tend towards institutionalisation and ritualism, that the purposes and support of higher education are basically conservative, that socialisation of higher education staff is extensive and effective ...   (Knapper and Cropley, 1991: 93)

Duke is more optimistic that the ivory towers are being demolished, albeit because of external pressures rather than an internal desire to change:

Universities are thus beginning to learn that to survive they must function as much more open systems, with regular traffic permeating throughout all the porous membrane which has replaced the ivory walls.   (Duke, 1996: 76)

Adult and continuing education departments are central to influencing change towards lifelong learning in universities (Duke, 1992). However, in some European countries the starting point is more advanced. In Sweden and Denmark, for example, a shift in societal attitudes and culture has already taken place. High participation rates by adults in education ensures that it is viewed as normal for adults to study. Boundaries between initial and higher education are less distinctive than other European countries. Concepts such as non-traditional adult student and adult students become meaningless.

The following section draws on work on the access of adults to universities undertaken with European colleagues in Belgium, Germany, Sweden, Spain and the Republic of Ireland. The study is confined to undergraduate level. Looking at how accessible European universities are in relation to non-traditional adult students raises questions about the extent to which universities are learning organisations. How far are policies and practices differentiated across Europe? Space limits discussions to a brief outline of three European countries; Spain, Sweden and the UK.

Spain

Historical and cultural traditions in Spain have had an influence on the development of adult and lifelong learning. The current situation is a political product of both the Franco and post 1978 democratic era. A political interest in popular adult participation arose after the transition to democracy:

> ... different proposals were made on how to solve the problem of illiteracy, encourage practical adult education and link non-formal educational activity with the objectives of the social and cultural involvement of the people.
>
> (Lopez, 1992: 2)

The transformation to an information society has placed education as the key to economic and social integration into Spanish society. In the 1990s a new educational law was introduced, the Law for the General System of Education (LOGSE). It differs from previous laws by promoting diversity rather than equality. The Government of the education system is divided between the state, the Autonomous Communities and universities. Spain has a dual university system with two types of universities: private and public. The former have strong links with industry and are aimed at the privileged groups in society who possess cultural and economic capital. In contrast public universities are overpopulated and provide students with less opportunities of getting a job.

Like Belgium, access to universities for adults is limited although the number participating (12% for 1987-88, Osborne, 1995) is higher. Priority has been with improving basic adult education while the high rate of university expansion concentrated on school leavers. Entry to university is restricted to those who have the school leaving qualification (PAAU). Adults (classified as those aged 25 and over) who do not possess this have to take an entrance examination, set by each individual university. It includes general and subject specific questions. There is one set date per year for taking the examination. Although the entrance examination is attracting a larger number of people hoping for career enhancement the pass rate is low. As the examination is based on formal knowledge, life experiences as used with APEL are ignored. The current nature of the examination acts as a cultural barrier to many adults. The main preparatory course is provided through a distance learning university, Universidad Nacional de Educacion a Distancia (UNED), an essential institution in a rural country.

The provision of courses preparing adults for entry to university is not extensive. Official Adult Education Schools and Popular Schools, which are independent of the state, offer a wide range of courses including preparatory ones for university:

> In its formal adaptation, it usually embraces six steps: literacy, new readers, certificates, undergraduate, graduate and postgraduate ... Usually the adult education centres also have activities of socio-cultural awareness.
>
> (Flecha, 1992: 194)

The curriculum of the Popular Schools is similar but their historical origins are political: they developed in opposition to the educational structure of the dictatorship. In rural areas Peasant Schools, founded by the Church, play a similar role. 'They have developed very interesting projects combining cultural activities with economic and social participation development' (Flecha, 1992: 194, 195). A brief mention also needs to be made about Popular Universities. These institutions receive a grant from the municipal government and like other adult education centres are concerned with basic adult education and social and cultural emancipation.

In Spain adult education policies have concentrated on basic education rather than access to higher education. The LOGSE Act of 1990 has created a need for adult and lifelong learning. The act increased the school leaving age from 14 to 16 thus changing the level of the school certificate (certificado). A large number of adults and young people, therefore, no longer possess the relevant qualification for the job market.

Adults are becoming increasingly aware of the importance of lifelong learning in Spain in order to meet the needs of the information society. Four regions or autonomies have, since 1990, approved laws in adult education: Andalucia, Catalonia, Galicia and Valencia. One effect of the law in Catalonia is the promotion of community development:

> The main emphasis on adult education is moved from the school system to educational concerns in community development. Thus, this law is not a regulation of formal education, but a common orientation to different kinds of adult education.
>
> (Flecha, 1992: 197)

In Spain the adult education movement was strongly influenced initially by the theory and practice of Freire and, since the 1980s, Habermas and the theory of communicative action and transformative practices. The present aim is to extend the influence of these laws to widen access of adults to higher education.

Sweden

In the mid 1970s the Swedish Government in discussing the Higher Education Bill stressed the need for the education system to be based on a model of recurrent education. It encompassed an individualistic view of the learner. The 1977 reform aimed to make the education system more democratic and accessible to groups who were traditionally excluded in society from participation in higher education by widening access routes. As Agelii and Bron point out 'Sweden is a unique country in Europe because it was here where the doors of higher education institutions became open' (1997: 11). European adult educationalists revere Sweden as a model country in terms of adult learning. Education and learning are core values in Swedish society. Abrahamsson (1996) maintains that the ideals behind adult education are about both social justice, equality and the development of a democratic society as well as contributing towards the economy and employment. Knowledge and education is thus regarded as beneficial for both the individual and society. The tradition of adult education is rooted in the folk high schools and study circles established in the 19th century. Today their popularity is as strong as ever.

Higher education consists of two types of institutions; a traditional university (universitet) and a university college (högskola). Provision in the latter is limited to undergraduate programmes although in future university colleges will have the opportunity to deliver PhD programmes and undertake research. Swedish universities do not differentiate between younger students and adults as adults are in the majority. Younger students are also older than their counterparts in other European countries as the leaving age for secondary school is 20. Universities also attract adult students by offering short courses, largely vocational in content, and for which credit can be gained. This situation led Abrahamsson (1986) to describe the process as the 'adultification' of higher education.

Adult education provision for those over the age of 20 is extensive and varied. The two main institutions are the municipal adult education (komvux) and the Folk High Schools. Komvux was initiated in 1968 for adults who lacked secondary school qualifications. Most of those who attend are in their 20s (1993 65% of students were aged 25 or under). The main aim of those attending is to be eligible for higher education. The Folk High Schools have more ideological roots, being linked to the Swedish popular adult education movement of the 19th century. The majority are privately financed. Each school has its own subject specialities. Recently there has been an increase in the number of Folk High Schools. There are also state schools for adults (SSV-schools) which supplement opportunities for adults in regions where a suitable komvux is not available. Often teaching is through distance learning. All three institutions are free. Financial aid is available through non-repayable grants from the government. Opportunities for vocational and employment training are also provided. The latter is a big growth area (Abrahamsson, 1996).

Despite the widespread provision of adult education access to university is fairly restrictive in the sense that adults have to either possess the school leaving certificate or sit an entrance examination. The latter is called 25/4 scheme. To be eligible a person has to be 25 years or over plus have four years work experience. About 35-40% of university students enter by this route. Unlike the UK there are no 'alternative' routes of entry which do not require formal qualifications.

The 1977 reform centralised and unified the system. Programmes for social work, teaching and nursing in colleges were given undergraduate study status. As a result the number of women undergraduates increased. The act established the practice of recurrent education which encouraged movement between work, leisure and education. Adult education policy has not stood still since the late 1970s. Rubenson (1993) identifies five policy phases since 1968. The early 1990s, with the arrival of the conservative-liberal government, saw the erosion of financial support for adults wanting to return to learn. A significant factor of the 1993 reform has been the decentralisation of the higher education system. One result has been the widening of subject choice at institutional level for adults. However, policy attention was focused on young people rather than adults. Access for certain social groups has been limited:

Higher education policy for the 1990s in Sweden differs again from the European policies by slightly closing its open access system for non-traditional students and giving more opportunity for traditional ones by creating more places for them. (Bron, 1996)

The educational values and culture are close to those required for lifelong learning in a learning society. However, Abrahamsson maintains that:

> The next decade will be a cross-roads for Swedish adult education. The former Swedish model of recurrent education still seems to have a high reputation in the OECD and the EC. It is, however, regarded as a bureaucratic construction within the neo-liberal culture of the present government. From a progressive policy point of view, it is important to ensure that adults will be able to use their rights to learn and develop across the lifespan ... It is, in fact, a crucial component in the development of a future European citizenship with or without the formation of a European Union.   (Abrahamsson, 1996: 179)

UK

Recent government reports (Kennedy, Fryer and the Green Paper) have brought the issues of lifelong learning and learning society onto the policy and public agenda. Current policy interest in HE stems back to an earlier Government policy document, 'Higher Education: Meeting the Challenge':

> places should be available for all who have the necessary intellectual competence, motivation and maturity to benefit from higher education.
>
> (DES, 1987: 7)

As in other European nations the number of those attending HE has increased. For example, the age participation rate (APR) for 18 year olds has changed radically since the 1970s from approximately 10% to 30% in the mid 1990s. In practice it has resulted in widening access for young women and more white middle class 18 year olds, the 'traditional' entrants. At the same time there has been a growth, since the mid 1980s, in the number of adults attending universities. In 1995-96 42% of the total undergraduate population were aged 25 or over (HESA statistics). Adults, however, are not evenly distributed across the university system. Most are to be found in the 'new' universities (the former polytechnics under the binary system) rather than in the 'old' universities. This increase reflects the growth in access routes to university whereby the traditional 'A' levels are no longer the only accepted pathway. Diversification of the student population and entry routes has raised questions about the massification of the UK higher education system and thus issues of quality and standards.

Other factors such as the introduction of a modular curriculum in some institutions and the establishment of a Credit Accumulation and Transfer system (CATs) have contributed to more adults accessing HE. The FE sector also plays a significant role in providing preparatory courses for HE such as pre-access and access programmes. The availability of part-time degrees has become increasingly important in enabling adults to study at university, particularly for those in full or part-time employment. HE in FE has also become important during the 1990s with colleges teaching franchised or partnership undergraduate degree courses. Boundaries between FE and HE have, therefore, become blurred (Fulton, 1993) being local makes FE attractive to adults who have been out of the education system for a long time:

> The accessibility of further and adult education establishments and their experience in attracting a wide range of students has made them an obvious location not just for access programmes but for franchise arrangements which take higher education outside of the academy.   (Parry, 1990: XXX)

'Adultification' is only apparent in certain institutions and departments within UK universities. For a number of years the Open University has provided an important, flexible alternative for adult learners, particularly those in full-time employment. The recognition of Access course credits as a third route of entry to HE removed a significant barrier to participation (Parry and Wake, 1990). Impetus for the inclusion of Access courses is rooted in the access movement and the establishment of the Forum for Access Studies in 1986. However, the Government's endorsement of Access as a mode of entry was due to economic rather than equity issues. Other alternative entry routes are now available such as APEL and vocational qualifications. It is also possible for adults to enter HE with few or no qualifications but it is not common. For example, the University of Warwick has a 2 + 2 degree programme for local adults who have been out of the education system for a long time:

> The programme provides new pathways into higher education for local adult students by offering an innovative degree structure, tailored wherever possible to the needs of non-traditional students who may lack formal qualifications but who are capable of studying for a degree.   (Merrill and Moseley, 1995: 36)

Research at Warwick studied the attitudes and experiences of adult students from the actors' perspective. By using a biographical approach it was possible to look at the learning careers of adults. The sample included social science 2 + 2, part-time and full-time degree students. The latter had mostly entered through the access route. Class and gender factors inhibited their initial schooling and most had been forced to leave school by their parents as early as possible although some had wanted to continue:

> I got no encouragement from my parents. In those days from a working class background the idea was that you worked for a few years and then got married (Sarah). The family needed the money a wage could bring, so I did not think of staying on at school. Times were hard and we did not have any money. (Peter)

In adult life several felt that they had missed out on education and viewed studying for an undergraduate degree as completing their education' and as one person explained 'a chance to redress my lack of education'. Another stated:

> I had a very interesting working life but I always felt that I missed out in more general education and certainly I would have been a very patient university student in my younger days.   (Adam)

At the start of their university career participants had a very narrow perception of lifelong learning - for them education and learning stopped with the acquisition of a first degree. However, when interviewed at the end of their degree courses attitudes had changed. They had a wider vision of learning. Many wanted to continue studying at postgraduate level although financial constraints prevented the majority from doing so. Despite the struggle which studying entailed, particularly for married women, all enjoyed the learning process. Leaving university marked a watershed in their lives. Being able to return to learn as adults empowered their lives: 'I feel that this is a very exciting time in my life and that my life is and will continue to change as a result of my studies'. Biography and lifelong learning thus interacted as the 'notion of lifelong learning points to the learning individuals in the shaping of their biography' (Walther and Stauber, 1998: 13). In looking to the future many were concerned about changes to the grants and benefits system and that opportunities for lifelong learning would be limited to those who could afford it:

My overall view is that in the near future many mature students who, for one reason or another, didn't have good educational opportunities when they were younger will feel that university is not a financially viable option for them. The current situation will worsen thus denying ambitious hardworking people the chance of success in higher education.

(male adult student in Merrill and McKie, 1998: 7)

However, the importance of lifelong learning was transmitted to their children and friends who they hoped would participate in education. Local non-traditional adults have been allowed entry alongside the high achieving 18 year olds and are proving capable of equally good academic standards. At an institutional level, departments with a higher adult participation rate are more supportive of access policies and initiatives than departments with a low adult participation rate.

Interest and enthusiasm for lifelong learning in universities has been revitalised by the publication of Dearing, the Green Paper and Fryer Report. What outcomes and changes the documents will generate is yet unknown. However, if adults perceive finance to be a stumbling block to returning to learn, lifelong education may only become a reality for certain socio-economic groups thus increasing inequalities and cultural capital between groups.

Lifelong Learning and European Universities: Concluding into the Future

The expansion of European universities in the 1980s and early 1990s has now stopped. Consolidation is now the order of the day. Although universities have opened their doors to more students they continue to be largely the preserve of the young and those from higher socio-economic groups. In most countries and in most institutions the number of adult students in higher education remains low, restricted mostly to the 'low status' universities and non-university higher education sector. Admissions criteria (Spain, Belgium) and the non-availability of part-time courses (Belgium, Germany) are experienced as obstacles by adults who feel that they are capable of studying for a degree. Most European universities have moved only slightly towards becoming learning organisations providing lifelong learning opportunities for both young and adult students.

The role of universities in lifelong learning also has to be considered within the wider macro context of society. Definitions of what a learning society should be are fragmented on ideological grounds of economic verses social factors and individualistic verses collective views of education. Education as a market place with learners as consumers choosing and taking responsibility for their own learning is now a dominant view within political and education spheres. For Edwards (1997) the use of discourse of lifelong learning redefines the traditional boundaries of adult education:

> ... the emphasis has shifted away from a focus on the provider towards one on the learner and learning in the anticipation that this will result in a greater permeability of boundaries of adults.   (Edwards, 1997: 107)

Ainley (1994) argues that the idea of a learning society is used as an instrument to improve competitiveness on the global markets. However, the belief in collectivity, community and society has not been completely forgotten. Ranson (1994) stresses the civic and social benefits of a learning society in reasserting democratic traditions and citizenship:

> The conditions for a learning society are, in the last resort, essentially political, requiring the creation of a polity that provides the fundamental conditions for individuals and the communities in which they live to develop their capacities and to flourish ... the good (learning) person is a good citizen.
>   (Ranson, 1994: 110)

If higher education in Europe is to play an essential role in the development of a learning society which emphasises equality, social inclusion and community, cultural and structural changes have to occur. Elitism and inequalities have to be challenged. The model for Watson and Taylor (1998) is a complex and multi-layered one:

> The appropriate culture and approach of the Lifelong Learning University is inherently pluralist: thus it may be that no single, simple model of liberalism is appropriate. The democratic imperative requires both functional involvement and personal development perspectives: even more, it requires a radical, critical educational programme and the involvement of large numbers of individuals and key sectional groups in the community.
>   (Watson and Taylor, 1998: 141)

Some universities in the UK, through Continuing Education departments, have reached out into the community to work with black, working class and women's groups (Preece et al., 1998). However, there is still a long way to go to achieve ideological, cultural and structural shifts which will generate lifelong learning opportunities for all adults rather than just for those who already have educational, cultural and economic capital.

References

Abrahamsson, K. (1986) *Adult Participation in Swedish HE*, Stockholm, Almqvist and Wiksell International.

Abrahamsson, K. (1996) 'Concepts, organisation and current trends of lifelong education in Sweden', in Richards, R., Hanson, A. and Raggett (eds) *Boundaries of Adult Learning*, London, Routledge, Open University Press.

Agelii, K. and Bron, A. (1997) 'Mature Students' Access to Stockholm University', in Merrill, B. and Hills, S. (eds) *Access, Equity, Participation and Organisational Change*, European Society for Research on the Education of Adults (ESREA), Leamington Spa, University of Warwick.

Ainley, P. (1994) *Degrees of Difference: Higher Education in the 1990s*, London, Lawrence and Wishart.

Alheit, P. (1996) 'I provocative proposal: from labour society to learning society', *Lifelong Learning in Europe*, 2, 3-5.

Antikainen, A., Houtonen, J., Kauppila, J. and Huotelin, H. (1996) *Living in a Learning Society*, London, Falmer Press.

Barnett, R. (1996) 'Situating the learning university', *International Journal of University Adult Education*, XXXV (1), April, 13-27.

Bron, A. (1996) *Definition of Non-Traditional Adult Student in the Swedish Context*, Stockholm, University of Stockholm.

Castells, M. (1996) *The Information Age: economy, society and culture*, Vol.1: The Rise of Network Society, Oxford, Blackwell.

Coffield, F. (1998) Lifelong Learning as a New Form of Social Control (to be published).

Department of Education and Employment (1995) *Lifetime Learning - A Consultative Document*, London, HMSO.

Department of Education and Employment (1998) *The Learning Age*, London, DfEE.

Department of Education and Science (1987) *Higher Education: Meeting the Challenge*, Cmnd 114, London, HMSO.

Dohmen, G. (1996) *Lifelong Learning: Guidelines for a Modern Education Policy*, Bonn, Federal Ministry of Education, Science, Research and Technology.

Duke, C. (1992) *The Learning University: Towards a New Paradigm*, Buckingham, SRHE/Open University Press.

Duke, C. (1996) 'What has the "learning university" learned?' *International Journal of University Adult Education*, XXXV (1), April, 74-7.

Edwards, R. (1997) *Changing Places? Flexibility, lifelong learning and a learning society*, London, Routledge.

European Commission (1991) *The Memorandum on Higher Education in the European Community*, Brussels, EC.

European Commission (1995) *Towards the Learning Society*. White Paper on Education and Training, Brussels, EC.

Faure et al. (1972) *Learning to Be: The World of Education Today and Tomorrow*, Paris, UNESCO.

Field, J. (1996) 'Universities and the Learning Society', *International Journal of University Adult Education*, XXXV (1), April, 1-12.

Flecha, R. (1992) 'Spain', in Jarvis, P. (ed) *Perspectives on Adult Education and Training in Europe*, Leicester, NIACE.

Knapper, C. and Cropley, A. (1985) (1991, 2nd edition) *Lifelong Learning and Higher Education*, London, Croom Helm.

Longworth, N. and Davies, W.K. (1996) *Lifelong Learning*, London, Croom Helm.

Lopez, V.A. (1992) 'Popular Universities in Spain', *International Journal of University Adult Education*, XXXI (2) July, 1-7.

Merrill, B. (1997) 'Lifelong Learning and European Universities: Rhetoric or Future Reality?', in Burgess, R. (ed) *Beyond the First Degree*, Buckingham, SRHE/Open University Press.

Merrill, B. and McKie, J. (1998) 'Money and the mature Student', *Adults Learning*, Vol.9, No.6.

Merrill, B. and Moseley, R. (1995) 'Access and partnership: the 2+2 degree programme at the University of Warwick', in Wisker, G. (ed) *Franchising: Flexibility and Fruitful Partnerships*, SEDA Paper, 92.

Parry, G. (ed) (1990) *Wider entry to engineering in HE, proceedings of a conference on HE*, London, Royal Society of Arts.

Parry, G. and Wake, C. (1990) *Access and Alternative Futures for Higher Education*, London, Hodder and Stoughton.

Preece, J. et al. (1998) *Beyond the Boundaries: exploring the potential of widening provision in higher education*, Leicester, NIACE.

Ranson, S. (1994) *Towards the Learning Society*, London, Cassell.

Rubenson, K. (1993) 'Adult education policy in Sweden, 1967-91', in Edwards, R., Sieminski and Zeldin, D. (eds) *Adult Learners, Education and Training*, London, Routledge/Open University Press.

Schuller, T. (1996) 'Modelling the lifecourse: age time and education', in Papaioannou, S., Alheit, P., Laurisden, J.F. and Olesen, H.S. (eds) *Community Education and Social Change*, Roskilde, Roskilde University.

Scott, P. (1995) *The Meanings of Mass Higher Education*, Buckingham, SRHE/Open University Press.

Trow, M. (1989) 'The Robbins Trap: British attitudes and the limits of expansion', *Higher Education Quarterly*, 43 (1): 55-75.

Walther, A. and Stauber, B. (1998) 'Lifelong Learning - an open concept between visions and divisions?' *Lifelong Learning in Europe*, Vol.1, Tübingen, Neuling Verlag.

Watson, D. and Taylor, R. (1998) *Lifelong Learning and the University, A Post-Dearing Agenda*, London, Falmer Press.

3 Lifelong (L)earning and a 'New Age' at Work

RICHARD EDWARDS

Abstract

This chapter charts some of the assumptions underpinning the policy focus on lifelong learning in the United Kingdom government's 1998 Green Paper, The Learning Age. It argues that the 'new age' of lifelong learning is itself a manifestation of a certain new age, culturalist discourse wherein values, attitudes and affect displace evidence and rigour in the construction of policy. This is examined in the context of some of the contemporary changes in employment and work. The chapter argues there is a parallel between the culturalist harnessing of attitudes through lifelong learning to the goal of a learning society and those to be found in measures to develop learning organisations. This promotes a culture of lifelong (l)earning, wherein earning and learning increasingly are fused, within which there remain a range of tensions and possibilities.

Introduction

Internationally, the notion of lifelong learning has been given greater prominence in policy in recent years. Indeed it would appear to be one of a range of 'policy epidemics' (Levin, 1998) that are changing educational structures and provision worldwide. Globalisation and the integration of national economies are held to have led to greater emphasis being placed on the competitiveness and efficiency of organisations and nations (Edwards and Usher, 1999). Central to supporting that competitiveness has been the argument that people need to be able to develop their skills and capabilities to deal with change, to become lifelong learners - on the assumption that many of us are not of course. This agenda has been furthered by concern for social exclusion and, particularly in the United Kingdom, the restricted profile of participation in education and training post-school. Opportunities to develop skills and qualifications are argued to

31

be central components in combating social exclusion as well as contributing to economic competitiveness.

The importance of lifelong learning - and its associated concepts, such as learning organisations, learning cities, learning societies and learning nations - is illustrated by a number of recent publications and events. For example, the European Union adopted 1996 as the European Year of Lifelong Learning. Also in 1996, the Economic and Social Research Council in the United Kingdom set up a Learning Society research programme. In 1997, the Dearing review of higher education (National Committee of Inquiry into Higher Education, 1997) and the Kennedy (1997) report on widening participation in further education both positioned the different sectors as contributing to lifelong learning. A review of higher education in Australia (Department of Employment, Education, Training and Youth Affairs, 1998) came up with a similar position. The British Labour government established a Task Force on lifelong learning which reported at the end of 1997 (Fryer, 1997). In 1998, the government published its Green Paper on lifelong learning and its responses to Dearing and Kennedy (Secretary of State for Education and Employment, 1998). Each in different ways posits the necessity for change which is already and will continue to have a major impact upon institutions, managers, practitioners and indeed learners. As the Green Paper expresses it, there is to be a 'renaissance for a new Britain', a new age, an age of lifelong learning.

This chapter attempts to chart some of the assumptions underpinning the focus on lifelong learning through an examination of certain aspects of the Labour government's Green Paper. It argues that the 'new age' of lifelong learning identified within the latter is itself a manifestation of a certain 'new age' culturalist discourse wherein affect displaces rigour in the construction of policy. In other words, and as has been argued elsewhere, policy discourse is not simply rational or technical (Ball, 1998; Stronach and MacLure, 1997). Drawing on previous work (Edwards, 1998), I then go on to explore some of the changes which can be argued to characterise the new age, in particular focusing on changes to employment and within the workplace. Here I suggest there is a parallel between the culturalist harnessing of attitudes through lifelong learning to the goal of a learning society and those to be found in measures to develop learning organisations. Finally, I return to the question of policy and suggest that the new age discourse promotes a culture of lifelong (l)earning wherein earning and learning increasingly are fused. The aim then is to demonstrate that, in contrast to views of lifelong learning as simply a form of reductionist vocationalism, there is a wider cultural agenda in play, although one in which there remain a range of tensions and possibilities at work.

The New Age, the Learning Age ...

Despite the rhetoric of the centrality of lifelong learning to the constitution of a leaning age and society, uncertainty surrounds the contemporary context within which it is framed. This means there are questions as to the nature of such a society and how it is to be achieved. Notions of the post-industrial society, the postmodern moment, the information society are only some of the many attempts to describe and name contemporary times. What is common and central to most of these characterisations is the increased rate of change in the world. This is itself both a reflection of and contributor to conditions such as disembeddedness, risk, speed, disorganisation and hyper-reality (Giddens, 1990; Beck, 1992; Baudrillard, 1996) which many would argue characterise contemporary times, however it is labelled.

Lifelong learning is posited as a necessary response to this contemporary condition. Given uncertainty, and with the answer seen as the acceptance and need to cope with change, there has emerged a greater emphasis in policy and practice on the need to harness and deploy people's capacities to learn and to continue to learn throughout life. This is mostly framed as an adaptive strategy rather than an active form of participation in the shaping of change. Here lifelong learning is seen primarily, but not only as reactive to an already set context - an answer - rather than also being proactive in relation to the desirability of that context - a question. Thus, in the government's Green Paper:

> we are in a new age - the age of information and global competition ... we have no choice but to prepare for this new age in which the key to success will be the continuous education and development of the human mind and imagination. (Secretary of State, 1998: 9)

Lifelong learning itself is not a new notion, having a long history in the world of adult education with its never entirely compatible concerns for personal development and social inclusion. However, it is harnessed now into a more powerful discourse, as an adaptive strategy for coping with change. In the process, it has in different ways both displaced and embraced its adult education roots. We find that lifelong learning has been adopted both at the national and supra-national levels as a framework for policy and practice, increasingly with the espoused normative goal of supporting the development of a learning society, where the latter is primarily, though not solely, framed within human capital theory. Thus, 'learning is the key to prosperity ... investment in human capital will be the foundation of success in the knowledge-based global economy of the twenty-first century' (Secretary of State, 1998: 7). Here, the goal is not one of social engineering in a modernist systemic sense, but of enabling individuals to look after themselves in conditions of uncertainty through a process of 'self-improvement'. 'The Learning Age will be built on a renewed commitment to self-improvement and a recognition of the enormous contribution learning makes to our society' (Secretary of State, 1998: 8).

While other formulations of lifelong learning might be displaced, they are not absent however. As with other concepts, there is no fixed and taken for granted meaning for lifelong learning (Edwards, 1997). In other words, multiple discourses invest the terrain of lifelong learning with different meanings. Thus, as well as being a key to prosperity, it also

> helps make ours a civilised society, develops the spiritual side of our lives and promotes active citizenship ... That is why we value learning for its own sake as well as for the equality of opportunity it brings. (Secretary of State, 1998: 7)

Lifelong learning is positioned as contributing to a set of social as well as economic goals, contributing to what others refer to as social as well as economic capital (Schuller, 1998). This is a powerful discourse, the evidence basis for which remains largely common-sense. While it may appeal to the affective and value domains with its view of 'progress' through learning, it is most certainly unproved as a set of assertions.

In a sense then, a discourse like this seeks to promote the very thing which is said to be lacking - a culture of lifelong learning. The new age of lifelong learning therefore seems to be conducive to a type of new age discourse, wherein the harnessing of emotions, attitudes and values displaces the requirement for rigorous argument, evidence and debate. A culturalist set of assertions on the desirability and necessity for lifelong learning is posited as both the way forward and in a way which is consistent with this aim. This in itself is significant, for as I will suggest it is part of wider trends, reflexively linked to the new forms of workplace identity and workplace learning wherein there is a focus on attitudes and value as much as skill. It is also an appeal to the consumer of rather than simply actor in policy, or perhaps even the actor in as consumer of policy.

The affective dimensions to the discourses of lifelong learning are not in themselves surprising, for as Ball (1998: 124) suggests 'policies are both systems of values and symbolic systems ... policies are articulated both to achieve material effects and to manufacture support for those effects'. Thus, for example, we find assertions that

> learning offers excitement and the opportunity for discovery. It stimulates enquiring minds and nourishes our souls ... learning develops the intellectual capital which is now at the centre of a nation's competitive strength ... learning contributes to social cohesion and fosters a sense of belonging, responsibility and identity ... learning is essential to a strong economy and inclusive society.   (Secretary of State, 1998: 10-11)

An effective policy would appear therefore to be one which is affective, and maybe even infectious, given the current epidemic! It is an appeal which is appealing to many educators, employers and others, as is evidenced for example, in the title to the Kennedy report (1997), which boldly stated that 'Learning Works'. Questions remain as to what forms of learning by whom, when and where have these effects, and whether such effects can be identified as the outcomes of learning, lifelong or otherwise. In what senses does learning work and how? What sense does the new age of lifelong learning make when we put the claims for it alongside some of the more rigorous analyses of contemporary change, in particular changes in the nature and availability of paid employment?

A New Age at Work?

What is the nature of the new age at work in the paid workplace? Here we return to some of the characterisations outlined above, to which lifelong learning might be said to be an adaptive response. However, I want to suggest that lifelong learning is a far more differentiated discursive strategy through which to harness individuals to a culture of self-improvement through work, wherein learning and earning become linked integrally, and through which fresh forms of exclusion are inscribed.

In his influential characterisation of the contemporary 'risk society', Beck (1992: 142) argues that

> in the current and coming waves of automation this [industrial] *system of standardised full employment* is beginning to soften and fray at the margins into flexiblisations of its three supporting pillars: labour law, work site and working hours ... Flexible, pluralised forms of underemployment are spreading.

Destandardisation produces and is a product of greater flexibility. The latter takes a number of forms at the organisational and personal levels. There is often an implicit assumption in such debates that increased flexibility is associated with up-skilling and multi-skilling rather than down-skilling. Aronowitz and DiFazio (1994) suggest, as an addition to this debate, that there is a displacement of skill by knowledge with the growing use of information and communication technologies. Increased flexibility is posited as the inevitable direction for the economy to which policy, organisations and individuals must respond. To be competitive in an uncertain and risk-laden environment, organisations need to adapt reflexively to market changes. This requires workers to be flexible within the workplace, transferring from one task to another, and flexible between workplaces, transferring from one job to another. Employment itself becomes destandardised and risk-laden.

This engenders greater insecurity for members of the labour force, something which is enhanced by the volatility of un- and under-regulated globally integrated markets. Destandardisation results in trends towards increased differentiation between a core of relatively securely employed workers and a periphery of part-time and temporarily employed, under- and un-employed people. The condition of those at the periphery itself becomes a constant threat to the core, who themselves become subject to insecurity, if of a different order. Labour market flexibility may foster competitiveness - although this is debatable as a general proposition, as it does not in and of itself necessarily increase productivity - but on the basis of lowered conditions of employment and greater competition for the paid work that is available. Those with the most skills and qualifications witness an expansion of opportunity, while those with the fewest a contraction of employment (Glyn, 1996). The processes of differentiation both within and between nations are enhanced by policies to regulate and curtail the influence of Trade Unions and management approaches which undermine collective bargaining and individualise the employment relationship.

Within flexible organisations, core workers can expect opportunities to become multi-skilled, increasing their skills both vertically within the sector and horizontally as they learn to do jobs previously the responsibility of others. They can expect also to develop core skills, such as problem-solving, and interpersonal skills facilitating working in a team. By contrast, peripheral workers will be engaged in low skilled or narrowly skilled jobs requiring little training or retraining. Core workers enjoy substantial autonomy in their work, whereas Taylorist principles are applied to peripheral workers. Indeed, the control over peripheral workers could increase through the indirect surveillance of information and communication technologies.

This has significance for issues of gender, as it is primarily women who are employed in periphery jobs. While flexibility can be said to offer opportunities to many who would not otherwise have the opportunity to work, particularly women, it is also important to recognise that many flexible workers also lose out on benefits accruing to other employees. The continued marginalisation of women within the labour force therefore seems to be the dominant trend despite increased levels of participation. Handy (1985: 162) comments that

> a flexilife will not look like heaven to everyone. It is, in fact, the kind of existence that the last few generations of women have been well used to, moving between work and family, mixing part-time work with home responsibilities, balancing career priorities with a concern for relationships in the home and, in many cases, having to abandon one for the other.

More critically, Hart (1992) argues that the flexibility which has played a role in female labour and its devaluation is now sought from the generic worker. The dual impact is to bring more women into paid employment and demand greater flexibility from all workers.

With the destandardisation, flexibility and individualisation of employment and work have come moves towards a greater focus on the culture of workplaces associated with the notions of learning organisations and human resource development. To become more efficient and effective, it is suggested that workplaces become or need to become learning organisations. This is a central feature of contemporary organisational and management theory. To enable organisations to change, the workforce has to have networks of communication within which to channel information and views, the opportunities to learn associated with facilitating flexibility and change, and ways of participating in decisions about these processes. This requires members of the workforce not simply to be flexible in the use of skills, but to be engaged affectedly, to be 'empowered' to participate in shaping the organisation's goals and practices, to feel part of and participate in organisational culture.

Learning organisations therefore seek to promote a culture of lifelong learning and require it as an aspect of sustaining and developing themselves. The notion of learning organisations is most often associated with private sector employers and commercial environments. However, it has come to have a wider applicability, partly as a result of changes in the public and voluntary sectors in many countries, wherein organisations have had to restructure to become entrepreneurial like commercial workplaces. Burgoyne (1992: 327) identifies a number of characteristics of a learning organisation. These can be found to varying degrees within individual workplaces and may operate differentially within the gendered division of labour within organisations (Butler, 1996). Learning organisations require: a learning approach to strategy; participative policy-making; open information systems; formative accounting and control; mutual adjustment between departments; reward flexibility; adaptable structures; boundary workers as environment scanners; inter-organisational learning; a learning culture and climate; and self-development opportunities for all. It is not simply the provision of learning opportunities that distinguishes learning organisations from other types of workplace, but also the form and content that provision takes. Solving a problem, introducing a new product, scrapping an old one, reaching a different market have been constructed as requiring participants to see the future in a new way. Success in this rapidly changing environment is held to involve continuous learning and changes of behaviour. Organisations change only if the people within them change and are prepared to change. Increasingly, learning is focused around how it helps the organisation to achieve its goals, processes organised through the practices of human resource development, and their emphasis on values and attitudes as well as skills.

With this, comes changed workplace identities. Central to the latter is the engagement of the whole person and a commitment to continuous improvement. Here the workforce, like the workplace is deemed to produce a virtuous circle of flexibility and enterprise, practices supported by the constant reflexive process of change and development. In her study of a large manufacturing multi-national in the USA, Casey (1996: 320), for instance, argues that

> the archetypical new Hephaestus employee is one who *enthusiastically* manifests the values of dedication, loyalty, self-sacrifice and passion for the product and customer, and who is willing to the extra mile for his or her team.

This entails an active subjectivity aligned to organisational goals which encourages 'each individual to apply the idea of continuous improvement to themselves' (Yates, 1994), to produce what Casey refers to as 'designer employees'. Here the alienation of industrialisation is displaced by an enthusiasm for work. Self-improvement is the key to learning organisations as well as learning societies. This has been particularly marked in those organisations involved in practices such as employee development schemes, action learning sets, quality circles and the like. The downside of this for many is an intensification of work.

In his study of the retail sector in the UK, du Gay (1996) argues that workplaces are characterised increasingly by forms of governmentality associated with 'an ethos of enterprise'. As well as applying to workplaces, workers are subject to practices of management appraisal and development which position them as enterprising engaged in an 'enterprise of the self'. In this position

> no matter what hand circumstances may have dealt a person, he or she remains always continuously engaged ... in that one enterprise ... In this sense the character of the entrepreneur can no longer be seen as just one among a

> plurality of ethical personalities *but must rather be seen as assuming an ontological priority.*   (du Gay, 1996: 181)

Exposure to the risks and costs of their activities are constructed as enabling workers to take responsibility for their actions, signifying a form of 'empowerment' and 'success' within the organisation. Nor is this restricted to careers alone, as the whole of life becomes inscribed with the ethos of enterprise. Enterprising identity and the self as an enterprise for workers emerges as organisations become subject to measures of performance in the delivery of services and goods through a contract. Rather than being governed simply by bureaucratic and hierarchic procedures wherein decisions are taken elsewhere and handed down to be implemented, workers are given 'responsibility' for achieving certain outcomes efficiently and effectively which are then audited. Here

> discipline is now more immediate and everyday with little overt intervention on the part of the corporate bureaucracy. The employees police themselves. The decentralisation and internalisation of discipline deepens the processes of employee identification with the company.   (Casey, 1996: 326)

Yet this discipline is not simply imposed nor is it always complete. Even in relatively restricted skill areas such as restaurant waiting research indicates that:

> service encounters are shown to have a performative character and thus one can think of those kind of workplaces as a stage, as a dramatic setting for certain kinds of performance, involving a mix of mental, manual *and* emotional labour.   (Lash and Urry, 1994: 202)

There are many senses then to the culture of lifelong learning. Workers may perform their roles as enterprising and flexible workers as required by organisations, but nonetheless be reflexively conscious that it is a performance. The culture is never complete or homogeneous.

A culturalist approach to lifelong learning therefore governs not only organisations which need to be more enterprising, making the most of the opportunities offered by new technologies and new and emerging markets. The same is also true of the workforce. This is not solely about skills, but, more importantly, about values and attitudes. Here the aim is to displace the regimented and disciplined worker of the industrial age - trained 'docile bodies' (Foucault, 1979) - by more closely aligning worker subjectivities to the goals and missions of the organisation. Engaging with the subjectivities of the workforce is a way of releasing the motivational impact of the 'empowered' and enterprising worker rather than suppressing it through a concentration solely on technical skill or competence. Worker subjectivity is brought forth rather than suppressed and alienated and becomes subject to training in what some have argued to be the attempt to govern the soul (Miller and Rose, 1993). This both supports individualisation and reflexivity as a form of active subjectivity, but also attempts to govern it through particular and never completely successful strategies of human resource development.

The significance of workplace and employment change have been much discussed. Debates about fordist, neo-fordist and post-fordist forms of work organisation, lean production and mass customisation have rested on the implications of new technology and the requirements of workplaces and workers to be reflexive and respond to the diverse and changing requirements of the consumer market. For some, this is a positive move, as the compartmentalised labour of the production line in which workers repeatedly undertake a specified task gives way to team work with workers undertaking a variety of tasks and roles. The post-industrial artisan replaces the alienated industrial worker giving greater job satisfaction to individuals. In this view, the introduction of new technology 'frees' the workers from arduous labour and work becomes more 'humane'. However, others have distinguished fordism as a method of production and Taylorism as a form of work organisation. For Clarke (1996), fordism refers to a strategy of production in which there is a linear sequence of work, a moving assembly line, dedicated machinery and a maximum use of standardised parts. Taylorism, by contrast, is a management strategy in which work is sub-divided into its component parts and re-designed using work study techniques to maximise efficiency in production activities and keep close control over workers undertaking a narrow range of low-skilled tasks. Although commonly associated with fordism, Taylorist methods can be applied in small and medium sized firms and to small batch production. It is entirely possible therefore to introduce advanced technological methods of production and employ Taylorist methods in the management of workers, a view often associated with neo-fordism. This suggests that the reflexivity indicative of post-fordist work organisations may collapse into Taylorised reflexes more characteristic of work organisations such as fast food chains, with implications both for the forms of learning available and achieved.

Early notions of the post-fordist artisan have given way to more cautious assessments for there are a range of possibilities embedded in the pursuit of flexibility as a strategy for economic innovation and renewal. Indeed, the possibilities for innovation as a condition for and outcome of flexibility are at least somewhat dependent upon the pedagogic assumptions and management approaches within the specific discourses of flexibility. Johnson and Lundvall (1991) talk of reactive and active forms of flexibility. If flexibility is constructed as an adaptive process, the notion of learning associated with this is stimulus-response. People and organisations are positioned as reactive to externally imposed conditions. This raises the question of the possibilities for innovation within such an organisation. By contrast, if flexibility is constructed as an active process of learning they argue there are greater possibilities for innovation. Johnson and Lundvall suggest that co-operation and partnership rather than competition provide the best conditions for innovation.

This suggests two ideal types of flexible organisation. First, there is the adaptive type, developing flexibility in response to changing markets wherein competitiveness is pursued through competition, promoting insecurity without the latter being addressed, managing or regulated. Management may be delayered but remains hierarchical and Taylorist in its approach, a situation of low trust. Second, there is creative type seeking to develop and position themselves within markets, where competitiveness is pursued through co-operation, wherein flexibility and insecurity are managed as a single phenomenon. Each of these may be said to be a 'learning organisation', but with differing pedagogical underpinnings: the first, based on stimulus-response; the second developmental, with the degree of development circumscribed by the extent of participation in the decision-making processes of the organisation. Each promotes a different culture of lifelong learning with different possibilities inscribed within it.

(L)earning in the New Age?

A number of questions emerge suggestive of a proactive engagement with the uncertainty of change of which we are a part. First, to what extent is the new age of lifelong learning to be adaptive or creative, part of and contributing to a post-fordist or Taylorised social formation? We need to ask about the various cultures of lifelong learning which are in play. Here, the alignment of a certain culture of lifelong learning espoused in the Green Paper and that sought in certain trends within the workplace are suggestive of a culture of (l)earning where learning and earning are increasingly fused. Yet, as the discussion of workplace change demonstrates, this will impact differentially on and within different organisations and various parts of the labour force, resulting in different levels of fusion. However, given that social inclusion is propounded within a policy framework which promotes initiatives, such as the University for Industry, the New Deal for the unemployed, individual learning accounts and Learning Direct, it suggests primarily that the culture of lifelong learning constructs social inclusion through economic inclusion, to which the levels and types of lifelong (l)earning are irrelevant. They are a matter for self-improvement, for creative and enterprising selves.

Second, in seeking to produce an affective culturalist policy, are the new strategies of human resource development being deployed at national level in governmental policy practices? In other words, do the policy practices of consultation and the substance of the policy document reflexively mirror each other and attempt to harness active subjectivities to the goals of policy and to lifelong learning themselves? Does the space of policy provide a terrain in which evidence and rigour can be deployed against affect and with different effects? In a sense, such a terrain is inevitable, but it might also be a troubled one given the uncertainties of lifelong (l)earning. Indeed, we need to ask what strategies are necessary for different formulations to be affective and whether they have the potential to be as infectious as those already in play!

References

Aronowitz, S. and DiFazio, W. (1994) *The Jobless Future: Sci-Tech and the Dogma of Work*, Minneapolis, University of Minnesota Press.

Ball, S. (1998) 'Big policies/small world: an introduction to international perspectives in education policy', *Comparative Education* 34, 2: 119-130.

Baudrillard, J. (1996) *Selected Writings*, Cambridge, Polity Press.

Beck, U. (1992), *Risk Society: Towards a New Modernity*, London, Sage.

Burgoyne, J. (1992) 'Creating a learning organisation', *RSA Journal*, April: 321-330.

Butler, E. (1996) 'Equity and workplace learning: emerging discourses and conditions of possibility', unpublished paper delivered to the National Colloquium on Workplace Learning, University of Technology, Sydney, July.

Casey, C. (1996) *Work, Self and Society: After Industrialism*, London, Routledge.

Clarke, A. (1996) 'Competitiveness, technological innovation and the challenge to Europe', in Raggatt, P., Edwards, R. and Small, N. (eds) *The Learning Society: Challenges and Trends*, London, Routledge.

Department of Employment, Education, Training and Youth Affairs (1998) *Learning for Life: Final Report. Review of Higher Education Financing and Policy*, Canberra, Commonwealth of Australia.

du Gay, P. (1996) *Consumption and Identity at Work*, London, Sage.

Edwards, R. (1997) *Changing Places? Flexibility, Lifelong Learning and a Learning Society*, London, Routledge.

Edwards, R. (1998) 'Flexibility, reflexivity and reflection in the contemporary workplace', *International Journal of Lifelong Education* 17, 6: 377-388.

Edwards, R. and Usher, R. (1999) *Final Frontier? Globalisation and Pedagogy*, London, Routledge.

Foucault, M. (1979) *Discipline and Punish: the Birth of the Prison*, Harmondsworth, Penguin.

Fryer, R. (1997) *Learning for the Twenty-First Century. First Report of the National Advisory Group for Continuing Education and Lifelong Learning*, London, DfEE.

Giddens, A. (1990) *The Consequences of Modernity*, Cambridge, Polity Press.

Glyn, A. (1996) 'The assessment: unemployment and inequality', *Oxford Review of Economic Policy*, 11, 1: 1-25.

Handy, C. (1985) *The Future of Work*, Oxford, Basil Blackwell.

Hart, M. (1992) *Working and Educating for Life*, London, Routledge.

Johnston, B. and Lundvall, B. (1991) 'Flexibility and institutional learning', in Jessop, B., Kastendiek, H., Nielsen, K. and Pedersen, O. (eds) *The Politics of Flexibility*, Aldershot, Edward Elgar.

Kennedy, H. (1997) *Learning Works: Widening Participation in Further Education*, Coventry, FEFC.

Lash, S. and Urry, J. (1994) *Economies of Signs and Space*, London, Sage.

Levin, B. (1998) 'An epidemic of education policy: (what) can we learn from each other?', *Comparative Education* 34, 2: 131-141.

Miller, P. and Rose, N. (1993) 'Governing economic life', in Gane, M. and Johnson, T. (eds) *Foucault's New Domains*, London, Routledge.

National Committee of Inquiry into Higher Education (1997), *Higher Education in the Learning Society: Summary Report*, Norwich, HMSO.

Schuller, T. (1998) 'Three steps towards a learning society', *Studies in the Education of Adults*, 30, 1: 11-20.

Secretary of State for Education and Employment (1998) *The Learning Age: a Renaissance for a New Britain*, London, The Stationery Office.

Stronach, I. and MacLure, M. (1997) *Educational Research Undone: the Postmodern Embrace*, Buckingham, Open University Press.

Yates, P. (1994) 'In search of new ideas in management', *The Guardian*, 3 March.

4 Adult Education with Theological Reflection: A Multi-Disciplinary Approach through Open Learning

CELIA DEANE-DRUMMOND

Abstract

This article is rooted in the particular experience of designing an adult education masters programme for adult educators working in specifically Christian contexts. It looks at the changing philosophy of adult education in universities and how such a development coheres with trends towards a postmodernist culture. Issues arising from the mode of delivery of the programme through open learning are discussed, including some of the restraints and problems encountered. The way such a process influences theoretical issues in the newly emerging theology of adult education is explored.

Introduction

It is widely recognised that adult education embraces a wide collection of methods and frameworks of knowledge that makes it difficult to define its parameters. Historically the early 20th century pioneers in adult education were those with strong Christian ideals. Albert Mansbridge (1876-1952), for example, rooted his concern for adult education in Christian socialism. He was particularly anxious to reach out to the underprivileged and the working class (Alfred, 1991). The origin of the concept of lifelong learning can be traced to Bail Yeaxlee, who was a deeply committed Christian. He believed that all those who engaged in lifelong learning would automatically be propelled towards Christian values and this would lead to a harmonious, egalitarian social existence (Cross-Durrant, 1991: 48-9).

Cross-Durrant suggests that while the Christian basis for adult education was naive, the idea of a philosophical basis for adult education is acceptable. Her view reflects the gradual removal of religious concepts from adult education policy to such an extent that even those wishing to teach Christian adult education only have wide access to university courses that are based on alternative secular philosophies. Since then the proliferation of alternative approaches to adult education have fostered very different values. For the present example it is relevant to consider the particular framework in which the programme that is being discussed is set, before moving on to consider particular practical aspects concerned with the method of delivery through open learning.

A Framework for Development

Adult education and theology: can there be connections?

The debates around the validity of combining adult education with theology are part of a wider debate about the relationship between education and theology. John Hull has shown that education need not make people religious, as the early pioneers hoped, but to exclude religion is to exclude a defining attribute to being human (Hull, 1984). One of the most vociferous critics of this approach, Paul Hirst, has portrayed theology as dependent on faith commitment and uncritical passing on of beliefs (Hirst, 1974). Hull has exposed this view of theology as naïve and limited. Theology is, however, distinct from philosophy in that it includes a practice, a 'doing' as well as 'studying', a religious consciousness, as well as analysis of religious behaviour. Since these earlier debates there has been a more determined effort on the part of theologians and educators to explore the connections between education and theology. Issues of particular importance include the relationship between religious tradition and education (eg. May, 1990), the church and education (eg. Foster, 1990), or more recent explorations of feminist and cultural issues (eg. Mullino-Moore, 1990; Matsuoka, 1990). Other more recent collections examine particular tensions in the relationship between Christian theology and religious education (Astley and Francis, 1996).

It is relevant to ask about the range of *philosophies* of adult education before moving on to consider their possible connections with theology.

Elias, Merriam and Knowles have identified six broad categories namely: liberal, humanist, progressive, behaviourist, radical and analytical (Elias et al., 1995). The liberal tradition, with its emphasis on transmission of knowledge for its own sake, has characteristically been contrasted with vocational training. However, there are other philosophies worth considering such as progressive, which puts emphasis on the learner's needs rather than the teacher. The behaviourist uses particular criteria for assessment in order to regulate the outcome and much vocational training operates with this philosophy. While assessment criteria are still characteristic of most validation documents of even liberal courses of education approved by universities, there needs to be a greater awareness of the philosophy behind such statements and the message that this will give to potential students. Furthermore, what is the relationship between vocational training and education? Can adult education combine approaches or does one necessarily exclude the other? Dolly suggests that the two can co-exist in a creative way (Dolly, 1995).

Humanists argue for choice and development of learners as *persons*, rather than controls by external agencies. Tutors become facilitators of learning. The changing model of priests as those who enable the religious development of the laity reflects this more humanist approach to learning in Christian contexts (Willis, 1993). Course design needs to take the emphasis on persons into account and allow sufficient contact to cater as far as possible for the needs of individuals. Radical philosophy of adult education has the transformation of society in view, rather than simply its reform. Radical philosophy has its echoes in theologies of liberation, pioneered by Latin American liberation theologians, such as Gutiérrez and Boff (Gutiérrez, 1988; Boff and Boff, 1987).

While radical reform was the keynote of much of the earlier university-based adult education, there are signs that it is being replaced by a commitment to 'improved work prospects', 'wealth creation' and 'individual development' (Benn and Fieldhouse, 1996). This is also apparent in a North American context, where economic priority and market forces are replacing community and explicit social responsibility (Griffith, 1996). Does this represent an acceptable shift in values for adult education? John Hull believes that the dominant culture today is one that is captive to money, rather than any higher ideals (Hull, 1996a). The Christian voice needs to be heard in this context and join with others who would wish to resist these changes. We will be returning to this issue again later. Why has this come about? One of the reasons may be the drift towards postmodernist views, which seems to leave a lacuna of uncertainty. Elias's volume (1995) did not discuss postmodernist philosophy and it has surprisingly little attention paid to it in other books dedicated to the exploration of the philosophy of Christian religious education (Astley, 1994).

Adult education in a postmodern context

The traditional liberal approach to adult education arose in the cultural context of modernity, which has its origins in the Enlightenment. This period was marked by industrialisation, capitalist world market economy, the growth of science and technology and overall optimism about progress undergirded by a certainty in the foundations of knowledge (Featherstone, 1990). Postmodernism, by contrast, is characterised by changing socio-economic structures towards flexibility of labour markets, globalisation and integration of national economies. The resultant uncertain market for goods and services leads to customised markets replacing mass production and the pressure to develop local identities in the face of the homogenous forces of globalisation. Parallel shifts in the philosophy of knowledge leads to distrust in any foundation for knowledge, the rejection of all universals and a scepticism towards transcendental claims. The power and purpose of education is now no longer certain, but more fluid and open to change. Lyotard has suggested that information technology is critical in turning knowledge into a commodity (Lyotard, 1984: 5). Hammersley believes that in practice this forces educational institutions to move from a professional to a market orientation (Hammersley, 1992: 172). We will be returning to the way that this is particularly relevant to distance education in the section below.

What would adult education in a postmodern context look like? First of all, it has to take into account the consumer culture (Usher et al., 1997: 15). The significance of consumer goods is that they are *signs* of individuation. Adult education is about the creation of self-identity and worth in competition with other demands on time and leisure. The modernist ideal search for truth is being replaced by a freer, experimental and more open approach to learning. Leirman and Anckaert have shown that one of the problems experienced by adults was a sense of *lack of meaning* and there was little optimism that adult education could meet this challenge (Leirman and Anckaert, 1993). They suggest that in a postmodern culture the search for meaning can only be carried out at the grassroots level by individuals who share their experiences with others. This emphasis on local development is important in terms of fostering appropriate contexts where learning can take place. While at first sight these trends might seem to work against the development of adult education and theology, deeper reflection suggests that this is not necessarily the case. In a postmodern context acknowledgement of the religious is once again one voice among others that deserves to be heard. Both theology and adult education face the challenge of postmodernism. There are a number of issues of relevance here.

The first issue to consider is what are the values implicit in postmodernist approaches to education? Andrews has traced the tradition of university education to the monastic ideal, where academics take on some of the features of the apostolic tradition (Andrews, 1996). Civic universities were seen as a welcome break from the male, elitist, introspective and residential formula of traditional establishments. While the comparison was partly historical and partly analogical, the association of ecclesiology and, by implication, theology with the kind of narrow restrictions imposed by monastic life becomes a prevailing mythology. Further evidence for this attitude can be found in Taylor's critical stance towards the fact that the structure of education in schools is still influenced by the Church of England, even though church membership has declined (Taylor, 1998: 5). However, theology is itself influenced by postmodernism so that it becomes a more dynamic, open approach (Lakeland, 1997: 85-6). In addition, the Church of England's education programme is making steps to come to terms with different aspects of postmodernity (Board of Education, 1997). Some of the values implicit in postmodernism can be welcomed, others, such as the attachment to consumerism need careful evaluation. The way this might contribute to a theology of education will be discussed in the third part of this article.

A second related issue to consider is: Is it legitimate to include education in values and spirituality in adult education programmes? A postmodern approach would seem to affirm the latter, though it raises some interesting areas for debate between religion and education. Halstead and Taylor, for example, have made a case for 'values education' from a secular perspective (Halstead and Taylor, 1998). This distinguishes values from spirituality, though spiritual and moral development in children are normally considered together (SCAA, 1996). The latter document refers to the importance of spirituality for 'adult life'. The reluctance of adult educators to deal with this issue adequately outside specifically Christian adult education no doubt reflects the perceived break from ecclesiastical authority and the reluctance to taint education with religious concepts. Ironically, many university departments of theology and religious studies are similarly reluctant to teach spirituality because it is considered to be too closely associated with religious practice and against the liberal tradition of education based on secular ideals. However, in view of the current search for meaning in adults, mentioned above, it seems that clearer teaching on spirituality from different religious perspectives would be a welcome development. Obviously, any practical research into the religious beliefs of others has to be conducted with a sensitivity that respects the 'other' and the most suitable research method is one that is participatory. This echoes what Usher et al. have suggested as a postmodern research method, one that 'oversteps the limits' and is both constructing and constructed through a reflexive, open approach by the researcher (Usher et al., 1997: 191).

The Design and Management of Materials

The development of open learning

We will now turn to the more specific case study of the development of a programme in adult education with theological reflection in the light of the current shifts in adult education and its possible relationship to theology. The programme entitled *Adult Education with Theological Reflection* was developed as a joint venture between a university college affiliated to a secular civic university in collaboration with the Church of England[1]. Paradoxically, perhaps, the university college itself was founded by the Church of England, but relies on its academic credibility by validation through a university founded on secular values. The project was partly funded by an education charity that has religious foundations. This open partnership between the Church and the college could be seen as a new departure for a civic university, especially in the light of the discussion above. Yet we will argue that the changing shape of education in both churches and university is such that theology represents a *widening* of horizons, rather than their restriction. Throughout the development of the programme the college and the board of education worked closely together to refine and develop materials that drew on the skills of staff from both communities. While those who were trained in an academic setting found it more difficult to design packages that were interactive and 'user-friendly' for students, those who were experienced as trainers found the academic resourcing more difficult. However, the partnership is proving very fruitful for both parties in creating packages that overall are both academically credible, but also stimulating for students. Unlike the mass produced open learning programmes, the staff concerned find that they have many functions to fulfil, such as that of designer, writer, lecturer, student tutor/counsellor and so on.

The programme was originally intended for students wishing to study at masters level. We believed that prior to the development of open learning resources it was essential that the content of the modules be tested through face-to-face teaching. The added investment in time proved invaluable. Not only were we able to obtain constructive feedback and comments from students taking this programme in the taught mode, but also those very comments could be incorporated into the final open learning package.

We are using the term open learning in preference to distance learning, because distance learning can sometimes be seen as more rigid in its structure and content (Rowntree, 1992: 13-29). Jarvis has criticised distance learning as a mode of teaching that he believes relies on the 'Fordist' philosophy of mass production, dominated by market forces (Jarvis, 1997: 111-120). His assumption that all distance learning is necessarily mass-produced for vast numbers of faceless students with writers removed from their students is misleading in the present context. The total enrolment number is relatively small, about 15 students each year. This allows for much more individual attention than he implies. Jarvis argues that the packaging and marketing of knowledge is centrally controlled and carefully regulated. However, by taking into account students comments from a taught course the material presented is more flexible and open to student input compared with a conventional lecture course. Overall, the advantages of learning at a distance, in particular the *access* to learning that this allows, outweigh the disadvantages. Most of the major problems encountered with distance education seem to be associated with mass production (Henri and Kaye, 1993). We have encountered fewer difficulties because of its relatively small scale; as such this is perhaps the open learning most appropriate for a postmodern, rather than modernist culture.

It is widely recognised that one of the difficulties of designing open learning materials is the provision of accurate feedback to students after particular activities (Rowntree, 1994: 101). The input from students on the taught programme facilitated the development of suitable feedback, as well as providing a 'humanising' element to the packages themselves. The disadvantage of this process is that some of the students who took the taught programme felt hard done by, as they perceived that they were the 'guinea-pigs' on the programme. Nonetheless, most welcomed the opportunity to have access to high quality resources of the type not normally available for taught programmes. They were also charged fees commensurate with other taught courses, which gave them substantial financial saving.

Those who register come from a variety of backgrounds within adult education/theology contexts and include non-stipendiary ministers, adult education officers/advisers, training managers, area coordinators for development agencies such as Christian Aid, priests and ministers from a variety of churches including the Church of England and the United Reformed Church, training officers for clergy, lay readers and training officers. Not all those who express interest in the programme are working in religious contexts, but all have a concern to bring together adult education theory and practice with Christian theological perspectives.

Particular account has to be taken of the type of learners in any open learning programme. Evans notes the difficulty of designing open-learning materials when the students are still unknown (Evans, 1994: 120). However, the flexibility of the content is such that it can take account of the diversity of student interest. Most modules draw on the particular working context of students as an element in the learning process. In practice we found that a small percentage of students had neither the time nor the necessary skills to work consistently at masters level. We therefore introduced an additional programme validated at the final year undergraduate level three, that is an advanced certificate and advanced diploma in adult education with theological reflection (CAS/DAS). All modules have learning outcomes provided at level three and masters level M, so that students know what is required of them at each level. Students who begin to work at Level M can transfer to the CAS/DAS programme and *vice versa*.

A multi-disciplinary approach

One of the advantages of this programme is that it draws on two fields of study in a creative synthesis of ideas. As we noted above, many of those who register for the programme are involved in adult education in church contexts. They may have acquired their theological knowledge through local church work and practice. Others are more specifically trained as church ministers from a wide variety of church backgrounds.

One of the core modules entitled *Theology of Adult Education* was designed specifically to help students learn the skills of theological reflection. A drawback of this component is that there is relatively little written material on the specific relationship between adult education and Christian theology. In a sense the students are inevitably working at the frontier of knowledge in this area. Most students have enjoyed the challenge and apply their skills successfully to other core modules, such as *How Adults Learn* and *Understanding Process in Adult Education*.

Another aspect of this programme worth highlighting is the development of a way of working intermediate between academic liberal education and vocational training. As Janice Dolly points out, there need to be new avenues developed which serve to build bridges between education and training (Dolly, 1995). Most adult educational programmes still tend to be either vocational for professional development, or focus on the academic knowledge content for its own sake. Lierman and Anckaert have devised a classification scheme for adult education which transcends the liberal/vocational divide (Leirman and Anckaert, 1993). They have suggested two broad categories of adult education, that of personal development towards communication, relational skills and participation in culture and society *or* education in view of health, family life and professional work. However, this programme seems to defy classification in this schema as well, since it encourages personal development and relational skills, but is also relevant to the professional life of many of the students. There is a specific requirement for skill development and assessment at the summer school held in September each year, which is a compulsory component for two of the core modules of study.

Students are encouraged to draw on their experience at their place of work and use this specifically as a resource for their assignments. This is not quite the same as work-based learning, since students do not negotiate their own learning outcomes. Nonetheless, learning outcomes are flexible enough so that students' written assignments are attuned to their particular contexts. In general, the religious context of the teaching practice of the students means that their learners are attending on a voluntary non-fee-paying basis, rather than for a particular qualification. These learners have highly variable educational backgrounds and interests and reflect the breadth encompassed in life-long learning communities.

The bridge between training and education is only really feasible because of the network of local tutors, who help students link their work practice with the specific academic requirements. In general the tutoring scheme is highly successful, though the variable number of students in a given area year by year can be disconcerting for tutors. The number of students in each area is less than six and in some cases one-to-one tutoring is operative. However, for the elective modules, normally taken in the second or third year of study, all students are given a choice of group tutorials in two different locations with a particular specialist for that module. The advantage of this scheme is that it allows students who have begun working together at the summer school to continue fostering these relationships.

Theology and Adult Education: An Exploration

Those working at the interface of theology and adult education seem to opt for either a community-based model for learning or an emphasis on individual development (Slee, 1993). The classical approach looks to the individual learner who is involved in a quest for meaning. The goal of education in this case is to work for the creation of an autonomous self-reflective person, who shares the skills of a critical, analytical thinker, but is open to challenge (Hull, 1990). Theological ideas that cohere with this approach stress the uniqueness of the human person as made in the image of God.

Those who adopt the more community-based approach envisage education as the work of a community by a network of people in relationships. The goal of education becomes the transformation of society through prophecy, protest, and action. The role of the individual in this case is to be a contributor to wider structural change. Theological ideas that cohere with this approach stress the idea of God in relationships. This may be expressed through notions such as the traditional Christian understanding of God as Trinity, or more radical perspectives, such as God as the liberator of oppressive relations between humans or in relationship to the earth.

The first model is associated with a stress on the idea of development and growth for the individual person, while the second is associated with the idea of social transformation and change. The philosophy of the first seems to be rooted in the modernist optimism about the capacity of the human being for self-transformation. The second is more an anti-modernist position that has its roots in Marxist philosophy and socialism. We are less convinced that the social reform strategy of the second category can be termed postmodern in the way that Slee describes, since by its very nature postmodernism refuses to accept any grand narratives.

The programme we have described seems to defy either categorisation. On the one hand, it allows for the development of the individual and is tailored to suit particular student aspirations, while, on the other hand, it provides work both with and for a community of persons in a Christian context. Those workers in the church, such as Anglican lay readers, can have their work accredited through an academic institution. It thus has a function in empowerment, which is then carried forward through the particular Christian education of adults that forms the basis of practice for most, if not all, the students. The informal, small gatherings of students and their tutors generate their own community basis for education, one that allows free exploration that draws on imagination in a way that is difficult in large classes. The sharing of relevant experience rooted in the life of the communities where the students work, either as paid or unpaid workers, reinforces the grounding of research in practice. To date, almost all the students have chosen research dissertations that are open and participatory, exploratory and search for connections between theory and practice. As Usher et al. point out, the researcher and the research in a postmodern context develop stories about the self and others (Usher et al., 1997: 224-5).

The problem with taking postmodernism to its limits is how to introduce a critique without the presumptions of the grand narrative. At the other end of the scale, how do we avoid becoming immersed in a sea of relativism? If theology is to be a public theology it needs to take account of the academy, religious communities and society. The dilemma is that in claiming neutrality towards all religious viewpoints it is easy to slip into a detached way of being that seems to transcend all religious traditions, but in the end only serves as a strategy for domination (Ford, 1995: 156). Usher et al. argue that postmodernism enables a questioning of objectivity and value neutrality in making knowledge claims, but does not necessarily reject these claims for what they are, namely socially formed, historically located cultural constructs, thus 'partial and specific to particular discourse and purposes' (Usher et al., 1997: 7). In this sense postmodernism is not anti-rational or relativistic.

From a theological perspective it becomes virtually impossible to engage in any theological reflection without making some reference to claims of universality, at least in terms of belief in God. Hence, while Christian theology can become more cautious about an arrogant attitude towards other religions, it still needs a public face that is prepared to witness to the scandal of the universal significance of the particular event of Jesus Christ. Any denial would be meaningless from a Christian perspective. Christian theology challenges, then, the postmodern notion that all our religious statements are *just* social and cultural constructs. There is a 'more' as well, which gives theology its particularity in a way that swims against the tide of modern philosophy.

In the expression of this 'more' we find Christian spirituality, which is a core element in the human search for meaning. Hull points out the ambiguity of the term spirituality; it can be other-wordly or secular and political, it can be based in reason or intuition (Hull, 1996b). Christian spirituality has variegated forms and expressions, but all emerge through reference to the 'Other' that is God. The temptation for Christianity in a capitalist modernist society was to create a spirituality that was highly individualistic. Today spirituality is more likely to be influenced by other voices such as the new age, feminist or green spirituality. The adult educator has to be sensitive to the varied spiritual experiences to be found in Christian communities and respect that faith is for them always from the inside, rather than the outside.

How do we distinguish between these competing voices which seem to strike at the core of religious experience? We would argue that the theology that is most relevant in this context is that of the wisdom tradition. Wisdom in its human aspect is the art of discernment, of distinguishing one from another, not simply by reason, but through an inclusive holistic engagement with all the senses. Wisdom which emerged in the Hebrew tradition included the insights from other cultures, but helped to steer the daily lives of ordinary people in a way that was honouring to God. Wisdom, furthermore, develops with age and is thus particularly relevant for adults who come to the task of learning with their own life-experiences. Wisdom in the Judao-Christian scriptures gradually came to be seen as the personification of the feminine, one created at the very beginning in order for creation to emerge. Wisdom is both transcendent, with God, but is also involved in the life of the world. Wisdom can become the basis for the construction of a theology of creation (Deane-Drummond, 1997).

Once we see wisdom as the means through which we understand a theology of adult education some of the difficulties of postmodernism can be confronted. Wisdom will embrace the local grounding of projects in local communities and the marriage of theory and practice. Wisdom resists attempts to be captive to the consumer money culture, while recognising the need to be practical in the development of new proposals and projects. Wisdom gives those who work in the context of religious communities self-respect, it no longer matters whether particular religious beliefs are fashionable or not. Wisdom is patient in trying to understand the needs of the learners and fit tasks that are appropriate for the individuals involved. Wisdom, finally, is not anti-rational, but refuses to allow reason to be the dominant paradigm in decision making. Wisdom encourages a multidisciplinary approach, so that insights from education, business studies, vocational training, theology, philosophy and the social sciences can be drawn out in a co-operative way, rather than through hostility and competition. Is wisdom another meta-narrative? No, as wisdom itself is multifaceted and only through different lenses can different problems and difficulties be resolved. There is rarely simply one solution to any situation; wisdom suggests, rather than forces the outcome.

To conclude. The changing face of adult education needs to take into account all aspects of human experience, including the religious. The prevailing philosophy of our culture is that of postmodernism and the development of adult educational programmes needs to be aware of this cultural matrix. The design of open learning programmes that are customised for particular groups of individuals can serve to widen access to learning and offer a real basis for learning that is relevant to the work place. A multidisciplinary approach to adult education offers a new and dynamic way of enlarging the horizons of those engaged in adult education. A theology of wisdom is offered as a fruitful approach to explore the relationship between adult education and theology, one that takes into account the postmodern context, but refuses to be governed by it.

Note

1   For further details of the modular components of this programme, see Deane-Drummond and Ineson (1998).

References

Alfred, D. (1991) 'Albert Mansbridge (1876-1952)' in Jarvis, P. (ed) *Twentieth Century Thinkers in Adult Education*, London, Routledge, pp.17-37.

Andrews, J. (1996) 'Communities, Universities and the Wider Educational Scene', in Elliott, J., Francis, R., Humphreys and Istance, D. (eds) *Communities and Their Universities: The Challenge of Lifelong Learning*, London, Lawrence and Wishart, pp.107-117.

Astley, J. (1994) *The Philosophy of Christian Religious Education*, Birmingham, Religious Education Press.

Astley, J. and Francis, L.J. (1996) *Christian Theology and Religious Education: Connections and Contradictions*, London, SPCK.

Benn, R. and Fieldhouse, R. (1996) 'Notions of Community for University Continuing Education', in Elliott, J., Francis, H., Humphreys and Istance, D. (eds) *Communities and Their Universities: The Challenge of Lifelong Learning*, London, Lawrence and Wishart, pp.25-36.

Board of Education of the General Synod of the Church of England (1997) *Tomorrow is Another Country: Education in a Post-Modern World*, London, Church House Publishing.

Boff, K. and Boff, C. (1987) *Introducing Liberation Theology*, Tunbridge Wells, Burns and Oates.

Cross-Durrant, A. (1991) 'Basil Yeaxlee and the Origins of Lifelong Education', in Jarvis, P. (ed) *Twentieth Century Thinkers in Adult Education*, London, Routledge, pp.38-61.

Deane-Drummond, C. (1997) 'Sophia: The Feminine Face of God as a Metaphor for an Eco Theology', *Feminist Theology* 16, pp.11-31.

Deane-Drummond, C. and Ineson, H. (1998) 'Theological Reflection', *Adults Learning* 9 (6), pp.20-22.

Dolley, J. (1995) 'Building Bridges Between Education and Training: the Changing Context of Learning', *Adults Learning* 7 (1), pp.24-26.

Elias, J.L., Merriam, S.B. and Knowles, M.S. (1995) *Philosophical Foundations of Adult Education*, 2nd edition, Malabar, Kriegar.

Evans, T. (1994) *Understanding Learners in Open and Distance Education*, London, Kogan Page.

Featherstone, M. (1991) *Consumer Culture and Postmodernism*, London, Sage.

Ford, D.F. (1995) 'Concluding reflections: Constructing a Public Theology', in Young, F. (ed) *Dare We Speak of God in Public?* London, Mowbray, pp.151-161.

Foster, C.R. (1990) 'Education in the Quest for Church', in Seymour, J.L. and Miller, D.E. (eds) *Theological Approaches to Christian Education*, Nashville, Abingdon Press, pp.83-101.

Griffith, W.S. (1996) 'Communities, Universities and Change: Recent North American Experience', in Elliott, J., Francis, H., Humphreys, R. and Istance, D. (eds) *Communities and Their Universities: The Challenge of Lifelong Learning*, London, Lawrence and Wishart, pp.78-92.

Gutiérrez, G. (1988) *A Theology of Liberation*, revised edition, London, SCM Press.

Halstead, J.M. and Taylor, M. (1998) *The Development of Values, Attitudes and Personal Qualities. A Review of Recent Research*, London, OFSTED.

Hammersley, M. (1992) 'Reflections on the Liberal University: Truth, Citizenship and the Role of the Academic', *International Studies in the Sociology of Education* 2 (2), pp.165-183.

Henri, F. and Kaye, A. (1993) 'Problems of Distance Education; in Harry, K., John, M. and Keegan, D. (eds) *Distance Education: New Perspectives*, London, Routledge, pp.25-31.

Hirst, P. (1974) *Moral Education in a Secular Society*, London, University of London Press.

Hull, J. (1990) 'Christian Nurture and Critical Openness', in Francis, L. and Thatcher, A. (eds) *Christian Perspectives and Education: A Reader in the Theology of Education*, Leominster, Fowler Wright, pp.306-319.

Hull, J. (1994) 'What is Theology of Education?', in Hull, J. (ed) *Studies in Religion and Education*, Lewis, Falmer Press, pp.249-272.

Hull, J. (1996a) 'Christian Education in a Capitalist Society: Money and God', in Ford, D. and Stamps, D.L. (eds) *Essentials of Christian*

Community, Essays in Honour of Daniel W. Hardy, Edinburgh, T & T Clark, pp.241-252.

Hull, J. (1996b) 'The Ambiguity of Spiritual Values', in Halstead, J.M. and Taylor, M.J. (eds) *Values in Education and Education in Values*, London, The Falmer Press, pp.33-44.

Jarvis, P. (1997) *Ethics and Education for Adults in a Late Modern Society*, Leicester, NIACE.

Lakeland, P. (1997) *Postmodernity: Christian Identity in a Fragmented Age*, Augsburg, Fortress Press.

Lierman, W. and Anckaert, L. (1993) 'Moral Issues in Adult Education: From Life Problems to Educational Goals and Post-Modern Uncertainty', in Jarvis, P. and Walters, N. (eds) *Adult Education and Theological Interpretations*, Malibar, Kreiger, pp.259-272.

Lyotard, J.F. (1984) *The Postmodern Condition: A Report on Knowledge*, Manchester, Manchester University Press.

Matsuoka, F. (1990) 'The Church in a Racial-Minority Situation', in Seymour, J.L. and Miller, D.E. (eds) *Theological Approaches to Christian Education*, Nashville, Abingdon Press, pp. 102-121.

May, M. (1990) 'Tradition and Education', in Seymour, J.L. and Miller, D.E. (eds) *Theological Approaches to Christian Education*, Nashville, Avingdon Press, pp.27-42.

Moore, M.E.M. (1990) 'Feminist Theology and Education', in Seymour, J.L. and Miller, D.E. (eds) *Theological Approaches to Christian Education*, Nashville, Abingdon Press, pp.63-80.

Rowntree, D. (1992) *Exploring Open and Distance Learning*, Milton Keynes, Open University Press.

Rowntree, D. (1994) *Preparing Materials for Open, Distance and Flexible Learning*, London, Kogan Page.

SCAA, (1996) *Education for Adult Life: The Spiritual and Moral Development of Young People, Discussion Paper Number 6*, London, The School Curriculum and Assessment Authority.

Slee, N. (1993) 'Endeavours in a Theology of Adult Education', in Jarvis, P. and Walters, N. (eds) *Adult Education and Theological Interpretations*, Malibar, Kreiger, pp.325-346.

Taylor, M. (1998) *Values in Education and Education Values: A Guide to the Issues*, London, Association of Teachers and Lecturers.

Usher, R., Bryant, I. and Johnson, R. (1997) *Adult Education and the Postmodern Challenge: Learning Beyond the Limits*, London, Routledge.

Willis, P. (1993) 'Teaching - Catechism and Preaching', in Jarvis, P. and Walters, N. (eds) *Adult Education and Theological Interpretations*, Malabar, Kriegar, pp.67-87.

5 Identity, Risk and Lifelong Learning

ROBIN USHER

Abstract

In this chapter, lifelong learning is understood in terms of its significations in relation to the risk society that characterises the postmodern condition. The contemporary role of the education of adults is examined within the context of uncertainty that is a consequence of that condition. It is argued that changing conceptions of knowledge and the need to understand knowledge in terms of its location in different social practices means that lifelong learning cannot be seen simply as a structure of provision but as a signifier with many different significations. This poses the need for practitioners working in the field of the education of adults to rethink their conceptions of adult learning and their role as institutional providers of such learning.

Introduction

> The reflexive modern society is a learning society with lifelong learning as its
> hall-mark.   (Wildemeersch, Finger and Jansen, 1997: 18)

The field of practice that is the education of adults is a complex one which in the last decade or so has undergone a process of intense change. The changes have been such that many would agree that 'the entire project of adult education seems to have lost much of its historical legitimisation, and is surrounded by serious doubts about the direction that could or should be taken' (Wildemeersch, Finger and Jansen, 1997: 14).

Whilst the intensity of the change may be debatable, it seems to be the case that the education of adults both as a field of practice and an area of theorisation is now characterised by an uncertainty which takes the form of a questioning of what is distinctive about this field and what, in the face of this change and uncertainty, are its values and purposes. At the same time, however, this questioning and doubting is happening at a time when a greater number of adults, from a diversity of backgrounds, are entering an increasing variety of programmes than ever before, and where 'adult learning' is being foregrounded in a hitherto unprecedented way.

In the face of the challenges posed by late modernity or the condition of postmodernity, it can be argued that the hitherto structuring educational paradigms, theoretical groundings and practices are in urgent need of reconfiguration. In order to make sense of the change and uncertainty that characterise the contemporary scene, new conceptual resources and a different discourse about the education of adults is needed - whose purpose is a radical redescription located in contemporary culture and society rather than a set of abstract transcendental principles about lifelong learning.

Thus in the first part of this chapter I will highlight some of the key features of postmodernity and the accompanying contemporary socio-economic and cultural changes which are impacting on the educational scene. I will then go on to consider the contemporary nature of knowledge and from this argue that we urgently need to understand 'lifelong learning' but not in the way it has been hitherto understood - for example, as a set of principles about education, as a description of psychological processes or as a structure of provision. The activity of adult learning, located in different discourses and played out through different social practices of the postmodern, is learning which could be inside or outside educational institutions, not necessarily within the modernist educational project, and not necessarily bounded by what educators would traditionally define as the transmission of 'appropriate' and/or 'worthwhile' knowledge.

I will argue rather that 'lifelong learning' needs to be understood more as a signifier with many possible signifieds or meanings - and I would also argue that this is a way of understanding 'lifelong learning' that is more appropriate in the light of the significant place of signification in postmodernity. Essentially, I want to argue that 'lifelong learning' needs to be understood in terms of its *significations* (the meanings it has and the meanings it gives) in relation to its positionings within contemporary social practices. To elaborate a little without giving too much away at this stage - the traditional enterprise of institutionally-based and provision-led adult education is, it could be argued, at risk - a situation itself attributable to the characteristics of the postmodernity and the risk society in which adults now live. So the very identity of the education of adults as a structured field of study and practice has become problematic, precisely at a time when learning has become an important aspect in the formation of the socially located identities of contemporary subjects.

The Postmodern Condition

Postmodernity (or 'late modernity') is associated with such contemporary trends as the growth of service-sector employment, 'post' industrial social formations and post-Fordist models of production and work organisation and management. A revitalised and reconfigured capital accumulation based on globalisation and new communications technologies has led to the reformation and globalised integration of national economies, with market mechanisms as its most predominant social feature.

With the reconstruction of the workplace has come a discourse that foregrounds the 'workplace as a site of learning', and the social re-definition of skills where skills become performance-based 'competences'. There is also an increasingly fragmented and unequal, core-periphery labour market where those without skills, cultural capital, access to information or market power can usually expect only a marginalised existence. All this has created a demand both for a multi-skilled workforce and for access and compensatory measures, with corresponding opportunities for, and new directions in, the education of adults.

The development of communications in its widest sense, from travel to the increasing reach of the electronic media, underpins globalisation as global integration - an integration which induces a consciousness of the world as one place. But this integration is not at the expense of the local - far from being suppressed the local is actually stimulated by globalising processes. What results is a paradoxical situation where on the one hand globalisation devalues community and communitarian values, inducing the disembedding and disorienting effects that characterise the uncertainties of the risk society, whilst on the other hand its effects in stimulating specificity and encouraging difference enhances these very values, albeit in a reconfigured form.

In the cultural sphere, there has been a blurring of the boundaries between high culture, popular culture, the market and everyday life (Lash, 1990; Featherstone, 1991; Harvey, 1991). Postmodernity leads both to a culturalisation of the material world of goods and products and a materialisation of the world of culture. In effect, everything becomes 'culture' - witness for example, the redescription of the workplace in terms of 'culture'. Images and information - signifiers as cultural artefacts - become pre-eminent hallmarks of economic growth and innovation.

In this postmodern condition, a culture of consumption coupled with marketisation becomes central to the economy and to social life as a whole. Modernist centres of production - the factory, the assembly line, large-scale manufacturing - become increasingly displaced by centres of consumption - financial services, small-scale specialised enterprises, shopping malls and superstores, entertainment complexes, heritage and theme parks. Here lifestyle concerns manifested through consumption rather than production become significant. The influence of fashion, image and 'taste' pervade an increasingly all-embracing consumer culture and affect all social groups.

When cultural change becomes so closely linked with economic change, the resulting emphasis on the individual as a consumer means that socio-cultural distinction overlays socio-economic division. Even those with little or no capital are swept up in this signifying culture of consumption. It is here perhaps more than anywhere that hitherto guiding paradigms of institutional adult education are proving to be most inadequate. To anticipate, 'lifelong learning' becomes not simply an aspect of economic instrumentalism nor an assertion of enlightened humanism but also a way of constituting meaning in a consumer culture where learning becomes a sign to be consumed in the marking and defining of identity and difference.

The Risk Society and Individualisation

Beck's metaphor of the 'risk society' (Beck, 1992) aptly designated the uncertainty of contemporary social and personal life in the postmodern condition. There are two aspects to this. On the one hand, the consequence of modernity and its modernising thrust has been the unprecedented growth of globalised and unabating dangers and hazards - 'risks' which are unbounded by either time or space, which affect everyone but for which no one can be held accountable. As Lash and Wynne (1992) point out, it is the very incalculability of the risk that is the issue and which induces the uncertainty that characterises the risk society.

The other consequence of modernity is its individualising thrust. For example, an important feature of this contemporary postmodern scene is the redrawing by the state of its traditional boundaries of responsibility - one aspect of this being the withdrawal by the state of comprehensive welfare provision. This is an example of the more general trend whereby, paradoxically, structural change itself 'constrains' people to become progressively free of structures (Lash and Wynne, 1992). Consequently, the choices to be made in directing lives become more and more the responsibility of individuals - people must reflexively construct their own biographies. For individuals, matters of identity - who they are - become questions in need of an answer rather than those answers being structurally ready to hand.

There is therefore an uncertainty that arises from the erosion of social and normative frames of reference (the structures) that traditionally gave meaning to people's experience and coherence to their lives. Shaped by the moral horizons of the life chances appropriate to one's class, family, neighbourhood, religion, ethnicity, sex and age, these frames of reference provided a stable social identity even whilst imposing strict limits on the freedom to develop lifestyles, desires and aspirations that transcended those horizons.

In the contemporary risk society, the permanent and stable identification with the meaning perspectives and frames of reference of specific communities has become problematic. The pluralisation of society has challenged the unequivocal norms and values that once constituted the core of family life, class culture, etc. In the risk society, subjects have many different and contradictory options at their disposal for organising their lives and giving meaning to their experience.

Furthermore, as Giddens (1990) points out, as the range of information and media through which it is available multiply, so individuals reflexively produce more information about themselves as a condition for their on-going development. Given the explosion in the availability of information and the proliferation of signifying images, making choices and constructing biographies becomes both necessary and yet at the same time increasingly difficult. All this produces a situation where the very need to make decisions actually makes such decisions less secure - a situation of disembeddedness which overlays and accentuates the uncertainties produced by globalised risk.

Thus identity necessarily becomes a matter of reflexivity or self-reflection. Given that we all now have a reflexive biography, people, as Beck points out, learn to behave as the individual centre of action, as personal planning bureaus with respect to their own life courses, their competencies, orientations and relationships. Giddens in the same vein talks of the development of self-identity as a trajectory that individually has to be planned - in effect, a lifelong learning project - where subjects reflexively incorporate their experience into a self-narrative. The failure to do this leads to an exclusion from the opportunities that the risk society offers with respect to self-actualisation and identity development.

However, the need to function as a planning agency for one's life course coincides with conditions that seriously endanger the development of a stable and coherent identity. In the first place, the choices made are necessarily contingent. There are a lot of possible choices and where there is uncertainty identity development is a troubled and disjunctive process. People have to build continuity into their biographies amidst the bewildering change and multiple options they experience in the different and often contradictory social and cultural contexts in which they are situated. Secondly, identity development becomes strongly individualised and privatised. Where there is a de-differentiation between the public and the private, meaning and identity become disconnected from the public domain (or more accurately the public domain blurs into the private) and become matters alone of individualised concern.

Thirdly, through the communications revolution image and images have become all-pervasive. People become engulfed by images, to the extent where the distinction between reality and image breaks down in a condition of hyper-reality (Baudrillard, 1988). The hyper-real is a world of constantly proliferating images or simulacra (copies detached from their original but which still have meaning independently of their original) which become a desirable reality to be consumed. The way the world is experienced changes and it becomes experienced as fragmented and decentred. New forms of experience proliferate, experiences that are not rooted in a stable and unified self and a hitherto 'solid' sense of reality. Hence there is a continual shaping and reshaping of subjectivity and identity. In postmodernity, sensibilities are attuned to the troubled pleasure of constant and new experiencing where experiencing becomes its own end rather than a means to an end, a way of cultivating the desire for a constant making and remaking of subjectivity and identity.

Reactions to this risk society are of course many and complex although existential anxiety and concern is likely to be significant. But the argument I have just been making about the relationship between the image and the real would imply that this is not the only possible reaction. When fixed reference points and solid groundings becoming increasingly detached and shaky, the difficulty of disembeddedness could also become something to be accepted rather than regretted - to put it another way, a condition of being *at home with homelessness* (Bauman, 1992).

Given then, this individualising aspect of the risk society, it is hardly surprising that institutional adult education has been forced to diversify by individualising its own offer, gearing itself to the specific circumstances and needs of learners and more and more provided in new tailor-made forms, like modular and contract education, self-directed learning, open and distance learning. On the one hand, these developments can be seen as a necessary and pertinent response to the challenges of the risk society, significant institutional adjustments to the highly individualised needs of today's society - but at the same there is also a confirmation and reinforcement of the ongoing processes of individualisation - which of course many adult educators, particularly those who see their work as education for social action and transformation, find very worrying - an example of why adult education is seen by many as being 'at risk', a risk compounded by the possibility that education is fast becoming a simulacrum of the rational activity it was once supposed to be.

Changing Conceptions of Knowledge

So far I have been talking about the condition of postmodernity. At the same time, it is also possible to talk about the postmodern *attitude* by foregrounding Lyotard's now famous definition of the postmodern as incredulity towards grand narratives (Lyotard, 1984) - an ironic incredulity which carries with it a questioning of the notion of an authoring centre or foundations of knowledge and a scepticism about any claims that certain kinds of knowledge, by their very nature, must be accorded canonical status - ie. that some knowledge is *intrinsically* worthwhile and some is not. The decentring of the world that is a characteristic of postmodernity implies a *decentring* of knowledge - another aspect of disappearing fixed references and traditional anchoring points. At the same time, as knowledge continually assumes the form of information in computer networks and memory banks, it is subject to constant change whilst becoming more rapidly, almost overwhelmingly, available - itself mirroring the conditions of rapid change and bewildering instability of the risk society.

All this has paradoxical educational consequences. On the one hand, it has contributed to an erosion of the 'liberal' curriculum and an emphasis on performativity, on learning opportunities that optimise the efficiency of the economic and social system. On the other hand, the decentring of knowledge has resulted in a valuing of different sources and forms of knowledge (including knowledge that would not have traditionally been considered worthwhile) and a corresponding devaluing of specialist discipline-based knowledge.

As the means by which 'worthwhile' knowledge is generated and transmitted through dedicated institutions, educational discourses and practices have had a powerful role in the development, maintenance and legitimation of modernity. Education is a defining characteristic of modernity where it has been conceived as the social institution endowed with the mission of furthering social progress, and conferring on individuals the means of rational empowerment. It is the site where ideals of critical reason, individual autonomy and benevolent progress are disseminated and internalised and so it is here that the project of modernity is most obviously realised - a project that has emphasised mastering the world in the cause of human betterment by means of 'objective' knowledge and rational scientific approaches. The grand narratives which Lyotard tells us we now greet with incredulity are nonetheless inscribed in the very practices of education, whether in its liberal, progressive or radical variants. Goals, definition of needs, curriculum, pedagogy and organisational forms have been structured by the implicit social engineering of the project of modernity. Thus the contemporary sense of crisis, the questioning of roles and consequent self-certainty that is felt by many can be seen as a microcosm of the more general crisis of modernity.

Clearly, therefore, education generally does not fit easily into postmodernity, nor can it adapt readily to the contemporary scene. One reason for this is the way that it reflects changes in how people relate to the world - the decentred self of the risk society, the more fluid positioning of subjectivity, challenges both the assumption of the bounded yet autonomous 'natural' self that brings itself and the world under the control of reason which is at the heart of modernist education - this is why I referred earlier to education now as a simulacrum.

Secondly, in questioning the status and indeed the very existence of foundational knowledge there is also a challenge to scientific rationality, to existing concepts, structures and hierarchies of knowledge and to the part education plays in maintaining and reproducing these. If there are no sure foundations and no Archimedean points from which knowledge is generated and assimilated but instead a plurality of partial knowledges then the very foundations of discipline-based education are themselves undermined. Without foundations and a faith in scientificity, the certainty and determinacy for which modernity strives is no longer so certain, and with this a curriculum based on the dissemination of 'true' and certain knowledge and a pedagogy based on the authority of the teacher as 'master' of a discipline - all these become highly problematic.

Thirdly, the undermining of the modernist project in relation to education undermines the grand narratives of progress and hence the meaning of progress which that narrative embodies and disseminates. The modernist notion of progress is both teleological and totalising. But the postmodern attitude is one that foregrounds *change without teleology* implying that change at either the personal or social level can be partial, discontinuous, it can take a multiplicity of forms and fulfil a variety of ends, or even simply be its own end.

Lyotard (1984) argues that the difference between modern and postmodern conditions lies in the *purpose* of knowledge. In modernity, the generation and dissemination of knowledge is justified in relation to the grand narratives which themselves are the basis for the development of state-supported educational practices and of educational institutions, curricula and pedagogy that embody and disseminate them. In postmodernity, knowledge has different and multiple purposes. Given that it is no longer so closely related to legitimating grand narratives, these purposes are complex and to some extent contradictory, a reflection perhaps of the ambiguous tendencies characterising the postmodern. However, one clearly discernible tendency (and one which is often emphasised to the exclusion of any others) is to do with knowledge being valued for its 'performativity'. This is usually taken to mean that the purpose of knowledge is the optimising of efficient performance. This is the most influential way of understanding 'performativity' although as we shall see later, it is by no means the only way. This contemporarily influential view of knowledge is closely linked to the post-Fordism and the information-communications revolution I mentioned earlier.

Given the individualisation inherent in the risk society, educational processes themselves become individualised, reconstituted as a market relationship between producer and consumer. Knowledge becomes commodified and is exchanged on the basis of the performative value it has for the learner as *consumer*. Hence the contemporary demand for education that is 'value-adding'. The marketisation of knowledge in the form of information spreads from the commercial realm into educational practices. Educational institutions increasingly find it difficult to claim a monopoly in the generation and dissemination of knowledge. When knowledge takes the form of information, it circulates through networks that evade the control of educational institutions (Plant, 1995). Moreover, educational institutions become part of the market, in the business of selling knowledge as a commodity and therefore reconstructing themselves as enterprises dedicated to marketing this commodity and to competing in the knowledge 'business'. Not only do they become geared to producing the personnel of post-Fordism, they are themselves expected to behave in post-Fordist ways (Ball, 1990).

The valuing of knowledge in terms of its performativity suggests that there is a co-implication of contemporary discourses of individualistic learner-centredness and current trends towards the marketisation of learning opportunities. Given this situation, it is hardly surprising that a 'vast market for competence in operational skills' is created (Lyotard, 1984: 51). The activities of professionals become, and this is obviously significant for the situation adult education practitioners find themselves in, increasingly governed by managerialism and the criteria of efficiency and effectiveness. Skilled performance embodied in 'competences' become an increasingly significant part of the agenda and an increasingly important and valued outcome of learning. Hence vocational and professional training become prominent and competency qualifications become a generalised standard to measure the meaning and significance of educational activities.

But at the same time, it would be mistaken and over-simplistic to not take account of other trends and even of countervailing tendencies within the trends mentioned. In modernity, education is concerned with shaping a certain kind of disciplined subjectivity and the pursuit of certain pre-defined goals; in postmodernity knowledge is also involved with shaping subjectivity albeit in a different and less stable way. As education in the postmodern becomes detached from legitimating grand narratives, it also becomes increasingly implicated with specific cultural contexts, on localised and particularised knowledges, on the needs of consumption and the cultivation of desire and on the valuing of a multiplicity of experience.

Consumption and Knowledge in the Postmodern

This is probably an appropriate point to bring these various tendencies together and complicate the picture even more by introducing consumption. This is a difficult topic because whilst there is a reluctant acceptance that consumption figures importantly in people's lives, any importance it may be accorded is often accounted for in terms of the language of manipulation and false consciousness. I would argue that although it is certainly the case that not all may consume equally, it is also the case that all are affected by consumer culture and consumerist discourse and images. Furthermore, this is not to be accounted for simply by pointing to manipulation and the inducing of false consciousness since it neglects the dimension of desire that is manifested in consumption and to which even oppressed groups are not immune.

Postmodernism as social theory has had much to say on the nature and significance of consumption in postmodernity and on how people develop their identities through consumption (Urry, 1994). Within consumer culture, there are tendencies favouring the aestheticisation of life and hence an emphasis on lifestyle, a whole range of practices that revolve around the eclectic and the aesthetic. Certain sites become centres of aesthetic consumption - urban areas, re-developed and gentrified, shopping malls, museums, theme and heritage parks - all providing spaces for new experiences and the forming of new identities.

Consumption, or the active use of goods and services, enables people to establish and demarcate a distinctive social space. But consumption is not so much about goods but about signs and significations. Consumer objects function as a classification system, as markers of difference, that codes behaviour and differentiates individuals. Consumer culture is therefore an economy of signs where individuals and groups communicate messages about social position and worth.

Now, it is easy enough to see the education of adults in the contemporary moment as being simply that of supplying the multi-skilled and flexible post-Fordist worker for the globalised economy. Yet this would be simplistic since there is also a need to examine the consequences for the education of adults of consumer culture. First, long-term changes in affluence have enabled an increasing number of adults in Western society to exercise choice in the purchase of goods and services, how they spend their money and how they use their time. Second, the notion of citizens as consumers (of learning) stands at the heart of contemporary policy developments. This is partly an ideological shift and partly to do with a growing private sector of providers. Linked to this is the widespread development of video and audio cassettes and increasingly sophisticated multi-media programmes available commercially which provide adults with a range of self-study options previously unavailable. Third, educational activities have become consumer goods in themselves, purchased as the result of choice within market-place where educational products compete with leisure and entertainment products. The boundaries between leisure, entertainment and education have blurred as for example, people increasingly learn from television programmes aimed at entertaining, and educational activities geared to consumer satisfaction produce outcomes previously associated only with leisure and entertainment. Fourth, and getting back to a point made earlier, consumer culture is marked by individuation and it is this which also characterises contemporary trends in adult learning. In order to explore the changing relationships between consumption, individuation and adult learning, we need to look much more closely at areas such as personal development and cultural creativity. The fact that there has been a growth in activities related to the fashioning of a new identity is no coincidence.

Patterns of adult participation in education and the increased significance of non-institutional adult learning cannot be understood then without reference to consumption. Taking account of it means that we have to consider the education of adults in the context of a cultural economy of signs where consumer choices are social communicative acts and where education is increasingly used by adults as a marker - an expressive means of self-development, a central part of the process whereby individuals differentiate themselves from others. For adults, therefore, it is only important for learning to be identifiable as 'education' if to be an 'educated person' is important to their identity, if it acts as a means of positioning themselves in some significant way. Hence the increased significance of learning in shaping subjectivity and identity.

One thing which emerges very clearly and very significantly from this is that consumption is a complex and multi-dimensional process which can be active and generative as well as passive and reproductive. In particular, we need to understand the significance of the cultural meanings of consumer behaviour, the role that consumer choices have in certain social practices where meanings and identity are developed. In general terms, this is an argument for locating adult learning within a socio-cultural paradigm of postmodernity or the risk society.

To illustrate this point more fully I shall relate consumption to certain contemporary social practices all of which involve adult learning but where 'learning' has a different signification in each. First, lifestyle practices. These work through an expressive mode of learning. Learning is individuated with an emphasis on self-expression, marked by a stylistic self-consciousness. Aestheticisation (the self-referential concern with style and image) and the constant and pleasurable remaking of identity necessitates a learning stance towards life as a means of self-expression and autonomy. Every aspect of life, like every commodity, is imbued with self-referential meaning; every choice an emblem of identity, a mark of difference, each a message to ourselves and to others of the sort of person we are. As we have noted, consumption is a signifier of difference - of the need to make oneself different and to identify with those who are different. Lifestyle practices, given the emphasis on novelty, fashion, taste and style, are practices of consumption, and moreover of a consumption which is potentially unending since as desire can never be satisfied, there is always the need for new experiences and hence new learning.

Second, confessional practices. These work through the bringing forth of one's self which becomes an object of knowledge, with one's inner life the terrain to be explored. The assumption is that there is deep hidden meaning buried 'inside', which once discovered, opens the door to happiness, psychic stability and personal empowerment. Again, this is a process where one is never done, one can never know all there is to know about one's 'hidden' inner self, where one can never finally realise all one's inner potential, and where there is constant need to change in order to adapt to a changing self and a changing environment. Hence there is a lifelong process at work here. In confessional practices, it is the self that is 'consumed' in a process based upon a never ending fascination with the self, its deepest secrets and its hidden potential. Difference is signified in terms of an open, well-adjusted, fulfilled and empowered person, 'in touch' with self as against those who are out of touch, repressed and incapacitated.

Third, vocational practices which work through an ostensible adaptation to the needs of the socio-economic system. The emphasis is on a pre-disposition to change and to not seeing particular skills as something to be owned and defended. Here what is consumed is pre-defined and 'relevant' (ie. applicable) knowledge and skills but which are at the same time disposable and ephemeral - thus one can never be prepared enough vocationally and in relation to one's position in the labour market since the market and one's position within it is constantly changing. Here then, consumption signifies difference (in relation to others) in the sense of being motivated, trained and effectively positioned in the market.

Fourth, critical practices. These work through the foregrounding of action in the 'here and now' as against theorising or contemplation or waiting for the right moment. They are located in a multiplicity of sites and can take a myriad of forms. They are not confined to educational institutions although these can be sites of critical practices. At the same time, critical practices do not occur within the productive order alone. They very often involve struggles against the dominance of consumption, particularly against the globalised risk which as discussed earlier is an inevitable feature of a consumption based economy but they do this by utilising techniques of ludic subversion and the creation and manipulation of seductive images. Resistance against the dominance of consumption and its consequent endemic risks are in a sense a non-consumption which itself signifies and therefore functions as a mark of difference. Critical practices are non-teleological and given also that there are always sites of resistance, to that extent they are always incomplete and never-ending - in the risk society there is always scope for resistance.

Thus all these practices involve lifelong learning, although this has a different signification within each practice. Of course, what I have described is probably not 'lifelong learning' as it would be understood conventionally by adult educators. This returns us to our original problematic. Adult educators tend to see 'lifelong learning' as a set of transcendental principles that they have formulated but which they understand as empirically related to a set of cognitive processes inherent in all adults. In other words, there is a tendency to reduction, to a naturalisation of lifelong learning and a consequent failure to locate it in contemporary social developments and practices.

This now brings us back to the postmodern condition of knowledge. Earlier, I pointed out that there was a powerful tendency to see this condition as one where knowledge was valued for its performativity alone with a consequent failure to understand the complexity of the place of knowledge and performativity within different social practices. Performativity has been mainly understood as signifying 'efficiency' or even more simplistically as 'relevance', but another and perhaps more fruitful alternative is to see it as signifying 'efficacy' because by doing this we can more adequately relate knowledge to the social practices of the postmodern condition. Thus:

• in lifestyle practices, efficacious knowledge signifies creating and re-creating identity and difference;
• in confessional practices, efficacious knowledge signifies gaining access to inner life and potential;
• in vocational practices, efficacious knowledge signifies advantageous positioning in the market and the workplace.

Critical practices are a little more difficult to relate to the significance of efficacy. They overlap with lifestyle, confessional and even vocational practices. They are firmly located in marketisation and the contemporary culture of consumption, recognising their immersion in the conditions of the present but in a reflexive, ironic and resistant way. They do not involve commitment to a universalistic 'cause' and a utopian project. They work by helping to surface local and very often subjugated knowledge and getting people to think about their situation through role-play, workshops, street theatre and popular carnivals - in effect, through *performance*. Performativity as 'efficacy' is not the efficacy of commitment to totalising projects of transformation but rather something much more modest although no less effective:

• in critical practices, efficacious knowledge signifies 'giving voice' to specific, subjugated knowledge, of empowering through a learning that is both participative and performative.

In the light of all this therefore we can say that performativity does not necessarily and simply signify 'efficiency' in the reproduction and maintenance of a market-dominated capitalist system. Whilst there are certain activities where performativity does mean this, there are others where it means something completely different. Certainly, 'performativity' does permeate all the knowledge practices of lifelong learning but it does so in different ways and with different significances and significations. To assimilate lifelong learning to one sense alone of performativity is to ignore the complex signifying characteristics of lifelong learning.

Reconfiguring Lifelong Learning

I have discussed the influence of the market and of individualisation in postmodernity. At the same time, postmodernity also provides space for rising social groups such as the new middle classes, for new postmodern social movements, and for hitherto oppressed and marginalised groups such as women, blacks, gays and ethnic minorities to find a voice, to articulate their own 'subjugated' knowledges, and to empower themselves in a variety of different ways (including through critical practices) and according to their own specific agendas.

The postmodern emphasis on reinvention means taking into account a diverse range of interests and locations within the social formation. The instability introduced by the risk society has provided a means of challenging dominant values and norms of knowledge. By undermining the certainty surrounding canons of knowledge, universal messages and the efficacy of enlightened pedagogues, opportunities are presented, 'risky' though they might be, for diversity and for new and innovative practices which switch the emphasis from 'provision' to learning opportunities, from the 'student' to the learner.

The education of adults is increasingly becoming more diverse in terms of goals, processes, organisational structures, curricula and pedagogy. This both reflects and is a contributor to a breakdown of clear and settled demarcations between different sectors of education and between education and cognate fields - and of which lifelong learning is a manifestation. Furthermore, the very notion of 'lifelong learning' implies that education can no longer claim a monopoly over learning simply because it is a formally constituted field since a multiplicity of activities in many contexts involve learning and hence can be deemed 'educational'. Lifelong learning foregrounds the simultaneous boundlessness of learning, ie. that it is not confined by pre-determined outcomes or formal institutions, and its postmodern quality, ie. its inherent discursive and socio-cultural contextuality.

As Edwards (1994) points out, when students are positioned as consumers demands are made on educational providers which they find difficult to cope with. The very notion of 'student' is reconfigured as indeed are notions of what constitutes 'provision' and 'providers'. When students become 'learners' changes follow in both the control and content of curricula and in the position and authority of teachers. That learners should make choices based on desire (including the desire to be optimally positioned in the market) rather than on a search for enlightenment and the mastery of a canon of knowledge can no longer be automatically considered perverse and uneducational. To do so is to claim that this is not what education is 'really' about and this itself is based on the assumption that there is an ideal model of education and that education is itself directed by a set of transcendental ideals. It is to see adult learning from a purely educational frame of reference as the systematic selection and delivery of learning experiences predefined by the professional educator and teacher. But in the postmodern condition it is possible to argue that this is a dangerously oppressive and totalising discourse which assumes learning is a 'gift' bestowed by enlightened pedagogues. Whilst institutionally-based adult educators might well want to foreground the empowering potential of education, there is also a need to see educational forms contextually rather than transcendentally, and therefore a need to re-assess the place of pedagogues within this.

To try and conclude then. For many institutionally-based educators, adult education seems to be at risk - although this is rarely attributed to the impact of a contemporary risk society. Certainly, its identity is less secure and bounded than it ever was. Yet this is happening in a situation and at a time when 'adult learning' is playing an increasingly significant role in the formation of the individual identity of adults. The key to the 'risky' changes within which the education of adults is caught up, and the re-description or re-configuration that is consequently needed, must foreground lifelong learning both as an interpretive concept and a signifier of a field of practice. But the term 'lifelong learning' now has multiple meanings given its location in different contemporary social practices, and these significations have a differential impact upon adult educators.

My own view is that in order to move forward, the education of adults needs to reflect the diversity of adult learners, their multiple and shifting identities and the plurality of their motivations, and to be capable of operating in a variety of learning settings and contexts within the present -

in other words, it must embody difference not simply as an ideal but as a reality. To borrow and slightly relocate the words of MacKenzie Wark (1997) - the education of adults should not have a fixed idea of itself but know the many pasts from which it descends and be aware of its potential, of the things it can do and be.

References

Ball, S.J. (1990) *Politics and Policy Making in Education*, London, Routledge.

Baudrillard, J. (1988) *Selected Writings*, Cambridge, Polity Press.

Bauman, Z. (1992) *Intimations of Postmodernity*, London, Routledge.

Beck, U. (1992) *Risk Society: Towards a New Modernity*, London, Sage.

Edwards, R. (1994) 'From a Distance: Globalisation, Space-Time Compression and Distance Education', *Open Learning*, 9, 3: 9-17.

Featherstone, M. (1991) *Consumer Culture and Postmodernism*, London, Sage.

Harvey, D. (1991) *The Condition of Postmodernity*, Oxford, Basil Blackwell.

Lash, S. and Wynne, B. (1992) 'Introduction', in *Risk Society: Towards a New Modernity*, London, Sage.

Lyotard, J.-F. (1984) *The Postmodern Condition: A Report on Knowledge*, Manchester, Manchester University Press.

Plant, S. (1995) 'Crash Course', *Wired*, April, 44-47.

Urry, J. (1994) 'Time, Leisure and Social Identity', *Time and Society*, 3, 2, 131-150.

Wark, M. (1997) *Virtual Republic*, Sydney, Allen and Unwin.

Wildemeersch, D., Finger, M. and Jansen, T. (1997) *Adult Education and Social Responsibility*, Frankfurt, Peter Lang.

6 Higher Education Courses in the Community: Issues Around Guidance and Learning Support for Non-Traditional Students

JULIA PREECE

Abstract

This chapter explores the relationship between community education, guidance and higher education goals, such as the development of autonomous learning skills. Issues surrounding preparedness for formal education provision are analysed with reference to interviews with community tutors and student focus groups. The chapter concludes by suggesting there is a need to bridge the existing self sufficiency and self awareness gap between the flexible aspects of facilitated community learning and the more formalised and rigidly presented support mechanisms of institutional systems.

Introduction

> If somebody were to say how much time do you spend helping, guiding, I wouldn't know, it's just there, it's practically in every sentence;   (Bill, tutor)

> I think the university and the youth service are probably about the same thing in a lot of cases.   (Mandy, youth tutor)

Recent policy documents (Dearing, 1997; Kennedy, 1997; Fryer, 1997; DfEE, 1998 and its Scottish and Welsh equivalents) have all raised the profile of lifelong learning as a desirable goal for the total UK population. The principle argument is that individuals need to be equipped with the skills necessary to cope with the demands of a fast changing world. The focus for this new 'learning age' has inevitably fallen on those who are not perceived to be currently participating in such a culture. Widening participation is the watchword of the educational world. The part to be played by each sector (initial, further and higher education) is described variously in the above reports, but there is a general recognition by Fryer and the DfEE that community based participation is likely to be the key starting point for new, post-compulsory education learners. Whilst Kennedy, and particularly Fryer, advocated a more comprehensive service for adults and future learners, the DfEE Green Paper is berated for scant mention of guidance or learner support as a means of helping learners make more informed choices about their own learning goals (Watts, 1998: 6-7).

The notion of guidance itself is a relatively new phenomenon. Indeed only recently has the role of guidance been seen as a part of the higher education provider's responsibility and then only as an information resource (Dearing, 1997; DfEE, 1997). There is, moreover, relatively little empirical evidence of what guidance means in practice, particularly for new learners (but see Houghton, 1998; Chapman and Williams, 1998 and Houghton and Bokhari, 1998). There is even less discussion on the guidance implications for higher education institutions in terms of widening participation in spite of a number of recent Higher Education Funding Council projects which specifically support guidance schemes (McNair, 1998). This chapter explores the relationship between the aims of community education, higher education and guidance. It then looks specifically at how a range of grass roots community educators explain their guidance and learning support strategies for achieving the goals outlined in the literature. The chapter concludes by suggesting there is a need to bridge the gap between institutional support systems and the perceived development needs of learners in community settings if their learning potential is to be realised.

The literature on educational guidance, community education and higher education often shares similar goals. Writers on each topic refer to notions of empowerment and learner autonomy; even the concept of 'emancipation' has been known to appear across all three domains. Recognition of this relationship between the three activities, however, is rarely made - if at all. Whilst the role of higher education in the community has often been expounded (Elliott et al. 1996, for example), the explicit nature of community learning in terms of an educational guidance experience is rarely stated (Houghton, 1998; Houghton and Bokhari, 1998). These links can be made more explicit now that guidance is beginning to be articulated as a holistic activity which engages a range of resources in which higher education has a role to play in a mass higher education system.

> Advice, tutoring, guidance, counselling or mentoring ... Traditionally the services have been seen as distinct, often without any structured links between them. However, they share a common concern to help individuals to relate their learning to their lives, and as higher education copes with increasing and increasingly diverse demands, it becomes more important to review their place in higher education and their relationship to each other. (DfEE, 1997: preface)

It is this new higher education discourse of diversity and learning relevance which opens up the possibility for exploring whether community education's long tradition of working with diversity has something to offer the higher education system as a whole. Higher education policy strategies are increasingly looking, on a global scale, to the economic argument for lifelong learning, increased access and more complex progression routes. This necessitates a more responsive system of guidance and support within learning environments (Walter, 1996). Indeed the urgency of a coherent support framework to meet this scenario is fuelled by evidence of an ongoing mismatch between non traditional student expectations and what staff usually offer in a higher education environment (McGivney, 1996; DfEE, 1997; Mayo, 1997).

A key issue in the debate is the notion of leaner autonomy. Much of the mismatch between official guidance quality assurance discussions (HEQC, 1995) and the reality of guidance work occurs through an assumption that the person in need of guidance is already a self directing learner with a clear understanding of their goals and an awareness of how and when to seek guidance as and when needed (McGivney, 1990; DfEE, 1997). Yet this notion of learner autonomy is almost an ideal state and one which Barnett (1990) claims is the end goal of higher education itself:

> An educational process can be termed higher education when the student is carried onto levels of reasoning which make possible critical reflection on his or her experiences, whether consisting of propositional knowledge or knowledge through action...   (p.202)

The mental acts marked out by such terms as analysis, synthesis, evaluating, criticism and even imagination are higher order acts.   (p.85)

These skills, or competencies outlined by Barnett are very similar to the skills which the educational guidance process claims to nurture:

> Giving them the skills to reflect on their personal academic and vocational objectives, to set goals, adopt appropriate learning strategies, cope with crises, review and manage their progression and beyond formal education ... in enabling individuals to take control of their lives as learners, workers and citizens in an increasingly uncertain world.   (McNair, 1996: 8)

So where does community education come in? Community education has a long pedigree of working with disenfranchised communities, utilising problem solving education, starting with issues of relevance to peoples' lives and developing in groups and individuals the skills of personal and collective autonomy so they can:

> Increase peoples' capacity to discover, define, pursue and achieve common objectives and in the process to develop more confident relationships with one another and the outside world.   (McConnell, 1997: 179)

Community education has traditionally adopted informal, inter-agency, facilitative approaches to learning. Therefore boundaries such as guidance, tutoring, mentoring and counselling are often already blurred in the practice of education. Community educators often work by feel and in responsiveness to the immediate circumstances and demands of their groups. Community education does not have the luxury of a formal institutional framework with contracted fee arrangements for learning. Education is on the learner's terms and if those terms are not met then the learners simply do not attend. Community educators therefore know a lot about diversity and difference:

> If it doesn't suit them and if they don't feel they are getting enough of what they personally are after they won't appear and so it is very important to be in a position to negotiate some of the content and some of the methods.
> (Carol, college community worker)

Whilst it is now freely acknowledged that many non traditional learners start from a community education base (Fryer, 1997), McGivney (1996) also points out that the informal, needs-led approach of community learning does not always prepare students for the exigencies of the formal system. Alternatively, put another way, formal institutions have yet to realise the degree of flexibility required to accommodate those students who have hitherto been excluded from their own special brand of provision for the elite (Fryer, 1997: 43). Carol identified for instance some of the implications for higher education if new students are brought into the system:

> HE was a terrible shock [to some FE students] because of the degree of inflexibility ... as further education has had to become more flexible ... I suspect HE is having to move in the same way ... and the sort of very hard edged traditional HE course ... seems to be being replaced increasingly with a lot more opportunities for people to go off and do a personal project ... a lot more individual tutor support and less of a sort of lecture format.

Research does not often engage with the kind of individual support students might need in order to be able to survive the transition to higher education. Whilst some may note, in retrospect, the differential in learning experience, they do so primarily through a deficit model of student. So for example, Fryer (1997) suggests that:

> To benefit fully from these larger and more complex institutions, learners need more developed skills of self management.   (p.8)

Whilst elements of this argument may be true, some researchers have tried to unpack the successful features of the community guidance experience, with a view to encouraging institutions to change (Dadzie, 1993), or give successful examples of institutional practice which adopts community education strategies of support (Houghton, 1998; Houghton and Bokhari, 1998). Houghton (1998) has described in detail how the key activities and principles of guidance outlined by McNair (1997) can be incorporated within an institutional setting, but emphasises the labour intensive nature of such a strategy. Houghton and Oglesby (1996) have also highlighted some of the shortfalls of HEQC (1995) guidelines for guidance which assume a common starting point of an adult who is already positioned to access institutional systems. They and Houghton and Bokhari (1998) identify a pre-pre entry phase, where:

> Guidance and learner support need to be fully integrated into the total learning experience and central to course provision from the planning through to the delivery stage.   (Houghton and Bokhari, 1998: 15)

using essentially a process of

> educative guidance strategies.   (p.16)

There is now increasing interest among HE providers in the idea of focusing on learner process rather than subject content as a means of achieving the critical awareness and learner autonomy goals outlined by Barnett. Tuckett (1996) for instance describes a *mature HE system* as a *lifelong learning kind of education* which:

> Would need underpinning by a coherent framework of learner support, delivered independently by HEIs and in partnership with others.   (p.48)

Seen in this light it may be that some aspects of the community education system of learning have potential beyond the pre-pre entry phase of learner support and could become more integral to the mainstream system. In order to pick the best of the community education learning experience and at the same time move community learners closer to the literature's self sufficiency goals outlined earlier in this chapter, however, it is necessary to understand more closely what is valued by the learner and what guidance and learner support strategies the community educators themselves value as part of their teaching process. It would not be possible, in the space of one chapter, to explore the totality of this issue. The remainder of this chapter, therefore, outlines some aspects of ongoing research into holistic guidance and learner support activities which might be understood in respect of a lifelong learning model of education.

The research was conducted with 10 community groups involving taped interviews with 16 tutors and/or key community workers along with diary records of focus group discussions with their learner groups. The respondents were participants in a community education project organised by a team of three action researchers at Lancaster University during 1995 and 1998. The groups all shared some form of disaffection from further or higher education system, though individuals in one group had attempted college or university courses in the past. The groups were often (though not always) self defining by some common cultural or other form of shared experience. For instance two groups consisted primarily of Asian women, one group consisted of a local Deaf community of adults, another of male prisoners. The research also included interviews with students and tutors in a rural community centre (Tracks), a youth organisation, family history study group and three self help disability associations (Growth, EXIT and CAPE). Key features of their learning experience were:

- course provision was part time and set up in partnership between Lancaster University and local agencies;
- tutors had a cultural or social empathy with their learner groups;
- single sex provision was made available where required;
- support facilities such as crèche, bilingual translation, transport and accessible venues were available;
- syllabus content was negotiated around a local or group interest but designed to fit in with higher education learning goals of critical analysis and included the teaching of study or other relevant academic skills or inquiry;
- student and tutor feedback informed future provision.

The Findings

All tutors felt they played a large role in helping the learners understand and articulate what their learning needs were. A general feature, therefore, of their guidance and learner support strategy was to build confidence:

> A lot of it is to do with lack of self confidence - 'I can't learn, I don't know how to learn', learning blocks in terms of like having the ability to think further and laterally, exploring different options, getting them to recognise their skills and what they have already got to offer as well.
>
> (Jatinder, Asian women tutor and course organiser)

Whilst this is not often cited in the guidance literature as a step towards learner autonomy, all of the tutors saw this as a primary goal, on which all other achievements would build:

> Because HEIs have equal opportunity statements, then they need to be looking at, broadly as possible what, how people need to develop in order to access HE and take advantage of it and some of that development needs to be in actually convincing people that they've got the skills to be able to cope with it.
>
> (Carol, college partner and course coordinator)

An academic might argue that it is not the place of HE to engender such needs in their students. Such an argument pre supposes, however, that all learners have received a standard starting base of positive educational experiences and that new learners simply require the means to make informed choices towards personally motivated goals. Such a vision of an HE learner negates the reality of many peoples' lives - a reality which has long since excluded them from the very HE experience now being offered. Each community group - and particularly their tutors - would identify common issues regarding a holistic guidance approach, but there were also distinctive issues around 'difference' which affected people's confidence to capitalise on their own potential. The most significant example of this confidence gap, coupled with a sense of cultural alienation came from the Deaf community. Their BSL translator interpreted a student's frustration which spilled over into the current day:

> When I was small they didn't understand me, it made me frustrated and angry, you know, the teacher the hearing teacher wouldn't understand us and would punish us and we were brought up that way, so that, I mean that affected us and that's why we had behavioural problems, that's why they labelled us, I mean it was the communication aspect and that's why I became frustrated, the teachers weren't aware what it is to be deaf.   (Andrea)

Similarly the need to untangle personal feelings and issues from the day's learning tasks was often cited as a common issue for tutors which transferred onto their daily teaching:

> A lot of it's to do with problems they're having in other areas of their lives really ... they obviously carry those worries with them whenever they come.
>
> (Rowena - tutor of Asian women's course)

These starting points produced the need in some cases to look beyond conventional vocabulary for guidance and in other cases to explain the reality behind those words in the community context. UDACE (1986) have described the main activities for guidance as informing, advising, counselling, assessing, enabling, advocating and feedback (in Houghton 1998: 20). Whilst these descriptions are clearly relevant to the community learner, their emphasis might vary. Furthermore, the interviews indicated there were more specific qualities of the holistic learning experience which needed to be taken on board. The focus in the remainder of this chapter, therefore, is on how the tutors developed their roles as encouragers and confidence builders, particularly through their understanding of equal opportunities principles. An early analysis of the tutor and student data suggests the main characteristics of the tutors' approach included aspects such as: 'personal relationships'; 'group relationships'; 'encouragement' and 'anticipation'. These features seemed important in terms of ensuring the success of UDACE's own list of guidance activities. The following pages will take each feature in turn with a view to discussing their implications for institutional practice in the widening participation debate.

Personal Relationships

The range of personal qualities cited most often by the respondents could be divided broadly into three categories - cultural empathy or understanding; availability and a way of behaving as tutor. The enactment of these qualities might be different, depending on the group, though they were all underpinned by a commitment to informality. Behaviour, for instance might include a degree of sharing experiences. Mandy, a tutor for the youth group was careful to emphasise her professional role as tutor but also stated a need to re-draw common teacher-student boundaries, exemplified by this reference to tutor roles on a residential course:

> They [the students] like the fact that tutors will take part and make fools of themselves by taking part in the rope course with them ... or whatever and that makes them feel more at ease and sort of treated more as humans.

Other strategies for older groups might be less challenging, with the aim of either making people 'feel comfortable':

We make them a cup of coffee and have a chat ...

or in the teaching style itself, as the family history focus group stated:

> We ask a lot of questions ... its to and fro ... very informal, if we're stuck we just ask, he comes back with questions, checks up, sets us little tasks to see how well we have understood, then follows up.

Being informal in itself was not enough, however. An important distinction, already identified by the Deaf community, was the need to relate in some way to people's sense of self. This ranged from a sensitivity to religious or disability differences:

> It's important that the tutor can interact and cater for their different needs, have empathy with the students;   (CAPE coordinator)

to an insight into the controlled and restricted lives of a prison environment. One group of prisoners, for example, highlighted the opportunity to see their tutor as someone who saw them as individuals, rather than prisoners:

> The tutor put herself across, explained herself, had time for us ... we felt we could trust her ... she wasn't judgmental.

A final feature of the tutor-student relationship was highlighted by almost every tutor interviewed - that of their availability. This included the willingness to give people a personal contact point out of hours:

> If they need advice ... I'd always give my number;
> (Surrinder, Asian Women's group tutor)

to making the community premises available:

> I usually say well if you can't get anywhere at home, come in here and write things;   (Tracks tutor)

or being available in the session itself:

> When I'm going round monitoring whatever they're doing, I end up sitting and talking to one of them and you know they tell me what's been bothering them

or why they can't manage to do the work ... and sometimes its automatic, they feel they can talk to me and I will always ask them especially if I know that they've been having problems.   (Surrinder)

Surrinder's comments raise a number of issues in relation to study and the context of study. Whilst not all students had 'problems' many did in their perceived context. The exigencies of study when it competes with daily lives requires a period of adjustment and support. The ability to cut off from the impact of competing claims during study is a hard earned skill. Successful community courses would facilitate these demands in order to nurture and embed UDACE's more structured 'enabling' forms of guidance.

An associated personal quality of tutors was the extent to which they encouraged new learners to achieve.

Encouraging

A universal theme articulated by all tutors was the issue of learner confidence. This meant that enabling students in itself was insufficient to ensure successful completion of targets. This ranged from straight forward enthusiasm generating:

> You've got to keep them sort of bubbling over all the time I think with a lot of moral support so they don't get too despondent and give it up ... pinpoint successes in their lives;   (Jatinder, Asian tutor)

to an ongoing commitment to building the inner self:

> Q. So if that adult support wasn't there, would that make it difficult for them to do assignments?

> A. I don't think they would do it ... if they didn't have the adult support here and people telling them that they could do it and they are good enough.
>   (Mandy, youth tutor)

The level of need to raise confidence through pro-active encouragement and support had significant implications for the degree to which students would seek out help independently. The expectation from formal guidance services is that the student will initiate his or her own questions and instigate his or her own requests for practical support (HEQC, 1995). The service is commonly predicated on a form of front-loading of information and advice in response to student requests. The tutors and even some of the students revealed that this model of guidance would simply disable students from the start:

> The people that come on these courses aren't the most supremely confident of people anyway. So ... they're not going to come out with everything that they need until you encourage them to.   (Brenda, CAPE tutor)

This often meant the tutors had to anticipate or find ways of responding to needs as and when they arose.

Anticipation

> Margaret knew what I'd achieved in the past so she knew if I was capable enough.   (Student, CAPE)

Tutors were constantly trying to move their students on from the dependency mode outlined by the above student. Sometimes this meant reconstructing the teaching environment, as one enterprise project tutor explained:

> The more confident would have taken all the major tasks and the mundane ones would have been left for the ones with less confidence - we didn't want that to happen so we paired them off.   (Janet, EXIT tutor)

Sonia, the prison tutor, explained that she constantly had to be aware of, and tuned into, issues during the learning situation that might hinder or affect student progress:

> You've got to have an ear working all the time that listens to and latches onto things ... so that you can pursue it later and also by looking at them.

Observation of tell-tale signs of need, as Sonia intimated, seemed to be a common strategy among tutors, though interaction was the most frequent method of anticipating needs beyond a personal knowledge of students:

A lot of the people don't know what their needs are until they come up against a problem. So its identified as you go along through the course, really just by chatting to people ... occasionally you kind of overhear them talking to each other and, er, sort of pick up on it.   (Jodie, Tracks tutor)

Guidance support did not, however, always come from the tutors. Many identified that the most effective means of developing independence and autonomy was through peer support.

Group Relationships

The opportunity for this kind of relationship emerged partly by the self selecting nature of the groups themselves. For instance, three groups shared an experience of disability. Whilst the project does not advocate the segregation of individuals as an ultimate goal, in the initial stages of confidence building it had advantages for some students, as one remarked:

I was happier people had disabilities ... we were all in the same boat, we can relate to each other, have a laugh about it.

Whilst many of the teaching strategies encouraged group work and mutual help, tutors saw that the shared experience of the learner groups could also generate more wide ranging opportunities towards an autonomous state of being:

It is also important students get support from each other - they get a life time of experience and ... many a time a student will say I tried this, or that worked for me ... if you can get the group to gel then the group can support each other.
                    (Christine, Growth tutor)

This strategy as an interim step towards independence was encouraged across the board, including amongst the relatively sophisticated family history study group:

They see me as a source of information but I am pleased that they actually do that with each other as well, there's a lot of information being transferred from one to another.   (John, family history tutor)

The sense of mutuality amongst most student groups meant that problems were often aired openly, resulting in not only the occasional by-passing of the tutor but also student role modelling, resulting in increased willingness to try new avenues:

> As its developed they've been going to each other and they've been sort of getting together and consulting each other ... they say 'Oh yeah, I remember how that felt but don't worry because if you go to such and such a place you can find out' ... they can see its achievable and its like you know, 'Oh, she can do it, its okay'.   (Enid, Tracks tutor)

Indeed one student remarked on her own growing awareness of how the course was generating a different way of learning for her:

> You need to get out of the old habits of learning where you expect the information to come to you.

Whilst the above experiences were also supplanted by more formalised assessments and access to specialist resources ranging from BSL translators to citizens advice bureaux, the strategies outlined here raise several issues for widening participation policy. The students were nearly all studying at Access level or near first year undergraduate level. Yet their needs were being identified and supported in complex and multiple ways in order to ensure they both achieved and developed as autonomous learners. Many tutors and students identified difficulties in finding your way round institutional settings - with comments like:

> It's quite a lot for some people who haven't been into adult education to walk straight into a college, find their way to student services;   (Janet, EXIT tutor)

and

> Nobody seems to know where they are going [in colleges and universities] and you think you are the only one who doesn't know ... the needs of adults are not readily addressed in college prospectuses. Adults need to know more, adults have other responsibilities.   (Bill, Growth tutor)

Conclusions

As the literature has already shown (McGivney, 1996), students often drop out prematurely when they do venture into the formal environment. This chapter has provided a number of indicators about student starting points. The anomaly that guidance and higher education both aim to develop self awareness and learner autonomy suggests that perhaps some stages of guidance need to take on more developmental strategies rather than assume an HE end state of mind before students have already begun their studies. Students' academic abilities are often undermined by systems which expect them to function at higher levels of independence than community provision requires. Group support systems provided through community courses, for instance, can often start to engender the kind of learner autonomy required by higher education. The process of development, however, cannot always be achieved with just one course and the capacity to block out other worries while studying requires considerable expertise. Perhaps two strategies might be considered to facilitate this learning gap. Community providers might, for example, be encouraged to develop more consciously the learning autonomy these tutors were obviously starting to develop. At the same time, institutions might take heed of recent college developments and Carol's comment about the slow change taking place in HE regarding flexibility. Guidance and learner support activities within the institutions should perhaps be understood more closely as teaching and learning activities which are built into the mainstream curriculum in such a way that students feel supported throughout their study time and learn more gradually to identify ways of addressing their own needs. Indeed the notion of higher education teaching which is centred more round learner facilitation than content based instruction is gaining momentum (McNair, 1998; Watson and Taylor, 1998). If community education, guidance and higher education share similar end goals, then it seems reasonable to suppose that one system can learn from, and complement the other.

References

Barnett, R. (1990) *The Idea of Higher Education*, Buckinghamshire, SRHE/OUP.

Chapman, I. and Williams, S. (1998) 'IT Based Guidance: reaching the parts that other guidance cannot reach?', in Preece, J. (ed) *Beyond the Boundaries: exploring the potential of widening provision in higher education*, Leicester, NIACE.

Dadzie, S. (1993) *Working with Black Adult Learners*, Leicester, NIACE.

Dearing, R. (1997) *Higher Education in the Learning Society*, London, National Committee of Inquiry into Higher Education.

DfEE (1997) *Getting the Most Out of HE: supporting learner autonomy, A DfEE Briefing Paper*, Moorfoot, DfEE.

DfEE (1998) *The Learning Age: a new renaissance for Britain*, Government Green Paper, London, HMSO.

Elliott, J., Francis, H., Humphreys, R. and Istance, D. (1996) *Communities and Their Universities: the challenge of lifelong learning*, London, Lawrence and Wishart.

Fryer, R.H. (1997) *Learning for the Twenty First Century, First Report of the National Advisory Group for Continuing Education and Lifelong learning*, London, NAGCELL.

HEQC (1995) *A Quality Framework for Guidance and Learner Support in Higher Education: the guidelines*, London, HEQC.

Houghton, A. (1998) 'Extending the Guidance Boundaries: an exploration of educative and empowering guidance strategies for learners who have been long-term unemployed', in Preece, J. (ed) *Beyond the Boundaries: exploring the potential of widening provision in higher education*, Leicester, NIACE.

Houghton, A. and Oglesby, K.L. (1996) 'Guidance and Learner Support: developing threshold standards', *Adults Learning* 7 (6), 146-147.

Houghton, A. and Bokhari, R. (1998) 'Guiding Differently', *Adult Learning* 9 (7), 15-16.

Kennedy, H. (1997) *Learning Works: widening participation in further education*, Coventry, FEFC.

Mayo, M. (1997) *Imagining Tomorrow: adult education for transformation*, Leicester, NIACE.

McConnell, C. (1997) (ed) *Community Education: the making of an empowering profession*, revised edition, Scotland, Scottish Community Education Council.

McGivney, V. (1990) *Education's for Other People*, Leicester, NIACE.

McGivney (1996) *Staying or Leaving the Course: non completion and retention of mature students in further and higher education*, Leicester, NIACE.

McNair, S. (1996) (ed) *Putting Learners at the Centre*, Gala, Moorfoot, DfEE.

McNair, S. (1998) 'The Invisible Majority: adult learners in English Higher Education', *Higher Education Quarterly*, 52 (2), 162-178.

McNair, S. (1998) Evaluation Report of widening participation projects funded by HEFCE 1995-1999.

Tuckett, A. (1996) 'A Mature HE System?', in Coffield, F. (ed) *Higher Education and Lifelong Learning*, Newcastle, University of Newcastle Upon Tyne.

UDACE (1986) *The Challenge to Change: developing educational guidance for adults*, Leicester, NIACE/UDACE.

Walters, S. (1996) 'Balancing Equality and Development in Universities after Apartheid: a focus on adult and continuing education', in Elliott, J., Francis, H., Humphries, R. and Istance, D. (eds) *Communities and Their Universities: the challenge of lifelong learning*, London, Lawrence and Wishart.

Watson, D. and Taylor, R. (1998) *Lifelong Learning in the University: a post-Dearing agenda*, London, Falmer.

Watts, A.C. (1998) 'Disappointment over the Scant Mention of Guidance', *Adults Learning* 9 (8), 6-8.

7 Mental Health and Adult Education

KATHERINE HUGHES

Abstract

Adult education is being encouraged to concentrate more heavily on providing for larger constituencies of students who have previously been excluded from education. At the same time social and economic changes and inequalities are putting increasing pressures on those students, exacerbated by cuts in funding. The mental health implications of these developments are considerable. In order to give the right sorts of support to those students and to help them in their struggle for an education, adult education needs to become more aware of mental health issues.

Introduction

Mental health issues and problems have never had such an exposure. Vast numbers of self help books are on sale; emotional literacy in an age of post-modern uncertainty, is given more serious attention; record numbers of counsellors operate in the workplace, colleges and community. Identity issues have become important and are often central to feminist, nationalist and post-colonial discourses. They have also more cynically been made important by advertising from the very global corporations that are simultaneously seeking to create more uniform tastes and wants.

However, at the same time as these often contradictory forces operate, tolerance of mental health problems in crucial areas such as the workplace has not necessarily increased. A recent study (MIND, 1996) found that 34% of people with mental health problems had been dismissed or forced to resign from their jobs. MIND has also found levels of ignorance and prejudice about mental health to be high amongst young people, especially college age students (MIND, 1997).

Major economic changes have been taking place in the local and global economy affecting most negatively the students which adult education is being encouraged to attract. The restructuring of industry and public sector organisations continues in a period of sharp international competition leading to higher unemployment, public service cuts, serious levels of poverty and widespread insecurity. At the same time, these changes make for a less sympathetic climate for the stress and mental suffering caused by the very processes of change.

The origins of this chapter lie with my impressions of higher levels of mental distress amongst students gained through experiences of teaching at Ruskin College and running the community short course programme. My argument is that more disadvantaged students are experiencing higher levels of mental distress and that adult education needs to take this seriously if we expect to offer positive and effective educational services to people who have been at the rough end of the widening inequalities of the past 20 years.

Ruskin, with its national (and to some extent international) catchment area offers perhaps a microcosm of some of the changes taking place in the labour market and society. Ruskin originated a century ago as a college for working men. Including women from the 1920s on, it served as an Oxford college for the labour aristocracy. Recent years has seen the devastation of male skilled manual employment with four million jobs lost since 1979 (Social Trends, 1998). The savage effects of unemployment and legislation has reduced trade union membership from 13 million in 1979 to six million today (Social Trends, 1998). Work itself has changed. Charles Handy (1994) argues that the fortunate few in core jobs will experience more intense workloads, greater expectations of flexibility, and long hours, and will be rewarded with security and large salaries. Other workers will have to put together 'portfolios' of work with commensurate insecurity and unprecedented pressures to adapt and reskill. Those who can barely gain a toehold into paid employment, are in low paid work with no prospects, or are outside work altogether, will experience the worst effects of stigmatisation, state bullying and poverty. The impact on relationships combined with women's higher expectations means overall one in five families headed by lone parents, more so amongst working class families. In Oxford, for instance 14% families on the Blackbird Leys estate are headed by a lone parent compared with 1% in the affluent North Oxford (Noble, 1994).

The student profile today has consequently changed considerably. Although many still have trade union and community experience, half of all full-time students are unemployed on arrival. The majority of part-time students are without paid employment. Most students (average ages 35-40) are single, often divorced. Many, especially amongst part-time students are lone parents. Married women, often still have partners unsympathetic to their efforts to gain an education.

Student prospects have also changed. Working class mature students in the past often saw adult and higher education as a route to social mobility. At Ruskin, skilled manual workers active in their trade unions knew that their sacrifices would lead to university and employment as a trade union official, teacher or even politician. There is no such guarantee today. In addition, cuts in fees, abolition of two homes allowance, increasing use of discretionary grants and reductions in student grants means record levels of debt (Bryant, 1997).

Strong impressions of greater levels of stress, mental distress, low self esteem, manifest in student autobiographies, pastoral pressures on staff time, greater levels of drop out, encouraged me to investigate. This seemed particularly important as in the wake of the publication of the Kennedy Report (1998), and that of Fryer (1997), adult education is quite rightly being encouraged to cater more for the needs of adults who have been excluded in the past. My hypothesis is that these students will come with greater numbers and intensity of problems. However they also come with the potential to rise above these and challenge their effects.

The language of mental health is a minefield and reflects the controversies and debates in the field. The term mental illness implies organic origins of problems such as depression, phobias or schizophrenia. While these are undoubtedly important it needs to be recognised that there are strong professional investments in this model. It also makes a sharper than justified distinction between the ill and well. Supported by media images of mental illness and its conflation with violent behaviour they encourage a public view of mental ill health that sees it in terms of 'us' and 'them'. Furthermore, they pathologise, localise and individualise problems that may well have a social component or in some cases be completely socially caused. The mental health charity MIND (1997) argues strongly for the wider term mental distress, which models mental health problems in terms of a continuum. Without denying more severe and intractable conditions, such an approach brings mental health issues into the lives of all of us and our communities.

Data and Analysis

I surveyed all Ruskin's full-time and part-time students of the year 1997-8. Questionnaires went out to 150 full-time and 100 part-time students identifying, in addition, age groups and gender. The exercise felt highly sensitive given the stigma involved to already often very disadvantaged students. I decided not to include race because of the issues of relatively small numbers and concerns about anonymity. Black students however identified the impact of racism in the generation of mental health problems. Many students articulated their welcome for the survey either directly to me or in their responses saying that it was about time these matters were taken seriously.

Forty full-time forms were returned and 33 part-time, a reasonable return given the preoccupation at the time with end of year assessment. The extent of the experience of mental distress which students themselves identified either currently or in the past proved significant. Of full-time students (overall 60% men and 40% women) 12 women and 15 men had experienced or were currently experiencing mental distress, seven women and six men had not. Of part-time students, (overall 60% women and 40% men) 16 women and 10 men had or were currently experiencing mental distress, five women and two men had not. Full time female students had experienced depression, clinical depression, anxiety and anxiety attacks, mental exhaustion and agoraphobia. Full-time male students mentioned anxiety, depression, manic depression, Post Traumatic Stress Disorder, stress and agoraphobia. Part-time female students mentioned severe stress, manic depression, clinical depression, breakdowns and anxiety. Part-time male students mentioned depression, a block on feelings, drug induced paranoia drug induced psychosis and obsessional compulsive disorders.

Part-time students have higher levels of mental distress. This is not surprising given that people with mental health problems are more likely to take part-time rather than full-time courses. It reflects too the encouragement into education of local organisations supporting people with mental health problems and more open entry criteria. It may also reflect the higher number of women in part-time education and their greater awareness of their own mental health problems. Less positively it also reflects cuts in services for people with mental health problems leaving them with nowhere else to go.

Of course it could be objected that those who felt more directly concerned would be likely to return the questionnaires. This is true, though it is unlikely that all those who did not return the forms has no relevant experience. The numbers anyway are high and suggest that these are concerns that adult education needs to take more seriously.

There is of course the question of whether there is actually more mental distress today or whether a complexity of factors has increased awareness and a willingness to articulate and value emotional disclosure. Overall figures are higher than many people realise.

> The number of people who have periods of mental distress is very large - with 12 million people having some psychiatric problems each year and at least 300,000 thought to be seriously ill at any one time.   (Philo, 1996)

Oliver James (1997) takes the view that in the West there is a major increase due to the nature of capitalist development which both creates the conditions in which people lose a sense of community and identification and feeds them in return the spurious solutions of material consumption.

> Put crudely, advanced Capitalism makes money out of misery and dissatisfaction as if it were encouraging us to fill a psychic void with material goods ... a sharp rise in aspirations and individualism since 1950, necessary for continuous economic growth has led to an all-consuming preoccupation with our status, power and wealth relative to others. We compare ourselves obsessively, enviously and self-destructively thus corrupting the quality of our inner lives ... at the same time our attachments are falling apart. 'Gender rancour' results from men's confusion and women's dissatisfaction leading to 'a holocaust of broken bonds'.   (p.xi-xii)

This comes close to a view of the post-modern self as described by Kerry Thomas (1996).

> 'Post-modern' refers to a time-period when the honeymoon with 'modernity'- science, technological progress and social freedoms is over. The post-modern self describes the self-hood that many people seem to be experiencing now, at least in the West: a mixture of disillusionment, boredom, confusion and celebration.   (p.327)

These perspectives are useful in identifying in wide-ranging and general ways aspects of the spiritual malaise affecting many and exploited by disingenuous consumption related solutions, at a time of rapid change, insecurity and social dislocation.

Other perspectives however would not leave matters there. Larry Atkins in the Guardian (25/8/98) points out that there are many who have benefited enormously from widening inequalities and technological transformations and who are not surprisingly optimistic about the future.

> Crucially, however, the optimists tend to be the rich and powerful people who have done rather well out of the less egalitarian and more deflationary years since 1973.

It would be difficult to argue that all in the West are equally affected by a spiritual lassitude and even if so, it is hardly likely to be unmediated by the effects of class, gender and race. The advantage of considering some of the structural aspects of mental health is that it can shift explanation from an over-reliance on individual pathology or personal failure to the wider social impact of oppression, exploitation and poverty. Such an approach has recently been cast in terms of an underclass carrying all too frequently the suggestion that people on the margins of society have created their own misfortunes due to their adherence to socially destructive values and behaviours (Murray, 1990; Dahrendorf, 1992). The argument here recognises the greater deprivations of many of the groups variously cast as the underclass, but challenges the idea of alternative values.

> ... we can say with confidence ... that the data available to us fail to confirm the notion of a culture of dependency.   (Heath, 1992, p.37)

It suggests too that as in the past, and perhaps more so today with the extent of economic restructuring, millions more are vulnerable to redundancy, sickness, an impoverished retirement, relationship breakdown. These are all situations that can lead to the stigma and damaging impact of social exclusion.

Sociologists David Pilgrim and Anne Rogers (1997) exploring the social processes by which certain people come to be labelled as mentally ill, examine studies that emphasise the importance of social class and conclude that ...

... it can be demonstrated unequivocally that social stress is correlated with social class ... in all social classes the greater the number of life events, both positive and negative, then the greater the probability of psychiatric symptoms appearing. But non-lower class people experienced a greater proportion of positive events and this led to them being buffered from symptom formation more often than the lower-class people. (p.15)

Richard Wilkinson (1994) argues that it is not only material deprivation that creates stress. After all, living standards for most people in the West are more affluent than in the past. The problem lies in the exclusion of certain groups from a psychological sense of sharing in the prosperity and an actual isolation for those excluded from work, bringing up families alone, or stranded by cuts in community facilities.

... the psycho-social implications of living in deprived circumstances as such, have a more important impact on health than any direct effect of the material circumstances themselves. (p.37)

Jane Hope of Oxford MIND agrees that while mental distress is widespread it does not affect all people equally. Leaving aside hereditary predispositions, certain groups are more vulnerable. They also have fewer means to create the conditions for recovery and face a greater likelihood of their problems being compounded by further negative events.

There's obviously a class thing here. I do think it's powerful. The way your life develops makes a difference to mental health. A lack of money and a lack of good housing, not being able to see the end of the tunnel can lead to mental health problems. Once labelled though, any feelings or difficulties are called their 'illness'.

Nairne and Smith (1994) introduce a feminist understanding to mental distress exploring the way patterns of gender-related mental health problems interweave with class. It is notable that for certain categories of hospital admissions, women have double the rate of affective psychoses and 90% neurotic disorders than men (Pilgrim and Rogers, 1997, p.23). Nairne and Smith argue that while women often blame themselves for their inability to cope with stressful circumstances, it is actually the pattern of their lives and social relationships which are making a major contribution to their disorders.

The oppression in every aspect of women's lives is real and in turn creates real distress and unhappiness. We are not encouraged to understand the problems in our lives as the manifestation of male dominance. Instead we are encouraged to believe the problems are of our own making ... Our economic dependence, usually on men and the lack of real alternatives for women mean we often feel obliged to do things for our keep despite the psychological cost. If we are economically dependent on the State we are kept on the edge of poverty ...   (p.110-111)

Brown and Harris' (1978) well known study of depression in women also identified social factors increasing vulnerability, including lack of paid occupation, lack of intimacy with a partner, relationship breakdown, being homebound with young children. Amongst working class women on many housing estates, depression was epidemic.

However, levels of affective and neurotic disorders in men are undoubtedly higher than recorded. Doctors' responses and men's reticence obscure greater levels of depression and anxiety. Studies of the psychological effects of unemployment suggest the effect of worklessness on men is major.

Being black can also increase people's vulnerability to mental distress. The psychological and material effects of racism and discrimination often combine with class and gender effects. Irish people for similar reasons also experience higher than average levels of mental distress and are over-represented in hospital admissions.

Racism is not confined to relations between white people and people not perceived as white. Anti-semitism is a form of racism and Irish people experience racism in Britain.   (MIND, 1993)

Racism existing in mental health services often compounds distress.

Studies over the past 20 years show that black people are more likely than white to be removed by the police to a place of safety under Section 136 of the Mental Health Act of 1983, detained in hospital under sections 2, 3 and 4 of the Mental Health Act, diagnosed as suffering from schizophrenia or another form of psychotic illness, detained in locked wards of psychiatric hospitals, given higher dosages of medication.   (MIND, 1993)

A tendency in mental health services to locate the mental health problems of black and minority ethnic people, such as schizophrenia, in their genes or culture obscures the historical material and psychological roots of racism and the effects of those. Against a background of increases in racist attacks on black people, the effects of industrial restructuring on employment and prospects and widespread evidence of higher levels of racism throughout Europe, it would seem reasonable to hypothesise an increase in levels of mental distress amongst many minority groups and a need to understand this increase and its treatment in structural and historical terms.

Debates about the increase in mental health problems cannot finally be resolved. Greater awareness itself generates more identification. So too does a view of society cast in individual terms and encouraged in that conceptualisation by the mental health profession. The MIND continuum model of mental distress furthermore includes most people at some point in their lives. However, it would seem reasonable to assume that people experiencing greater levels of poverty, insecurity, homelessness, racism, debt, unemployment, relationship breakdown are also going to suffer more in consequence.

In terms of tackling the issue of mental health in adult education, an awareness amongst adult educators of the various structural components of mental distress can open strategies for supporting students in generating their own understanding and actions for challenging some of the problems. This is important, because although people's willingness to speak out about their troubles is perhaps greater, it does not necessarily follow that the stigma and social and economic punishment for mental distress is any the less. The stigma surrounding mental distress has undoubtedly several causes. One is fear, and this was most commonly cited by students in response to the questionnaire.

They are frightened of the unknown - you can't see it.   (Female)

Because it is little understood, people shy away from it as if it were a contagious disease.   (Male)

Fear and also bad publicity - bad stories in the press. There's another fear - this could be me if ...   (Female)

Fear relates to the bewildering and often intractable manifestations of distress, to ignorance about its etiology and our own anxieties about the irrational and deep rooted 'devils' that may lurk within us.

Such understandable fear of what cannot be seen as might a physical impairment, is projected into the language, widespread and derogatory, that is used less to communicate more to keep the fears at bay. Greg Philo (1996) collates a glossary of 164 terms used in relation to mental health the great majority of which are offensive - barmy, ga-ga, loony, nuts, potty, soft in the head, psycho. Such language is used frequently and routinely amongst a population who would not dream of making such references to women (chicks, olds bags, bitches) or black people (wogs, coons, niggers), physically or mentally impaired people (cripples, morons, retards) or the elderly (old croaks, geriatrics, wrinklies). Perhaps it feels more acceptable because subconsciously we all feel implicated and afraid, but this does not bear much scrutiny. Destroying people through language is only one step away from destroying them socially or even physically.

> If thought corrupts language, language can also corrupt thought.
>
> (Orwell, 1957: 154)

The media plays an important role in legitimising fears and strategies for holding them at bay. The extent to which popular drama relies on themes of often crude and violent insanity is quite remarkable. A survey of a week's television viewing is salutary. Newspapers routinely refer perjoratively to politicians or criminals in terms of mental insanity. The Sun (1/9/98) describes Tony Benn's suggestion for helping the ailing Russian economy as ...

> Barmy Benn lashes out at cash lifeline.

Greg Philo analyses the content of the popular press that frequently conflates mentally ill with violent (eg. Sicko kids blamed for bloodbath that wiped out family, Daily Sport, 19 April 1993) and concludes ...

> Such representations can clearly affect audiences. They can alter perceptions of the 'dangerous' nature of mental illness as well as affecting beliefs about the risks of random attacks by the 'maniacs who are presented as populating the world'. (p.80)

As well as almost respectabilising fears, the implications are also that mental illness is closely associated with violent and unpredictable behaviour, affects a minority and has no everyday implications for the rest of us apart from our safety from these people.

Stigma has an important economic component. Early capitalism had to break with the routines of seasonal cycles and different paces of activities of rural communities.

> ... as industrial capitalism emerged, these rules of action (market relationships) appeared as unnatural and hateful restraints; the peasant, the rural labourer in the unenclosed village, even the urban artisan or apprentace did not measure the return of labour exclusively in money earnings, and they rebelled against the notion of week after week of disciplined labour.   (Thompson, p.357)

Capitalism had (and in many countries still has) the immense task of moving people into the inhumanity of a factory routine. The task now to persuade workers used to the security of a 40 hour week to embrace the idea of several jobs throughout life and endless reskilling is perhaps equally great. Failure or unwillingness to adapt can become pathologised into stigmatised statuses including workshy, as dealt with by labour camps as in the 1930s (Guardian 12/8/98) or currently workfare type policies, or mental illness initiating a circumscribed patient role and the lifelong punishment of a negative mental health record. Mental health structures and processes then act as a form of social control. Pilgrim and Rogers (1997) argue that this is even greater for certain groups. Black men who are more likely to find themselves labelled as schizophrenic, when actually they are exhibiting the anger and suffering of people sharply affected by racism and social and economic exclusion.

> Coercive psychiatry, as part of the wider repressive state apparatus offers itself as a post-colonial, Europeanised alternative to repatriation. Ideas about banishment to another country can be replaced by the mechanisms of exclusion and control afforded by the mental hospital, prison and physical treatments.   (p.60)

Under these circumstances it is not surprising perhaps that MIND found levels of prejudice about mental distress to be very high particularly amongst the college age population. A recent campaign has been directly targeted at universities and colleges, home of future opinion leaders, industrialists, educators, medical professionals (MIND, 1997). This campaign is aimed at challenging myths about mental distress. These include the myths that mental distress sufferers differ from normal people like ourselves, that mental health sufferers are violent, that once affected conditions persist for life. Such myths are widespread deeply rooted, and of course very damaging.

Effects of stigma on adult students is considerable. Respondents to the questionnaire described these as following.

Stigma can lead to feelings of isolation, loss of long-term friendships, employers being less likely to employ someone.   (Male)

People with mental health problems are shunned and treated badly. They are made to feel inferior and no good. This can destroy any good effects treatments may have on the sufferer.   (Female)

Enforced socialising with others who may be more intolerant than usually of mental health problems, who are bigoted or racist, creates bigger problems.
                                                                          (Male)

Unless tackled detrimental effects on educational progress are almost inevitable. These are compounded where staff have little understanding of what students are dealing with and cannot offer appropriate support and allowances.

Time limits for assignments and too high expectations can cause problems.
                                                                          (Male)

Tutors needs to be supportive and boost students' confidence in their achievements. Special needs and individual forms of help might be identified.
                                                                          (Female)

Where supported the educational experience approached at an appropriate pace can be constructive and contribute to greater self-esteem and a more hopeful future.

Issues of mental distress in adult education cannot be shoved under the carpet. This is especially the case as most adult educators accept the philosophy that education involves relating to the whole person both in terms of the invaluable life experiences and learning that students bring with them and also the contradictions, dilemmas, traumas that accompany such problems as redundancy, abuse, prejudice, disability, relationship breakdown.

Mental distress needs to be tackled head on in adult education especially as adult education is one of the few areas in which people can experience the beneficial effects of community and integration. As Emile Durkhein (1970) notes in his study of suicide that suicide rates were dependent on the degree to which individuals were integrated into social groups. The protective effects of community were also noted by Jennifer Newton (1988) ...

> ... social support may play a major role in modifying the deleterious effects of stress on health. (p.148)

Students themselves identify this as important ...

> There needs to be an acceptance of people for who they are irrespective of illness and background. Proactive approaches in classes and using literature would help. (Female)

Staff development is another area which needs more action. This is not to turn adult educators into psychiatric nurses and social workers, which some of us perhaps feel we are in danger of becoming anyway! Educators need to be able to do what they do best which is to educate and support learning. However, it cannot be avoided that many of us are woefully ignorant about mental health issues. This means that we can ignore warning signs, fail to give support when it would have been beneficial, fail to know about or refer people to the appropriate agencies or professionals, become too involved in situations where we do more harm than good, or become too involved for our own psychological or professional good. We may also fail to take sufficiently seriously the need to proactively create a community that is informed and supportive.

Student ignorance about mental health issues is probably equally widespread. Myths abound, offensive comments and language are widespread with the inevitable damaging effects on individuals and the student community. Student education in mental health matters would make a useful contribution to building an understanding community. This can take the form of mental health awareness sessions with appropriate professionals, educational campaigns generated by mental health agencies in conjunction with students, specially designated notice-boards with up to date information and sources of help.

> People are better educated today about our bodies. People should be more educated about our minds. We can then be more responsible.
>
> (Jane Hope, Oxford MIND)

Counselling facilities can be of great help. At Ruskin half of the full-time students consult the college counsellor within any one year. The advantages of being able to talk at length and in confidence with a trained professional helps many through the challenges and stresses of struggling with education and also acts as a useful conduit for ideas as to how student community life can be improved. However, for most of adult education this is probably only a dreamt of luxury. Even where affordable, it cannot be a sufficient answer. Educational counselling facilities cannot substitute for services in the community and NHS and need to be clear about the limits as well as the extent of what can be achieved. They in turn cannot substitute for a wider understanding of mental distress amongst adult educators.

Mental health issues can also become part of the academic curriculum. The interest shown in studying Social Psychology at Ruskin has been remarkable. Six part-time courses have run with a full complement of students in one year. A full-time module has now been developed as well as an option, again fully subscribed. Such courses explore the interconnections between individual experience and social processes both comparatively and historically. Mental health issues are only part of such a course which provides a wider context for relevant understanding and crucially, debate. Such courses as well as providing confidence boosting qualifications can generate levels of understanding that allow students to conduct their own educational campaigns, consciousness-raising and ideas for action.

The wider issues and debates affecting mental health can also be introduced as part of the curriculum or community life. Campaigns around low pay, education and training, student grants, anti-racism, bullying at work, working hours, unemployment, domestic violence, provision for lone parents, pensions are all directly relevant to mental health and are increasingly being seen in part as such. UNISON's campaign (1998) about workplace bullying and NATFHE's research on workplace stress, (1998) MIND's policy campaign on racism (1997) and Age Concern's Debate of the Age (1998) are a few examples of current activities focusing on the relationship between social processes and the psychological effects of those.

Conclusion

Adult education is experiencing the greater involvement of students who are suffering from mental health problems. The government is encouraging more 'disadvantaged' students into education whose greater vulnerability relates to increased social and economic pressures that impinge more heavily on certain segments of the population. An underclass discourse that blames people for their own distress, individualises and compounds problems more readily isolating sufferers.

This challenge requires several responses from adult education.

Firstly, it requires a recognition that mental health matters need to be taken more seriously because without such an understanding students will be less likely to make educational progress thus compounding a sense of failure. Secondly mental health issues and debates need to be made more 'visible' as part of an equal opportunities approach. This would involve providing information, raising awareness and challenging discriminatory language and behaviour. It would also involve examining ways in which the structures and cultures of educational organisations support or are detrimental to the mental health of students and of staff. Thirdly, staff development needs to support staff in making interventions or referrals that are appropriate and helpful and in developing alongside students, services that are relevant and helpful. Materials from teaching unions can also help staff identify the extra pressures on themselves of student anxieties and the more general intensification and insecurity of work. Fourthly, student education about mental health can challenge some of the stigma, myths and self-blame attached. Workshops, seminars, noticeboards, course content, student campaigns are a few of the ways this can be advanced.

In increasing generally an awareness of how social and economic changes can have both positive and negative implications for mental health, adult education can make a further contribution to debates about social justice and social change.

References

Age Concern (1998) *Debate of the Age*, London, Age Concern.
Bryant, R. (1997) Funding nightmare ahead for social work students in *Professional Social Work*, October 1997.
Dahrendorf, R. 'Footnotes to the Discussion', in Smith, David J. (ed) *Understanding the Underclass*, London, PSI.
Durkheim, Emile (1970) *Suicide: A study in sociology*, London, Routledge and Kegan Paul.
Elliot, L. (1998) *Superpower update: US is morally bankrupt, Russia just bankrupt* in The Guardian 25th August.
Fryer, B. (1997) *Learning for the 21st Century*, National Advisory Group for Continuing Education and Lifelong Learning.
Hainge, M. (1997) *Mental Health and Young People Resource Report*, London, MIND.
Handy, C. (1994) *The Empty Raincoat*, London, Hutchinson.
Heath, A. (1992) 'The Attitudes of the Underclass', in Smith, David J. (ed) *Understanding the Underclass*, London, IPPR.
James, O. (1997) *Britain on the Couch- Treating a low seratonin society*, London, Century.
Kennedy, H. (1998) *Learning Works- Widening Participation in Further Education*, Coventry, FEFC.
McKie, D. and Wainwright, M. (1998) *Jobless hardened in Labour Camps* in The Guardian 10th December.
MIND (1996) *Not just Sticks and Stones*, London, MIND.
MIND and Health Education Association (1997) Mental Health for Young People Campaign, London, MIND.
Murray, C. (1990) *The Emerging British Underclass*, London, IEA Welfare and Health Unit.
Nairne, K. and Smith, G. (1984) *Dealing with Depression*, London, The Women's Press.
NATFHE News, June 1997.
Newton, J. (1988) *Preventing Mental Illness*, London and New York, Routledge and Kegan Paul.

Noble, M. et al. (1994) *Changing Patterns of Income and Wealth in Oxford and Oldham*, Oxford, Department of Applied Social Studies.

Orwell, G. (1957) 'Politics and the English Language', in *Inside the Whale and other essays*, England, Penguin.

Philo, G. et al. (1996) *Media and Mental Distress*, London and New York, Longman.

Pilgrim, D. and Rogers, A. (1997) *A Sociology of Mental Health and Illness*, Buckingham Philadelphia, Open University Press.

Social Trends (1998).

Thomas, K. (1997) 'The Defensive Self: A Psychodynamic perspective', in Stevens, R. (ed) *Understanding the Self*, Open University.

Thompson, E.P. (1963) *The Making of the English Working Class*, Great Britain, Camelot.

UNISON (1998) *Bullying in the Workplace*, London.

Wilkinson, R. (1994) 'Health Redistribution and Growth', in Glyn, A. and Miliband, D. (eds) *Paying for Inequality*, London, IPPR.

With special thanks to Jane Hope of Oxford MIND, and to the students of Ruskin College.

8   An Exploratory Examination of Changing Perceptions of Careership: The Implications for the Management of the Continuing Professional Development of Teachers

LORAINE POWELL

Abstract

The teaching profession is not immune to changes in the social and political culture which impinge upon and are reshaping attitudes towards career development. Given the changing psychological contract between employer and the employee, personal development is gaining precedence over organisational development. The paper examines whether self-development is essentially in conflict or in support of professional development. How other professions approach continuing professional development challenges the appropriateness of current INSET arrangements and TTA strategies. An exploratory survey of new teachers confirms their focus on 'employability', and schools constraining rather than facilitating their professional development.

Introduction

In health care, pensions, large corporations, society is shifting from collective to individual responsibility. In education, whilst the established patterns of structure and status represent a powerful historical legacy, environmental scanning cannot ignore the focus on self-directed behaviour. The changing nature of the psychological contract between employer and employee, in particular, influences the changing ways in which people, at the end of the twentieth century, think about their work and careers.

Do the rapidly changing patterns of employment outside the teaching profession affect young teachers' perceptions of a 'career', how do they view their ability to shape their own future? If national policies for continuing professional development continue to focus on meeting organisational needs to the neglect of personal development will social, political and financial pressures lead to conflict between an individual's professional goals and those of the institution? Who should set the agenda for continuing professional development? Other professions, for example, the RIBA, the Engineering Council have encouraged acceptance of CPD as part of professional life, safeguarding the standards of professional competence. The most developed model is that offered by the Institute of Personnel and Development (IPD) for professionals in personnel and training, where CPD is a condition of continuing membership of the Institute. Can the current mindset in Education absorb new habits of continuous learning, building appropriate elements of CPD into a more strategic framework in order to successfully meet organisational expectations alongside individual teacher aspirations?

Hopson (1996: 2) reminds us that before the 1830s, 'people did jobs', but they did not 'have' jobs. An individual defined him/herself by the skills they possessed and the families they belonged to. The linking of work to jobs, jobs to income, and reputation to job title was a product of the industrial revolution. Even today to many employees, including many teachers, a job provides a sense of self worth. Over the last decade attitudes towards lifelong employment, a career with regular promotions have been sorely tested. In Hopson's view (1996: 2) 'there is no such thing as a career path anymore, only crazy paving and, you have to lay it yourself'. When employment guarantees have gone, individuals focus on a range of professional and personal skills that they see as transferable to a number of employment situations, they need to develop their own employability.

For young teachers, part of Hopson's Generation X, the 18-29 year olds, employability is more attractive than employment, challenge and variety more attractive than security and money, self fulfilment more attractive than status. If so, what are the implications for continuing professional and personal development? Will the CPD policies being introduced by the Teacher Training Agency, in particular, meet the needs of Generation X? What are the origins of this culture shift?

Change and the Organisation, the Effects on Employees

Change has no conscience, however, the better change is understood, the more it provides individuals with opportunities. Corelli Barnet (1995) catalogued the world of uncertainty. Key factors are now well known; the globalisation of markets, intensifying competition, constant technological innovation, the decline of traditional industries, demand for higher quality and value, growing ecological problems and international recession. Organisations constantly need to respond to these environmental influences.

Restructuring and privatisation in the 1980s frequently led to: delayering management, reducing employees to a small body of core workers, contracting out and making use of part-time or self-employed workers. This in turn has put continual pressure on the public sector to imitate the private sector and become 'lean' organisations. Lean organisations are seen as dynamic, yet they are also fragile. Holbeche (1996) found in her research for Roffey Park that many organisations in the private sector are failing to take account of the strains flatter structures impose on people. Nearly three-quarters of employees reported increased work loads, over two-thirds stated that there was a consequent reduction in morale, whilst as few as one percent of employees within these new structures are motivated to behave in a way which will make lean systems work.

In terms of career development in flatter structures, staff reported that they were used to continuous change and were prepared to be flexible when renegotiating their terms of employment. The footloose worker with less loyalty to the company or organisation is matched by companies or organisations with less long term loyalty to their workforce. The Roffey Park research acknowledges the value of enhancing each individual's employability while no longer providing a 'job for life'.

This move, away from control dependency and compliance, towards partnership and autonomy brings us to a need to re-evaluate appraisals, reward systems and differentials that emphasise status and hierarchical systems. Empowering oneself, influencing the organisation from any level is critical to fostering initiative and employee satisfaction. Murlis and Wright (1993: 30) allege that employee satisfaction in the UK has plummeted over the last twenty years, and on a number of crucial indicators levels of morale are lower than in the mid 1970s. Only in teaching and the health service is there a possible cure for the 'motivation blues'. Here there is still a sense of doing a job well against the odds, a greater emphasis on personal integrity and taking pride in undertaking work for its own sake rather than simply for financial gain. Murlis et al. thesis is that employees generally get their motivation from satisfying their personal values rather than from anything the organisation can provide, yet systemic and structural change faces the public sector, including education. Staff here also are likely to respond to the same sort of stimulus engendered in the private sector.

Watts (1993) sees a structure emerging in society where education and employment are to a large degree mutually dependent. One works to learn, one learns to work. These symbiotic and continuing processes redefine the concept of career:

> Increasingly a career cannot be defined as a structure: it has become 'boundary less'.
> (Arthur, 1994: 300)

Wijers (1996: 187) draws attention to the practice in IBM where management had asked all its employees to reflect on themselves (self-assessment) and to ask themselves the question as to whether they could make a viable 'offer' within the company's internal labour market (self-marketing). In conclusion Wijers states that individuals must learn to perform three tasks, firstly to form an identity, secondly to determine a direction and thirdly to plan a career and steer themselves into it. Learning these skills 'gives people a hold on their career, an articulation of the future you want to create'. In exploring the context of career management in a climate of change, old habits and assumptions need to be challenged for differing success factors and new competences need fostering and maintaining. Maynard Keynes' view that worldly wisdom teaches us that it is better to fail conventionally than to succeed unconventionally, may well be prevalent in the reality of many organisations, but Prahalad and Hammel (1990: 89-90) stress the need for organisations to consciously audit human capital, especially the core competencies employees possess, and the use that is being made of these by senior managers. Their findings of productive companies highlighted the use made of those people identified as carriers of core competencies; the ability to handle diversity, flexibility, resilience, keeping goals in mind and seeing the essentials in a mass of information. The benefits to society and the economy of this approach is that the key resource (professional competence) is not only renewable but self-generating. Whilst 80% of our technological inventions have occurred since 1900, it is encouraging to detect in the new technologies, an element of 'full circle into the future', in terms of an emphasis on individual talent and organisational ownership structures which echo many of the developments of the late eighteenth and early nineteenth century (Naisbitt, 1995).

Market Influences on the Teaching Profession

However, the information society gives increasing power and influence to the many. It allows markets to move much faster and competition to become more intense. In 1994, the Institute of Directors asked its members what factors contributed most to competitiveness, 78% said education. This year also saw the publication of the Government's first comprehensive audit of the UK's competitiveness position in the White Paper, 'Competitiveness: helping business to win', and the following White Papers of 1995 and 1996. The contribution requirement of Education and Training is to provide a motivated, flexible and highly skilled workforce, meeting the new National Targets for Education and Training both for foundation levels and for lifelong learning. Following the White Papers is the Technology Foresight Programme which also sees education as having a pivotal role to play in developing competitiveness. The genuinely coherent modularised qualification sought, based on a broader Baccalaureate model, aims to make young people better able to adapt to technological change and frequent career changes. One outcome of the Foresight programme is the need to develop and maintain networks, partnerships and connections, for differing sectors of the economy. Teachers will have to work interprofessionally, as illustrated presently in Single Regeneration Schemes, and as they do so the facility to move between sectors, adopt cyclical career patterns is likely to grow.

In education as in business, policy developments are being expressed in the language of the enterprise culture. The market place, as seen through local management of schools, GMS, school marketing strategies, league tables has highlighted the importance of the external environment in determining strategy. Teachers increasingly like their counterparts elsewhere have to be able to handle not one single trend but simultaneous trends, their occupational identity is no longer assured.

The iron law of inevitability about market intensification brought with it a culture of restructuring. Grace (1992: 148) addresses this as the economy of teacher employment, where changed criteria regulate the appointment of teachers to the school, cheapness of appointment overriding quality of appointment. Restructuring the expectation for teacher appointments has led to a narrow conception of what teaching is. Hargreaves and Reynolds (1989) put the issue well, when they see the policy goal of education as having changed from what it enabled to what it delivered. Earlier Giroux and McLaren (1986) and addressed again by Grace, see the image of the teacher as a transformative intellectual as missing from present discourse. Despite this perceived reduction in costs, morale and power (Jenkins, 1991: 45-61), candidates still come forward for training. Rafferty (1991) would view this as the Government solving the teacher supply crisis by closing down the economy. Nevertheless HMI (1992: 1) report that the recruitment and appointment procedures for new teachers are generally satisfactory and often good. However they go on to say (p.4) that anxieties about future employment often have unsettling effects on new teachers. Temporary contracts of one year or less ranged from less than 10% to 100% in the LEAs surveyed. This striking variation in practice may well directly affect the way in which young teachers' decisions about their career plans are reached and implemented.

The continuing flow of young people into a profession where a significant number of schools operate on the verge of viability brings additional concern. Nias (1989) in a study of teachers' perceptions of their own careers refers to 'the dread of professional stagnation', as teachers simply lost heart as they had nowhere to go. Nias (1989) and Jenkins (1991) particularly see the deletion of the post of Deputy Headteacher being budget driven. As resources decline so too the resources devoted to staff development are devoted more to the interests of the school than to the individual. Fidler et al. (1991) point up this irony whilst Jones (1990) sees Headteachers facing a central dilemma of whether to give priority to the needs of the individual teacher, the justification cited that funding courses for individuals may only serve to enhance an individual's career in someone else's school. As headteachers become subject to the economy of teacher employment, governors and headteachers can make teachers redundant or award points above the standard scale for recruitment or retention of a post. Overall, given Levacic's (1993) reporting of the Audit Commission findings on teaching staff costs, promoted posts are declining at a time when in-service training and the professional development of teachers is becoming more competitive and more central to government plans for raising the quality of the teaching profession.

From INSET to CPD

INSET has been financed and organised in various ways over the last decade. In the early 1980s, Higher Education was the lead partner, providing long courses available to secondees. LEAs were levied and able to draw down from the uncapped pooling arrangements. It was expected that teachers undertaking degrees or diplomas would gain promotion or a new post. At a time of falling rolls, ACSET, the Advisory Council for the Supply and Education of Teachers established in 1984, viewed the pooling arrangements as overgenerous to LEAs in that they could recoup 75% of the budget for seconding a teacher, in response to the problem of a surplus of teachers due to a contracting service. A more focused INSET provision centred on the LEA and TVEI, with the introduction of TRIST (TVEI related in-service support for teachers) in 1986. However, rapidly the LEA as lead partner was supplanted from 1987 by a series of forms of arrangements GRIST (Grant Related In-service Training), LEATAGS (LEA Training and Grant Scheme), followed by GEST (Grant for Education Support and Training), which embedded INSET provision within the schools' remit. Thus, OfSTED in 1993 reported on school focused INSET provision. They found that a coherent strategy in schools for providing opportunities for management development and training is still lacking (p.3). Induction for Headteachers and their deputies is frequently inadequate. The teachers' perception of INSET were that it ... (p.5) 'boosted their self-confidence and had a significant impact on their personal teaching methods'. Almost all schools in the survey had school development plans in place. The best provided clear management targets and therefore a context for training and experience, they also gave the managers a better understanding of change. Training needs are identified by school development plans and appraisal, but neither of these methods is likely to be sufficient in the absence of external inputs which provide a view wider than that of the individual school. The external input was soon determined by the TTA (Teacher Training Agency). Gillian Shephard at the launch of the TTA's first Corporate Plan in March 1995 drew attention to the lack of a strategic approach to in-service education, given the investment of around £4000m per year. 'It is an area about which we know very little' - she asked the TTA to survey in some detail the cost and nature of current in-service training and development activities and to stimulate strategic thinking about the ways of directly managing this activity better in the long term. The external input, through government direction was apparent, but the Secretary of State acknowledged ...

> there is a difficult balance to be struck ... the priorities of the individual teacher as identified by appraisal ... the priorities of the school, as set out in the development plan of post-inspection action plans ... and the national priorities which emerge from those with an overview of the school system.

Given this lead and the absence of evidence of the national picture, a research study conducted by MORI (1995) for the TTA surveyed continuing professional development in a stratified sample of 7,800 schools. This more comprehensive view of human resource development activities within the schools sector highlighted the lack of consistency as to how much any one school spent on CPD, budgets ranged from nothing to over £25,000. Whilst teachers perceived CPD activities that they were involved in as useful, only 26% claimed they had had a great deal of impact on their work in the classroom. More importantly the survey revealed that different people had differing ideas as to the purpose of CPD and that few schools had any systematic means of evaluating CPD activities. In considering policy options, Anthea Millett in the TTA first annual lecture refers to both 'light touch' and 'heavy touch' strategies. The light touch would be built around national criteria, the heavy touch by way of a national framework or professional qualifications to provide assurance that teachers had successfully completed relevant training programmes. The resulting national standards of excellence targeted at four key points, namely: newly qualified teachers, expert teachers, experts in subject leadership and management, experts in school leadership and management, can be interpreted as the heavy hand. The implicit assumptions being that schools exhibit characteristics of modern rather than postmodern organisations. The proposals reflecting Clegg's (1992: 214) criteria of increasing specialisation and hierarchy, stratification, formalisation, standardisation and centralisation of action. This rigidity is in sharp contrast to more complex, fragmentary yet flexible features of postmodern organisations, the ascendant sociological framework at the end of the twentieth century.

The TTA in setting out its organisational focus for CPD, whether through Headlamp, the National Professional Qualification for aspiring Headteachers or increasing Key Stage 2 teachers' subject knowledge, is directly concerned with the impact on improving teaching and learning, a declared aim being that this will, according to Mrs Shephard in July 1995, still further enhance the status of the profession. The development of the profession rather than the personal development of teachers is paramount. Furthermore, the OfSTED Handbook in 7.1.B states

> an examination of the documentation, (syllabuses, schemes of work, lesson plans and records) will show ... the focus and extent of in-service training related to teaching.

Only two references refer to the needs of individual teachers, firstly in 7.6.1A. Opportunities are made available for teachers to update their skills and a staff development policy sets individual needs within the context, of the school's development plan. Secondly in Part 5 Technical Papers, Paper 9 ...

> Consideration should now be given to drawing up a staff development policy which links institutional needs to those of the individual teachers, and includes procedures for monitoring and evaluation.

Whilst those who work in other professions may share concerns over the inadequacies of training and development opportunities available to today's teachers and tomorrow's educational managers, the focus on externally directed qualifications and vertical career patterns is in contrast with emerging self-directed notions of CPD and career paths outside the teaching profession.

CPD and Career Development: Views from Another Profession

Postmodern organisations in the 1990s are more organic, less differentiated systems. Understanding how personal and professional development can be explored in the context of career management can bring benefits to the organisation. Theoretical models of career planning are important but work models, values, interests, skills, personality type, learning preference are factors in aligning organisational and personal vision. Developing organisational capability and capacity building through a greater emphasis on self-development, a focus on learning rather than training, is central to the CPD policies and strategies as propounded by the Institute of Personnel and Development. The Institute believes that professionals need to update their knowledge and develop their skills continuously and that the primary responsibility for this lies with the individual, not the employer. The emphasis on learning and therefore personal development can be massively enhanced by a planned and systematic approach. The IPD Directory (1996) and accompanying disk helps the member to identify current knowledge and skills and to set them against an assessment of the abilities needed to meet current and projected work and own career aims. The gaps between the two show the areas that need to be addressed by a CPD plan. The IPD requires members to produce, manage and periodically update a personal development plan, although the format is not prescribed. The three key elements are:

- The development objectives, divided into immediate and short term needs, and long-term career and development needs.
- Plans to meet these objectives: subdivided into work-based activities, formal learning and informal or personal action.
- A schedule of target dates for action and dates on which to review how effective the action has been.

They maintain, IPD Directory, p.54:

> CPD is only fully effective when it becomes part of the normal way you manage your career and is not seen as an additional chore.

They view the real test as whether the individual's CPD actually improves their professional competence and adds to the achievement of their personal career objectives. Clutterbuck (1996) writing in People Management in support of CPD acknowledges that most people in the UK do not have a defined programme of personal growth. ' Individuals lack the motivation, the tools and the support mechanisms to alter their career and developmental expectations'. His answer is to redefine learning in a much broader way (p.23). 'By focusing on the notion of personal value, success is not simply a matter of a career, but is about using an individual's natural talents to the greatest effect'. Clutterbuck's views are supported by an IES, Institute of Employment Studies Survey in 1995 which showed that when people have access to self-development material, they are twice as likely to choose personal rather than technical skills development. Its conclusion being that people are taking responsibility for their own development, either because they have an eye on their future employability, or because they are taking responsibility for their future careers. The need to develop coherent clearly stated policies on CPD led the IPD to produce a pack detailing the Institute's policy, which includes a system for professional development either on disk or on paper. Outcomes matter far more than inputs, the minimum level of CPD activity is recommended as 35 hours per year or the equivalent in learning hours/outcomes. This small but regular investment of time in learning is seen as an essential part of professional life and therefore a requirement for corporate membership. Presently the IPD is undertaking its first survey of corporate members to ascertain compliance with its declared policy. The feedback and outcome will be illuminative, but the aim is to help all members to embrace the CPD philosophy without fear of being judged.

CPD cannot be diverted from the wider employment relationships within an organisation. Here again its value to the individual is that one remains up-to-date as a professional working within an ever-changing world where the psychological contract is changing with regard to tenure in organisations, including education establishments. How far has the emerging focus on personal development and learning changed teachers' perceptions of continuing professional development and notions of a career?

Changing Approaches to Careership in the Netherlands

Working with Educational Careers Guidance in the Netherlands, Wijers and Meyers (1996) explored developing views, similar to those of the IPD, that individuals in modern society are increasingly becoming responsible for their own work allocations.

In the recent past, people reached a working position by means of institutional forces (Wijers et al., p.186). Schools traditionally also provided young teachers with an identity and a direction. This in turn ensured that the teacher reached and remained at a work destination that fitted his or her identity and direction. Currently however, those leaving initial teacher training are often confronted with the problem of getting a job, often repeatedly, until a permanent post is secured. Wijers concluded that teachers have no clear awareness of their direction and identity. The responsibility is with the individual to develop the skills necessary to gain, and retain a place to work. Wijers et al. (p.189) state

> individuals have to learn to tune the development of their qualifications to their talents, interests and motivation (identity) on the one hand and to future market demands on the other.

Whilst occupations such as teaching previously formed a relatively stable structure, changes in the world of work are affecting the deeper structures of established expectations including teaching.

The research in the Netherlands confirmed that teachers are expected to be flexible, creative, stress proof, possessing both learning capacity and social skills. Wijers (p.197) thesis is that individuals need to acquire 'actor competences' which can be considered as a specification of Drucker's (1993) concept of an educated person. Actor competences are qualities which enable individuals to appear on the social stage as actors, as persons who are no longer mainly passive, ie. they are aware of the social construction of reality, and are able to participate in the historical process (Berger and Luckman, 1966).

Particularly in the knowledge society, (Toffler, 1990), cultural and social forces are weakened and it is imperative that teachers determine their learning goals and plan their learning processes in order to keep abreast of the increasingly complex environment in which schools or educational organisations are forced to operate. Coming from a careers guidance perspective, Wijer's is reassuring in respect of accompanying changes in the role of the careers guidance counsellor

> from ferryman to pathway finder ... the adventure offered by pathfinding will compensate for the loss of security and clarity enjoyed by the ferryman.
>
> (p.197)

The Attitudes of Young Teachers in the UK towards Careership and CPD

As other professions such as personnel, architecture, the law see the acceptance of CPD as part of professional life, what of the teaching profession? Government initiatives, are well publicised, well funded and prescribe the training needs for the service. In the past responsibility has often been taken narrowly in the sense of 'who pays' for INSET. This exploratory small survey looks at the question of teachers attitude and commitment to CPD allied to a reassessment of their career planning. Is the emphasis on self-development, employability, building career resilience likely to lead to better job satisfaction than the government's proposed models, what can we learn from perceptions of career expectation of our young teachers?

Hopson's Generation X, identified as 18-29 year olds have matured in a society that has become more complex, experienced simultaneous trends both towards internationalism and individualism whilst being educated themselves in a system which emphasised greater self-learning at the expense of traditional teaching methods. On entry to the profession they must be aware of the social and economic constraints on education, not least as it affects their tenure, their promotion prospects and career development. The central purpose of the survey was to learn more about the views of those young people who have just entered the profession. The sample is drawn from teachers under 27 years of age who have entered and been in continuous service in the profession for less than three years, ie. post-September 1994. As a preliminary survey it was not practical to employ a random or stratified sample, for this relatively unexplored area of research. The ad hoc sample survey employed has been selected as a representative sample of a much larger population.

The sample is drawn from newly appointed teachers in three local authorities in West Yorkshire. The respondents had all been appointed to first posts, either temporary or permanent, in the Primary sector. A comparison group from the secondary sector would have been informative, but findings are restricted to those entering the Primary Sector, where traditionally the commitment to teaching as a career has been strongest. No account was taken of teachers entering different key stages, size of school or the schools geographical location. Sixty questionnaires were distributed via a snowballing strategy. Headteachers and Deputy Headteachers identified members of the population who identified other informants and so on. What was unexpected and striking about the distribution of questionnaires were the relatively few new teachers in any one school. The greatest number was two in any one school, whilst several schools who expressed an interest in the survey had had no new appointments for up to four years. Schools staff appear static rather than stable and this again raises questions for the profession.

The prepared questionnaire used both open and closed questions. Some questions were more appropriate to an interview schedule than a questionnaire, but the writer thought it important for young teachers to see themselves as researchers and was looking for reflexiveness ...

a capacity to review critically and reflectively processes and practices.

(L. Stenhouse, 1975)

Headteachers were briefed in person and by telephone as to the aims and use of the questionnaire and envelopes were provided for secure replies.

Of the 60 distributed, 31 replies were returned including 11 after the due date. Given the nature of the sample it was qualitative indicators that were being looked for. Evidence of

1. changes in the normative orientations in attitudes, beliefs, roles in relation to CPD and career development;

2. to gain insights into the factors affecting the processes of professional development of new teachers.

As Moser and Kalton (1971: 267-8) point out

non-response is a problem because of the likelihood - that people who do not return questionnaires differ from those who do!

Anonymity means there is no way of linking responses with individuals. In this limited time project no reminders were sent after the first distribution.

In reporting the results of the survey, provision was made for those having experienced differing forms of Initial Teacher Training, namely the BEd route or the Degree plus PGCE route. Other differences of sex and, length of service are not seen to be significant. The decision to use a narrative reporting style, ensured respondents were not identified, other than by training mode, and was thought the most appropriate strategy for communicating the process of critical review.

New Teachers Attitudes Towards Careership and Continuing Professional Development - The Survey Results

The findings are reported using a number or organising output measures, ie. accessibility, availability, awareness, appropriateness, efficiency and effectiveness, and acceptability. These could be looked on as 'partial performance indicators', however, the whole probably has another dimension. Nevertheless, the parts which appear provide an appropriate reporting system and characterise the exploratory survey of new teachers views on careership and continuing professional development.

Accessibility - over 60% of the respondents were on temporary contracts, with four on their third temporary contract within the first two years of teaching. As one would expect this was seen as the greatest barrier to their further professional development and short term goals are simply to obtain a permanent post. The dissatisfaction expressed by those on temporary contracts may also have been compounded by schools, who through time constraints or other factors, have been unable to set targets for development and career progression of this most vulnerable group.

For new staff with permanent posts, schools appear more ready to set targets for development but relatively few arise through the appraisal process. Timing of the appraisal process may be particularly significant here, but only one teacher commented on the relationship between appraisal and professional development and training.

Availability - findings here were related to time and the range of activities, provided through the school. Time spent on Continuing Professional Development, includes school based time and was expressed per term. The range was from 0 to 65 hours with an average of 27 hours. Schools presented a conventional menu with overall workplace learning ranging from 10% to 50% of allocated time, followed by courses and job rotation. Less than six teachers had had the opportunity of attendance at a Conference (5), Flexible Learning (4), Management Training (4) or Research (1). As might be expected no staff had participated in telematics or enjoyed a short secondment. The question however, was personal, ie. what type of action will you take to meet these objectives? The answers relate to what can be obtained in the school and perhaps give an assumption that the school is viewed by the cohort as the main provider and access point for Continuing Professional Development.

Awareness - Guidance on Continuing Professional Development for new teachers. The Headteacher is seen as the staff member who knows what is available, or has access to resources. Heads and Deputy Heads are named in preference to INSET Co-ordinators. Where the co-ordination is not a Head or Deputy, one person named the Careers Advisor within school, whilst on 25% of returns no evidence was given as to whom to approach for advice and guidance. One explanation may be that the survey was only conducted in the Primary Sector, where schools are relatively small and the scope for delegation less than in the secondary sector. Nevertheless, the findings suggest that the management of CPD is not seen as meriting additional points above the main salary scale and is not critical to the organisation of schools. If so, one would have expected new teachers to have more readily identified the post of responsibility from within the school staff.

Appropriateness - to career development. When asked whether secure employment or employability was preferred, employability was clearly identified as more important by 60%, a further 30% saw the two targets of being of equal worth, whilst only 10% preferred secure employment, hence approximately 90% of this small survey put the focus on transferable skills at this stage in their career. This is further reinforced through specified priorities for continuing professional development, where gaining greater personal confidence and competence had the highest priority followed by; to enhance career prospects, to improve performance in your current job, for managerial and organisational benefits and finally to increase your learning capacity.

The concern for employability and personal skills is allied to short and long term goals. A significant number of teachers commented they had little control over short term goals, as a consequence of temporary contracts, some temporary allowances and the constraints of time and heavy workloads on a first post. However, all returns did note long term objectives. Although at the start of their careers, the classroom is not the place to stay for some. Teacher training or curriculum development at a 'wider level than just one school' was mentioned frequently, for example, becoming a music manager or language coordinator. To be a Deputy or Headteacher was also considered by 40% of respondents although caveats were included such as viewing this post as 'working towards a more advisory role'. Given these standpoints, the primary teacher still expects a life time career in the School system. Cyclical careers, moving between schools and other employment attracted only one respondent. Nevertheless vertical careers perhaps have less attraction also, what seems to be emerging is a stronger emphasis on personal development, horizontal career moves and a higher concern for personal job satisfaction. This last factor relates to the question, 'do you regard the future with enthusiasm?' Interestingly respondents were split on this issue, some of those replying affirmatively interjecting, 'it depends what sort of a day I've had', 'I want to develop professionally ... but I am nervous as to whether events will work out as planned', whilst for others, 'there is a definite feeling of mutual support and extensive communication', 'most people are dedicated and value themselves as teaching professionals'. In summary, careers are becoming more personal, yet still primary teachers see their development and their loyalty within a schools sector setting.

Efficiency and Effectiveness of CPD - Few teachers have a written personal development plan although most new teachers do currently keep a personal record of their continuing professional development. Only one respondent makes a personal financial contribution to the plan whilst only a further two would be prepared to consider such a proposal. In relation to financing staff development to implement the school development plan, all replies were negative. No respondent commented on time as a resource or having a financial cost in relation to the latter. One might expect there were other priorities for financing at this stage in one's career, however the answers were reinforced by the offer of loan arrangements. Both the present government's Career Development Loan or a proposed Individual Learning Account received no endorsements. The central view is still that in the management of the profession, continuing education should be an entitlement in the best interests of the service. Finance was overwhelmingly seen to be the greatest barrier 'continual cuts in INSET funding', 'no money to fund an allowance for my present management role'. Improvements thus focused on the need for 'more funding', 'more non-teaching time', 'a personal training allowance, so I could receive support in my areas of need rather than in my area of responsibility'. There appears to be a substantial gap between expectations and what can be delivered. On the job training has been in practice a less expensive option, but teachers question its quality and comprehensiveness, the demand for high quality off the job training is seen not only as desirable but as enhancing the standards and status of continuing professional development.

Acceptability - Whilst personal financial commitment to lifetime training and self-development is, in general terms, absent it is nevertheless valued at this stage of a teacher's career. It is seen as 'essential, stop learning and you stagnate as a teacher', and as 'very important to keep up with changes', 'essential for self-esteem, self-worth and personal fulfilment'. The most extensive comments from the questionnaire were given in this section. Personal growth and development is again embedded in how they see the concept of career, ' a lifelong profession in which you strive for continuous improvement and achievement', 'a career is a job with an element of continuing professional development', ... 'of working with a dynamic fulfilling occupation with the option for change within that sector aided by professional development'. These personal and optimistic statements contrast with how they view others and their attitudes, 'a lot of disillusionment', 'I don't feel many teachers see it as a career, many appear to be looking for ways out', 'many of my colleagues are insecure and have resigned themselves to 'coasting', they do not see the need to continue to learn'.

For new teachers an awareness of the link between career development and continuing professional development has been well evidenced in the responses to this small survey. It seems important that this is embedded in policy management action taking account of the declared personal focus in the professional development of teachers and the development of the teaching profession.

Reframing Continuing Professional Development

The ways in which teachers as professionals try to update and refresh their own learning throughout their career is critical to any developed economy as we move into the next millennium. Professional bodies, including the IPD have recognised this need by taking action to promote and encourage CPD. Whilst individuals are seen to have a right and a duty to undertake CPD, there is a strong case for CPD becoming a shared responsibility.

In a survey of professional bodies, Welsh, L. and Woodward, P. (1989: 149) 58 respondents from differing professional bodies had CPD policies and a further 38 were considering introducing a CPD policy. Many have introduced CPD as a criteria for consideration of applicants to a fellowship or other upgrading of membership categories. As a consequence, higher status is afforded to such members. In education, without a Teachers General Council, there has been an apparent reluctance of professional bodies and the other pressure groups, including Unions to promote CPD as integral to teachers pay and conditions or as an expected contributor to explicit criteria for promotion. In this vacuum, the TTA has been able to establish crude benchmarks for a national system. The incremental progression from novice to expert to manager to entrepreneur is about to be enacted as a profound cultural transformation of the profession. However in assessing the emergent patterns and new settlements. Grace (1995: 212) sees 'the great issue for the 1990s and beyond is, are those central values to be those of market culture or of democratic culture?' Historically, professional bodies and schools have invested very little in any deliberate way in shaping the broader professionalism of their staff. The question of who is to set teachers' professional agenda is critical when educational institutions need to present themselves as strategically forward looking organisations. This paper comes to the conclusion that the only acceptable answer is that teachers working as individuals or groups, must set the agenda themselves, within stated policies on CPD, agreed between professional bodies and government, through the TTA. Without this, schools will continue to erect barriers to effective delivery whilst a centrally imposed model acts as a barrier to acceptance of the principle by many teachers, and consequently take up of CPD is not likely to transform professional performance.

Many professional bodies, such as the Royal Town Planning Institute place the emphasis on the individual to assess their own CPD needs and offer advice on how to develop a personal CPD plan. In education, the imminent review of appraisal could provide a gateway to this activity. We also have a growing expertise in mentorship. Through more efficient and effective use of the appraisal process and mentors who are able to extend the professional learning of staff, CPD could be central to job satisfaction and motivation of teachers.

Fidler and Fugh (1991) and Jones (1990) both refer to the barriers presented by the school. As INSET has come through the HE age, the LEA age to the School age, schools are currently accountable for the range of provision. Headteachers, aware of OfSTED criteria, the rise of whole school development planning, along with overall restraints on school budgets have, in many cases put the needs of the school before the needs of individual teachers. Teachers secondments are in the past, there is restricted freedom of choice in course provision, and GEST allocations in many local authorities need to be demonstrably linked to either the School Development Plan or OfSTED action plan before it can be confirmed as available for the school to spend. There is a dilemma for headteachers as to whether to give priority to the needs of the individual or the needs of the organisation. Research in this paper would suggest that where 'training' is aimed at schools or organisational development, rather than individual development, young teachers would not regard the training they receive as CPD at all.

There is a culture shift in the attitudes of new teachers. The survey demonstrates their changing expectations towards teaching as a career, they are ready to make an investment plan for their own training and development. This generation have grown up being told this is a climate of change, of growing unemployment, changing work patterns and therefore they have a different set of responses previously noted as flexibility, career resilience, their own employability. There is more of an expectation that they need to develop a range of professional and personal skills that are and will be transferable to a range of employment options as they occur in their future. A career is a personal career, something new teachers now carry with them rather than belonging to a particular profession.

The change in culture has brought a change in teachers' value systems in relation to CPD, thus changes in structuring career development must follow to stand any change of success. More dialogue, more participation, allowing teachers to identify with CPD objectives because they are their objectives, needs to be addressed by school managers and nationally by

Professional Associations and the TTA. Collaboration is essential to maximise individual strengths and responsibilities and at the same time give common direction to the profession. It may be healthier for education that teachers do not expect to spend a lifetime in the profession, that a personal view of a career opens up more opportunities for individuals and for this important area of social policy.

> ... keep interested in your own career, however humble; it is a real possession in the changing fortunes of time.

This Desiderata of 1692 would seem entirely appropriate for the new teachers of 1999.

References

Arthur, M. (1994) 'The boundaryless career: a new perspective for organisational inquiry', in *Journal of organisational behaviour*, 15, pp.295-306.

Barnett, C. (1995) *The last victory, British dreams, British realities*, London, Macmillan.

Berger, P. and Luckman, T. (1966) *The social construction of reality*, New York, Doubleday.

Clegg, S.R. (1992) 'Modern and post-modern organisations', in *Sociology Review*, April, pp.24-28.

Clutterbuck, D. (1996) 'A personal development plan for every citizen', in *People Management*, September, p.23.

Department of Trade & Industry (1994) *Competitiveness: Helping Business to Win*, London, HMSO.

Department of Trade & Industry (1995) *Competitiveness: Forging Ahead*, London, HMSO.

Drucker, P. (1993) *Post Capitalist Society*, New York, Harper Business.

Fidler, B. and Fugl, B. (1991) 'Managing in the 1990s', in *Journal of Educational Management and Administration*, Vol.19, No.2, p72-77.

Giroux, H. and McLaren, P. (1986) 'Teacher education as a counterpublic sphere: towards a redefinition', in Popkewitz, T.S. (ed) *Critical Studies in Teacher Education*, London, Falmer Press.

Grace, G. (1992) *School Leadership Beyond Education Management*, London, Falmer Press.

HMI (1992) *The induction and probation of new teachers*, DES.

Hargreaves, A. and Reynolds, D. (1989) *Educational Policies: controversies and critiques*, New York, Falmer Press.

Holbeche, L. (1994) *Career Development in Flatter Structures*, Horsham, Roffey Park Management Institute.

Hopson, B. (1996) 'Up is rarely the way', in *Lifeskills Magazine*, No.3, pp.2-5.

Institute of Personnel Development (1996) *Directory*, London, IPD.

Jenkins, H. (1991) *Getting it Right: a Handbook for Successful School Leadership*, Oxford, Blackwell.

Jones, J. 'The role of Headteacher in staff development', in *Journal of Educational Management and Administration*, Vol.18, No.1, pp.27-35.

Levacic, R. (1995) *Local Management of schools, analysis and practice*, Buckingham, Open University.

MORI (1995), *Survey of Continuing Professional Development*, London, TTA.

Moser, C.A., Kalton, L. (1971) *Survey Methods in Social Investigations*, London, Heinemann.

Murlis, H. and Wright, V. (1993) 'Decentralising pay decisions: enpowerment or abdication', *Personnel Management*, March.

Naisbitt, J. (1995) *Global paradox, the bigger the world economy, the more powerful its smallest players*, London, Brearley.

Nias, J. (1989) *Primary Teachers talking - a study of teaching as work*, London, Routledge.

OfSTED (1993) *The management and provision of in-service training funded by the Grant for Education Support and Training (GEST)*, London, DFEE.

Prahalad, G. and Hammel, G. (1990) 'The core competence of the corporation', in *Harvard Business Review*, 90, pp.379-391.

Rafferty, F. (1991) 'Lack of status fuels the exodus', in *Times Education Supplement*, 27 December, p.1.

Stenhouse, L. (1975) *An Introduction to Curricular Research and Development*, London, Heinemann.

Teacher Training Agency (1995) *Headlamp*, London, TTA.

Teacher Training Agency (1995) *Chairman's letter to the Secretary of State*, 24 March, London, TTA.

Teacher Training Agency (1996) *Annual Lecture at the Royal Society*, London, TTA.

Teacher Training Agency (1996) *Promoting excellence in Teaching - The Corporate Plan*, London, TTA.

Trapp, R. (1996) '3M's creative hothouse', in *Human Resources*, September/October, p.30.

Toffler, A. (1990) *The new power elite*, Aldershot, Gower.

Watts, A.G. (1993) *Promoting careers: guidance for learning and work.* National Commission on Education Briefing 15.

Welch, L. and Woodward, P. (1989) *Continuing Professional Development: Towards a national strategy*, Glasgow, Pickup.

Wijers, G.A. and Meijers, F. (1996) 'Careers Guidance in the knowledge society', in *British Journal of Guidance and Counselling*, Vol.24, No.2, pp.185-188.

9 Never Mind the Outcomes, What About the Experience: Lifelong Learning, Autobiography and Skills for Progression to Higher Education

ANNA PACZUSKA

Abstract

It is widely recognised that formal or classroom based learning makes up only a tiny fraction of our total learning. The Assessment of Prior Experiential Learning (APEL) is an approach to assessment and accreditation, which formally recognises that much of our learning, is unrecognised, unacknowledged, unpresented and unaccredited. Even before lifelong learning came onto the national policy agenda, APEL was already being used to enable mature learners to return to learning by recognising learning gained through social experiences and work, and had also been written into new programmes of national vocational qualifications launched in the late 80s and early 90s. Early initiatives encouraged formative processes but also stressed the need to focus on the learning gained from an experience, not on the experience itself. This chapter explores the relationship between the learning experience and how that influences the recognition of the learning outcomes.

The accreditation of prior learning will have an important role in the future, as more adults participate in education and training. APL is particularly relevant to people returning to work or changing careers. (Gilbert Jessup, 1991)

Experience: the accumulation of knowledge and skill through personal participation in events. Men think that experience described by men is more

143

valuable, yet it is often not even in a language derived from their experience ... it is removed from experience altogether by being cast in abstract and theoretical terms ... we need ... a language of experience and this must necessarily come from our explanation of the personal, the everyday, and what we experience.

(A Feminist Dictionary - Cheris Kramarae and Paula A. Treichler)

Introduction

Assessment of Prior Learning is now most commonly associated with the award of credits for work based learning towards vocational qualifications such as NVQs and vocational degrees. But the first use of APL or APEL in Britain was in a developmental continuing education context rather than a vocational one. The idea of identifying learning from past experience as a basis for progressing to new learning programmes was developed in the late 80s as a way of enabling mature students to gain entry to higher education. Portfolios were widely used as frameworks for assessment. These usually contained evidence of learning and ability based on autobiographical work. Achievement was identified and presented in the portfolios using a variety of developmental approaches. At the same time some schemes for enabling progression used an autobiographical approach to identifying achievement and learning from experience but were not formally titled assessment of prior learning schemes.

The first initiatives stressed that the value of APEL lay in the process it encouraged students to undergo: reflection, self and peer assessment and confidence building through the recognition of achievement. These processes enabled students to recognise a wide range of achievements for consideration as a basis for entry to higher education, provided a means to recognise achievements not recognised by conventional examinations and presented an opportunity for students to submit achievements they themselves valued regardless of whether these achievements were formally acknowledged by the qualification system.

This raises a number of issues related to promoting opportunities for lifelong learning. The experience of early schemes to enable adults to return to learning based on assessing their learning from experience suggests that though such schemes focus on the learning which resulted from experience and not on the experience itself, the nature of the learning experience is a profound influence on how students value their learning from experience, how they express and present their learning in different contexts and how different representations of learning are viewed and interpreted by assessors.

The Purpose of Self-Assessment

Autobiography is a starting point for reflection and self-assessment in a number of schemes to enable progression to higher education for mature returners. The approach is based on the recognition that the lack of formal qualifications is not the same as lack of learning and students are encouraged to look back over their experience, identify their learning and use it as a basis for progression. Sometimes the process of self assessment conforms to a structured approach through the assessment of experiential learning, but elements of APEL also exist on other courses or programmes. Access courses, whose programmes aim to increase self-awareness, confidence and enable student to produce CVs and Personal Statements as part of their preparation for higher education, use a similar approach though this is not formally described as APEL.

Autobiography and personal accounts have been at the heart of many instances of the use of self-assessment of past learning for mature students. At the School of Independent Study at North East London Polytechnic (now Middlesex University), new students were required to write autobiography as part of their course planning in a contract system of learning. The autobiographies were used to identify student qualifications for progression to their self-designed courses. This mirrors the approach of structured APEL procedures which also rest on reflective autobiographical writing to identify significant learning and present it for assessment.

At school level Progress Files, formerly National Records of Achievement (NRAs), have always encouraged students to look back over 'other experiences' to identify and self-assess informally learned skills. In each context, whether at school or post school level, the self-assessment process rests on two different though related aspects - formative and summative.

Formative Assessment

Part of the process of looking back is to enable students to understand their past experience and from this determine starting points for going forward. Autobiographical writing, according to one writer, is a development process which:

> ... acts as a catharsis and helps students deal with the many areas in their lives they have not dealt with.   (Redwine, 1989: 91)

The process is one in which feelings are an important subject for attention and indeed are a way of assessing or reviewing achievement. Boud (1985) found that as students reflect on their feelings they find pride in their achievements and also identify and remove obstructive attitudes and feelings. This happens because the students can take different approaches to past experiences and may re-evaluate them to identify even 'failure' as a learning experience. These reflections may be useful in personal terms although they would be difficult to couch in learning outcomes terms.

Redwine (1989) argues that autobiography helps students with three different kinds of learning: improved self-concept, a more realistic view of abilities and greater sense of ownership of achievements. This, she argues, helps students to succeed in their classes when they return to learning.

Humm (1990) points out that a central reason for focusing on autobiographical writing in programmes for mature students is its important function in establishing identity:

> Woman's autobiographies exploit rhetoric of uncertainty about themselves and about the role of woman, and record feelings not accomplishments.   (p.45)

This focus on feelings plays a part in fixing a starting point for future work and is also a motivating factor:

> As students evaluate where they have come from, they gain a new appreciation of where they are going. Their commitment to higher education during this re-evaluation is strengthened.   (Redwine: 89)

The value of the formative process in self-assessment is also acknowledged in the movement to promote recording achievement at school level. The

RANSC report (1989) argues for understanding of the value of the formative process and the relationship between process and document in recording achievement as an important part of gaining acceptance and credibility for records of achievement.

At all levels in education self-assessment is seen as a development process which enhances students' self-esteem and self-awareness and provides an opportunity to recognise a range of achievement, not just academic. This increases self-confidence, motivation and commitment and is therefore valuable in itself. Just how valuable the process is depends on how an individual views themselves at any particular time. The same set of experiences may be evaluated differently depending on the distance and circumstances in which the evaluation takes place. This variation in the way we account for the past may be the reason that autobiography has been designated as an 'invention of sorts' (Heaney, 1986: ix). But the word 'invention' is not intended to suggest that autobiography may be fiction rather the use of the invention 'reaches back to its old Latin meaning of discovery and to its Renaissance association with creative imagination' (Heaney: ix). In this sense autobiography is creative process, an 'invention' or discovery of self which can be highly motivating in deciding what to do next.

Problems arise, however, when students attempt to use analysis of autobiographical work (which is essentially formative and focuses on personal self-assessment) in a formal or summative way. To 'translate' achievement and informal learning into formal skills and learning outcomes or even academic 'credit' is not straightforward.

Adult students without formal qualifications have frequently gained a great deal of learning from experience. When they attempt to present their learning from experience to a higher education admissions tutor, however, the attempt to represent the past in a way which is appropriate to the formal requirements of assessment for entry to higher education is more successful for some autobiographies than others. The differences do not arise from individual differences in ability, or, as might be expected, even from different skills in self-assessment. Rather the differences lie with candidates' perceptions about what is being self-assessed, in their engagement with the formative process, and in assessors' perceptions of the relative value of different achievements and the way they are presented.

Gender and Achievement

Work on records of achievement has shown that attitudes towards achievement (and recognising achievement) vary according to gender. At school level boys are more 'achievement oriented' than girls. Boys tend to be more confident in recognising their worth while girls feel more confident than boys in personal reflection (Broadfoot, 1989). In self-assessment work on ROAs girls tend to dwell on the personal whereas boys tend to value and present skills and achievements. (Both, incidentally, tend to underestimate their achievements through self-assessment).

Gender differences in self-assessment are also evident among mature students. The use of biography in the contract system of education at Middlesex University (Humm, 1990) clearly indicates an institutional validation of the idea that autobiography can give students 'a developed sense of their individuality' from which students can understand their past experiences and evaluate the learning relevant for progression to higher education. Yet, as Humm's research shows, there are differences in the way people tell their autobiographies. This is essentially a difference in the ways different students choose to 'invent' themselves and their achievements. While the idea of lifelong learning implicitly acknowledges the value and diversity of learning from experience, this does not necessarily carry over into assessment practice. This has implications for the recognition of the 'worth' of different kinds of learning in academic terms. Humm's work, for example, indicates academic recognition appears to work against female autobiographies which are more likely to be judged more 'unsound' than male ones. This is based on what women choose to focus on in their accounts of themselves as opposed to men.

Humm explains how, in the research, men's work is more acceptable to assessors because:

> Men have made their lives into patterns of self-chosen events set in a rational pursuit of well-defined educational goals. Women's lives were always a part of the lives of others.   (p.40)

The differences between men and women according to Humm are reflected in language and syntax and indicate that men seem to possess or recognise the form of autobiography which tutors are happy to recognise and approve of at higher education level. Women's biographies focus more on childhood and are apparently geared to individual emotional needs as well as to the objectives set by assessors. The results at Middlesex were that women's biographies met with less approval from assessors: 80% of male biographies passed the validation compared to just under 60% of women's biographies (Humm: 40).

Humm's explanation for these differences in outcome is that there is a duality of objectives in female autobiography which deal with personal objectives as well as the demands of assessment. Her solution is to suggest that autobiography in this context should become a process of negotiation - between the student's subjective or developmental needs (to define an identity by retrieving the past) and the expectation of self-assessment and self-presentation held by the school.

A similar idea is inherent in the notion of a 'conversion curriculum' for returnees to education and in particular for mature women seeking to gain entry to science courses (Pam Percy et al., 1991). Here the suggestion is that among women returners, learning from experience is couched in such familiar everyday situations that it becomes invisible both to the student themselves and to the tutor who is assessing the student:

> ... much of the prior learning that women students bring with them is located in a discourse of domestic, local and specific science which is unfamiliar (or perhaps too familiar) to admissions and therefore dismissed.   (p.33)

The invisibility of women's prior learning to science tutors observed by Pam Percy raises two questions. First, is it possible to assist women, or students in general, whose learning is 'invisible' to tutors to successfully recover and represent their prior learning so it becomes visible to higher education? Second, how do we assess it? This second is particularly important in the light of work on Records of Achievement which shows that where teachers are not familiar with particular cultural models they may not fully recognise the achievements of certain pupils (Broadfoot, 1989).

A Language for Self-Assessment

It could be that some students need support in presenting their learning in an appropriate, recognisable language and form. A 'conversion curriculum' is one way of describing a language support programme which should enable students to translate their social, domestic and cultural experience into skills recognised and assessable by educators and employers. This support would be additional to current forms of preparatory study for progression to higher education and would focus on the new language of skills which is being introduced to both further and higher education. Students would be encouraged to 'translate' achievements gained from experience, breaking them down into skills, abilities and knowledge to match learning outcomes laid down by higher education. The task then would be to assess how far the skills presented by the student match the skills criteria required by higher education.

This focus on the outcomes in terms of skills and abilities sounds straightforward but could be problematic. Usher (1989) points out it means potential students wanting to take non-traditional routes into higher education would be faced with demonstrating competencies for progression to higher education when much of higher education itself does not know what exactly what skills and abilities are required for particular courses. At present criteria for progression are usually expressed in terms of qualifications in which the specific skills and abilities are implicit rather than explicit. Formal qualifications act as a proxy for criteria for progression but do not identify them.

The dilemma may be resolved by work which aims to generate threshold criteria for entry and progression to higher education through a national credit scheme for post-16 qualifications (FEU, 1992) but progress on this front is slow. It is not the skills and abilities which are in question, but equivalencies between the skills and abilities which are embedded in different achievements. Couching achievement in terms of skills, ability and knowledge is not in itself a major problem. A language has long been widely available through career guidance literature. In education, moves to identify core skills provided a basic vocabulary and ways of describing skills (HMI, 1989; BTEC Common Skills, 1991; BP, 1991) in the early 1980s. Skills have recently been redefined by the work round key skills which have explicitly looked at the way each post 16 qualification develops the required skills. Achievement summarised or accounted for in terms of skills could theoretically be equivalenced to skills embedded in a range of post 16 qualifications.

The problem is this limits and predetermines routes into higher education to those which can be equivalenced with existing qualifications.

The establishment of individual and flexible routes into higher education for mature learners was a major achievement. The development of self-assessment and the moves towards recognition of learning from experience helped to broaden non-traditional routes and extend and widen access to higher education. The irony is that the attempt to extend the number of pathways by noting down the diversity of experience that can lead to appropriate learning may now result in the creation of assessment hurdles which define the specific skills required for progression in rigid terms. This may result in less flexibility for so-called non-traditional students.

Is it possible then to write criteria or outcomes statements which are a generic rather than qualification equivalenced way of assessing a students' ability to succeed in higher education? In addition to avoiding 'A levelisation' by relating specifically to formal qualifications, such criteria or outcomes would also have to transcend the generally acknowledged tendency for admissions decisions to relate to social as well as academic criteria, to 'stand outside the social relations of entry practices' (Pam Percy: 34). The notion that outcomes statements can 'stand outside social relations' in this way is perhaps as idealistic as the idea that any assessment practice is either scientific or truly impartial.

The technical requirements which have to be fulfilled in any attempt at generating outcomes statements for progression which cater for learning acquired through a variety of experiences are probably similar to the problems which confronted the designers of NVQ competences described by Robert Wood et al. (1989). The need for validity and reliability and also for transparency and fairness is something which, as Wood et al. point out, most universities lack the 'built-in' apparatus to study systematically in their assessment systems (p.7).

To set up a set of criteria which fulfils the technical requirements, let alone co-ordinate those across higher education, requires an operation on the scale of a national examination and one that is potentially just as inflexible and exclusive as current national examinations for entry to higher education.

Language and Assessment

The point, perhaps, is the way learning from experience is presented through autobiography and the way it is interpreted by assessors.

Autobiographical writing has different functions, personal as well as public (Collins, 1984) and any autobiography will not fulfil simply one or other objective. Form is also an issue. As Humm's research shows, women write in a language that differs in syntax from that used by men and this appears to be a form less acceptable to assessors.

Such differences can be said to arise from gender based cultural differences. Some writers have pointed out that women's writing style is part of women's socialisation, which is essentially training in how to be socially subordinate. Cameron (1990) describes how some critics describe women's writing as a 'reflex of their powerlessness and men's power over them'. Other writers interpret the difference in a more positive 'women-centred way', interpreting the 'difference' as strength rather than a deficiency.

The differences are 'quantitative not absolute' but they require explanation and interpretation, particularly where autobiography writing is the basis of an assessment process. One strategy is to encourage women to develop more assertive styles in using language in the 'public' arena. Critics argue this imposes 'a male style' which may be effective in getting women heard but doesn't tackle the issue of getting the rules changed so that women's language is regarded equally with men's language. It does, however, raise the issue of how assessors recognise a diversity of achievement and how tutors cope with supporting students in presenting diversity.

For tutors it means enabling women, and indeed all students, to express themselves in an 'appropriate' language for a given situation. Students have to recognise and learn how language is different in different situations. In other words, students have to learn the skills for assessment.

Assessors could be aware of different ways of interpreting qualities they are assessing and that applies to gender differences as well as other criteria. It is difficult to say whether women's autobiographies are 'less acceptable' because they are being judged by men, because they are different in themselves, or because they are being used for a different purpose by the women themselves. The point is that students present their learning in different forms and in different ways. Theoretically the outcomes may be similar or equivalent but the way they are presented is mediated by the experience through which they are achieved. While the development of outcomes statements for assessing learning from experience was claimed to be a way of assessing the learning rather than the experience, or of acknowledging the learning regardless of where and how it occurred, a closer look makes it clear the experience as the context for learning profoundly influences how a student presents that learning. Can outcomes statements ever be flexible enough to cater for this, or do assessors themselves have to become more flexible in their approach?

Personal Skills

The acceptance of developmental diversity in self-assessment and presentation of learning from experience is important. The temptation when confronting a new issue is to attempt to fit new facts into existing models. This can lead to confusion and misinterpretation. It happened with personal skills. The observation of a preoccupation with personal issues by some students in post-16 work on recording achievement was interpreted in the light of expected outcomes and defined as personal development:

> ... the notion of personal development has been transformed into that of
> personal skills.   (Slater, 1985)

In this equation the 'personal' of the formative process became confused with the 'personal' of the summative process and a crude 'translation' was contrived. The two 'personals' are in fact quite different. The truly personal is about exploring feelings, emotions, identity, motivation and how they affect our learning. Personal skills may be necessary to do this, which includes skills such as critical thinking, hypothesising, questioning, reflecting back and so on (6), but personal skills can be learned in a number of ways and can be evidenced without the emphasis on formative assessment provided by self-assessment through autobiography.

There is a choice between two languages here: self is described in personal language, outcomes and competence are described in education or training jargon. Any confusion limits the freedom of expression assigned to autobiography and narrows the perception of achievements presented by autobiographical writing. This in turn confuses the function of autobiography in establishing identity. Personal language is the medium for expressing feelings. This expression of feelings is an important aspect to the 'return of learning' process. This language may not reveal or identify learning in the skills language valued by assessors.

Tutors encouraging students to self-awareness and self-assessment through autobiographical writing are faced with a contradiction. On the one hand, the discovery by the education system of personal knowledge and experiential learning is a major challenge to the dominant knowledge paradigm (Usher: 75). By exploring the personal, students can recognise their wealth of learning from experience and can be enabled to access higher education through reflecting on experience and generating autobiographical writing. The writing process can have considerable benefits in personal terms. On the other hand, there is a danger that self-assessment and self-evaluation is acceptable to higher education only if it displays 'personal skills' relevant to progression. This could serve to confuse and underplay the personal and emotional benefits of autobiographical writing.

Negotiation and Dialogue

Much of the way students present their learning depends on the tutor. Self-assessment is a process as well as an outcome, part of the curriculum as well as a judgement. Its outcome depends on the dialogue between student and tutor. This can take the form of enabling and facilitating reflection on experience as well as assessing outcome.

The difficulty is that the relationship between student and tutor is an unequal one, and this can influence the outcome of self-assessment. Mary James in her analysis of the tutor/student relationship in self-assessment makes the point that there are two different relationships or processes at work: 'dialogue' and 'negotiation' (James, 1990). She says the two terms are interchangeable but are, in fact, quite different. Dialogue is conversation, negotiation implies differences of views, perceptions and interests.

The introduction of student self-assessment is generally an attempt to motivate and empower students, but in Mary James' view, the process is generally marred by the reluctance of tutors to acknowledge existing power relations between tutor and student which ultimately results in student judgements being over-ridden by tutors. If this is the case then self-assessment becomes a sham.

Mary James points to three possible solutions to this dilemma. Students should be given access to a third party, or advocate, who would represent their views in the negotiation of the assessment outcome. Such an innovation would, perhaps, take into account different cultural approaches to achievement and different ways and languages for expressing achievement. Another way students' views could be strengthened in negotiation of assessment is through linking student assessment to teacher appraisal, making it a reciprocal, and symmetrical activity'. Third, James suggests 'assertiveness training' for students in order to enable them to present their views more forcefully.

The trouble with all these views, as James rightly points out, is that they are conflict models of assessment which involve an element of trade-off which really have nothing to do with education.

In conclusion, James attempts to analyse the source of the problem and identifies the combination of formative with summative as the confusing factor. She suggests that:

> ... one feasible solution might be to develop further the distinctions ... and put them into practice as entirely separate but complementary activities ... the process would then be plural rather than singular.

The solution suggested by James, to separate the formative and summative elements of self-assessment, makes sense in the light of the different functions of self-assessment already identified here.

Conclusion

As practitioners have observed, for mature returners to learning the process of writing autobiography as part of self-assessment is clearly perceived to have a beneficial function in understanding identity and gaining self-awareness and motivation. This is different from a formal process of self-assessment, skills identification and presentation of learning for summative assessment.

The two processes have often been integrated in programmes for adults returning to learning. The integration presents a number of difficulties: students may use different languages and forms of writing about the personal and assessors may not be able to uncover the learning inherent in some autobiographical writing. Negotiating agreement between students and assessors about the outcomes of self-assessment is not the same as dialogue about experience and is affected by the power relationship between tutor and student.

It is tempting therefore to look to separate formative and summative processes, and at the same time provide students with clear guidelines about the form, language and presentation needed for summative assessment. This among other things would make a clear distinction between personal development processes and the identification of personal skills. It would also place the self-assessment process in a formal relationship to summative assessment while allowing dialogue and discussion as part of the developmental process.

The problem is that the more formal the summative process becomes in courses for promoting lifelong learning and enabling mature learners to return to learning, the more like 'A' levels the progression curriculum becomes. The notion of an 'alternative' or 'complementary' route into higher education based on recognition of learning from experience is lost.

It may, however, be practically possible to separate the formative and the summative processes and deliver them separately. In work with post-16 students to uncover informally learned skills the autobiographical route was largely unproductive because younger post-16 students do not have the distance from which to look back on experience and 'invent' themselves. Instead, the skills recognition process may be embedded in other activities which encourage and support students in considering progression to higher education (Overbury and Paczuska, 1992). This support replaced some of the developmental functions of autobiography but allowed the formative and the summative aspects of assessment to be worked alongside each other but separately, in a different form. The question this raises is whether we want students to become skilled at self-assessment for itself, or whether self-assessment is simply a way of enabling students to return to learning and by looking back to identify whether they have gained the abilities needed to succeed in higher education.

The issue is important not only for admissions but also for higher education itself. Tutors in higher education are moving towards encouraging all students to acquire skills in self-assessment. The introduction of self-assessment to work-based programmes, for example, shows that skills in self assessment do not come naturally or easily and students need to acquire skills in self-assessment before undertaking their course:

It was discovered learners needed time to prepare themselves for self-assessment. The researchers proposed that learners' preparation should start from the moment when pre-entry information is sent out and last through the duration of the course ... it was felt strongly that therefore before the learner could interrogate his/her experience at the workplace, he/she needed to assess their own strengths and weaknesses.   (Tuck et al., 1993)

If self-assessment continues to gain popularity as an assessment method in areas where experiences may be diverse, resources will have to be directed towards 'facilitation and learning support' and 'courses will need to be redesigned to accommodate skill development and self-assessment time' (Tuck et al.: 45).

Programmes for enabling mature learners to return to learning and the preparatory curriculum are where the issues associated with self-assessment were first raised. Many of the schemes no longer exist but they raise issues about how we promote lifelong learning and how we enable mature individuals to assess their achievements and determine at what point they may rejoin the learning agenda. This requires a much wider awareness of the implications of different cultural interpretations of self-assessment. It has become an education truism to repeat that the outcomes are what matters, not where and how they were achieved. However, the experience in which achievement is rooted is what determines whether we recognise the outcomes as valuable or not.

References

Boud, D., Keogh, R. and Walker, D. (1995) (eds) *Reflection: Turning Experience into Learning*, London, Kogan Page.

Broadfoot, P. (1988) (ed) *Records of Achievement: Report of the National Evaluation of Pilot Schemes* (PRAISE).

Cameron, D. (1990) *The Feminist Critique of Language: a Reader*, London, Routledge.

Collins, M. (1984) 'Literature and New Courses in FE Colleges', in Miller, J. (1984) (ed) *Eccentric Propositions Essays on Literature and the Curriculum*, London, Routledge and Kegan Paul.

DES (1989) *Report of the Records of Achievement National Committee* (RANSC).

Heaney, S. (1990) 'Foreword' to Quinn, J. (1990) (ed) *The Portrait of the Artist as a Young Girl*, London, Mandarin.

Humm, M. (1990) 'Subjects in English: autobiography, women and education', in Thompson, A. and Wilcox, H. (eds) *Teaching Women, Feminism and Women's Studies*. Manchester University Press.

James, M. (1990) 'Negotiations and Dialogue in Student Assessment and Teacher Appraisal', in Simons, H. and Simons, J. (eds) *Rethinking Appraisal and Assessment*, Buckingham, Open University Press.

Overbury, J. and Paczuska, A. (1991) *APEL, Progression and Skills for Science: report of the BP Access Project*, London, South Bank Polytechnic.

Percy, P. et al. (1991) *Women's Attitudes to Science the Technology Courses*, London, South Bank Polytechnic.

Redwine, M. (1989) 'The Autobiography as a Motivational Factor' in Weil, S. and McGill, I. (eds) *Making Sense of Experiential Learning: diversity in theory and practice*, Buckingham, Open University Press.

Slater (1985) quoted in Chitty, C. (1985) 'Towards a New Definition of Vocationalism', in *Post 16 Education: Studies in Access and Achievement*, London, Kogan Page.

Tuck et al. (1992) *A Self-Assessment Model for the Integration of Work Based Learning with Academic Assessment*, University of Huddersfield.

Usher, R. (1989) 'Qualification, Paradigms and Experiential Learning in Higher Education', in Fulton, O. (ed) *Access and Institutional Change*, Buckingham, Open University Press.

Wood, R. et al. (1989) *Boning, Blanching and Backtacking: Assessing Performance in the Workplace*, London, Employment Department Briefing Series.

10 Towards a Learning Society: The Role of Formal, Non-Formal and Informal Learning

ROSEMARY MORELAND

Abstract

This paper argues that voluntary and community organisations are engaged in providing deliberate and planned learning to adults and that the nature of this learning is distinctive from that provided by statutory education bodies. It further argues that this is a grassroots response to gaining the knowledge and skills, which people feel are important to them. The paper draws on research carried out by the author, which attempts to place this learning within a larger lifelong learning framework.

Introduction

Recently, the terms 'lifelong learning' and the 'learning society' have been gaining popularity. A number of documents cite a range of social, economic, technological and personal factors which urge the necessity of encouraging a learning society. (DfEE, 1998; DfEE, 1996; Commission of the European Communities, 1993; Council for Europe, 1992; Council for Europe, 1987). The Council for Europe have sponsored a number of projects based on this theme throughout Europe and named 1996 as the European Year of Lifelong Learning. The recent UK government documents claim that adults (16 years +) need to be encouraged to take part in learning throughout their lifetime (DfEE, 1998; DfEE, 1996). They bemoan the low participation rate of adults in lifelong learning in the UK, as evidenced by the recent surveys by NIACE/Gallup (1997) and the Campaign for Learning (1996). Although these studies adopted very wide definitions of learning, the results are somewhat disappointing, in terms of positive attitudes towards lifelong learning. Whilst the UK government documents acknowledge the wide range of settings in which learning takes place, they appear to focus on the education and training of those over 16 years. Thus they adopt the term 'learning' as the more user-friendly option to education, without defining either term.

This chapter examines the terms 'lifelong learning' and 'the learning society' in order to understand more fully the views of society upon which they are premised. The chapter will also distinguish between the terms 'learning' and 'education', and suggests working definitions for each of these. The chapter draws on research carried out in Northern Ireland in order to explore the range of learning available to adults, in the community, in order to understand more fully their contribution to a learning society (Moreland, 1993). It will be argued that statutory education bodies are only one form of adult education provision and that there are many more which appear to be offering adults opportunities to engage in both planned and unplanned learning. Furthermore, distinctions between the nature of learning opportunities provided by the range of providers suggest that each of these have an important contribution to make to promoting a 'learning society'. The next section will examine some of the literature on 'lifelong learning' and 'the learning society', in order to understand more fully what is meant by these terms.

Lifelong Learning and the Learning Society

Whilst the two terms 'lifelong learning' and 'the learning society' are often used synonymously the 'learning society' stresses *where* learning takes place, while, 'lifelong learning' is more properly concerned with *when* it takes place. Strictly speaking lifelong learning includes all learning which takes place from 'cradle to grave', although in practice, it generally refers to learning which takes place beyond full-time, uninterrupted study. For example, it may include those who return to study after leaving school at 16, yet exclude those who continue through to university.

However, the European Lifelong Learning Initiative's working definition of lifelong learning is 'the development of human potential through a continuously supportive process which stimulates and empowers individuals to acquire all the knowledge, values, skills and understanding they will require throughout their lifetimes and to apply them with confidence, creativity and enjoyment in all roles, circumstances, and environments' (Longworth and Davies, 1996: 22).

This is an expansive and all-encompassing description of lifelong learning, which does not draw out any distinction between learning and education. Definitions of 'lifelong learning' differ therefore, according to the context and other terms, such as 'lifelong learning', 'recurrent education', 'continuing education' are also used to denote similar activities, although the use of the term education as opposed to learning is rarely explained. The rising importance of the concept of lifelong learning is implied by the increase in organisations and programmes aimed at promoting the idea of lifelong learning. For example, the European Lifelong Learning Initiative and the World Initiative on Lifelong Learning were formed to broaden the discussion around the topic and to initiate projects based on this concept (Longworth and Davies, 1996). Documents pertaining to the Council of Europe, the United Nations Educational, Scientific and Cultural Organisation, the Organisation for Economic Co-operation and Development and other international bodies increasingly perceive lifelong learning to have an important role to play in the 21st century (Longworth and Davies, 1996). However discussions around the idea of lifelong learning are not new. Indeed as far back as the early 1970s the UNESCO Institute for Education had proposed lifelong learning as '... the master concept for educational policies in the years to come for both developed and developing countries' (UNESCO, 1976: 182). Lengrand (1989: 9) states that the International Commission on the Development of Education came to a similar conclusion in 1973, when they stated that 'the idea of lifelong education is the keystone of the learning society'. Here again we find the terms 'learning' and 'education' being used interchangeably, and indeed the linking of 'lifelong education' with 'the learning society' suggests that the common ground between the two ideas was established as early as the 1970s, when both concepts came into usage.

Barnett (1998) has suggested that there are four versions of the learning society: the economic approach; enhancing quality of life; the democratic approach and the emancipatory approach. Barnett (1998) argues that literature on the learning society reflects one or more of these definitions and thus a fuller understanding of the possibilities of a learning society can only be gained by recognising each of these definitions. Barnett (1998) claims that the recent Report of the National Committee of Inquiry into Higher Education (1997) mainly adopts the economic approach to the learning society, with some reference to enhancing the individual's quality of life. This view is echoed by Ainley (1998: 559) when he claims that:

To the Conservative and succeeding New Labour government as well as the CBI, a 'learning society' is one which systematically increases the skills and knowledge of all its members to exploit technological innovation and so gain a competitive edge for their services in fast-changing global markets.

Although the two most recent UK government reports (DfEE, 1998; DfEE, 1996) claim a number of factors urge the necessity for promoting lifelong learning, the underlying premise of these reports stress economic factors. The second version of the learning society, Barnett (1998) suggests, is about enhancing the quality of individuals lives and he claims that this notion of the learning society is embodied in such terms as 'continuing education', 'education permanante' and 'lifelong learning', as well as mainstream adult education provision. A third version of the learning society, the democratic approach, links learning with citizenship and stresses the importance of learning in helping people to play more full and active roles in a participatory democracy. The final approach, which he suggests is not as fully developed in the literature, suggests an emancipatory view of the learning society, which enables society itself to become self-reflexive and self-learning. This fourth approach is left rather vague. The ideas of self-reflection and self-learning appear to link in with the desire to encourage adults to become autonomous, independent learners, a goal of the UK government's lifelong learning strategy (DfEE, 1998). Indeed there is a huge body of literature in the field of adult education which deals with these concepts (Schon, 1983, 1987; Brookfield, 1987, 1985a; Mezirow, 1985; Freire, 1974). Many of these deal with learning in a collective as opposed to individual approach, which Barnett (1998) suggests is an important aspect of the emancipatory version of the learning society. Whilst recent UK government reports on lifelong learning (DfEE, 1998; DfEE, 1996) do imply a vision of a learning society which is based mainly on an economic approach, they also incorporate the individual and collective learning goals implicit in Barnett's (1998) second and third approach to the learning society. This would suggest that in order to gain widespread support for the promotion of this concept, these documents attempt to include all visions of the learning society. However, it is important to recognise that different visions of the learning society arise from conflicting views about the nature of the present society and what it should be in the future. While a vision of the learning society may incorporate more than one approach, there is however a need to acknowledge the tensions which exist between the different approaches. Thus it can be seen that the terms 'lifelong learning' and the 'learning society' contain within them a number of related and sometimes conflicting ideas. Whilst there appears to be widespread support for these concepts, there is a need to clarify the meanings implicit in them. Similarly, the terms 'lifelong learning' and 'lifelong education' are often used synonymously and much of the writing in this area fails to distinguish between the two terms. The literature on lifelong learning or the learning society therefore must first clarify the definition of learning or education, which it adopts. The next section examines the terms 'learning' and 'education' in more detail and suggests a means of distinguishing between the two terms.

Education and Learning

A study carried out by Reed and Loughran (1984) examined a wide range of activities which are not normally considered educational, but in which they claimed a large amount of purposeful learning occurs. They argued that learning includes knowledge gained both consciously and unconsciously and drew a distinction therefore between the two. They adopt a broad definition of education as:

> any intentional, overt and organised effort to influence a person or group with the aim of improving quality of life.   (Reed and Loughran, 1984: 2)

They conceived of learning as a vast system, which includes both planned and unplanned learning and defined learning therefore, as '... any modification in an individual or group that results in behavioural change' (Reed and Loughran, 1984: 2). In a similar distinction, Cropley (1980) contrasted deliberate learning, in which there is a conscious intention to learn, with spontaneous learning, which is devoid of explicit goals. However he pointed out that one type of learning is not necessarily more effective or valuable than the other.

In much of the writing in this field, then the terms 'learning' and 'education' are not defined or else they are used synonymously. Even when they are defined, there is sometimes a lack of consistency. Ironside (1989) attempted to break down the concept of lifelong education into formal, non-formal and informal education. The formal he sees primarily as the institutionalised education system, including professional training, and non-formal therefore, is any organised form of education, which does not take place within the formal system. Finally, informal education is defined as:

> ... the lifelong process whereby all individuals acquire attitudes, values, skills and knowledge from daily experience and from the educative influences and resources in their environment.   (Ironside, 1989: 15)

Applying Reed and Loughran's (1984) distinction between planned and unplanned learning, this is more appropriately a definition of informal learning, which includes knowledge gained non-purposefully, outside of any programme, for example leisure reading, exchange of job-related information with a colleague. As it takes place informally, the educational component of this concept would be restricted to the purposeful gaining of knowledge outside of any programme, for example, trying out a new recipe, reading a history book to find out more about a particular event or period. This discussion highlights the need for a tightening up of definitions and a clarification of terms. This paper uses the term 'learning' to refer to both planned and unplanned learning, whilst the term 'education' refers only to planned learning.

Formal, Non-Formal and Informal Learning

The wide range of settings in which learning takes place has been previously mentioned. Some educational writers have drawn distinctions between formal and non-formal education (Simkins, 1977: Fordham, 1979). Ironside (1989) has attempted to provide a definition of formal, non-formal and informal education, although this lacks consistency. Reed and Loughran (1984) constructed a five-point scale of Lifelong Learning, which ranges from more formal through to less formal. This allows for greater fluidity of movement, acknowledging the overlap, which occurs around the boundaries. However, their definition of informal learning as purely accidental leads to their failure to identify situations in informal settings, which specifically aim to facilitate learning.

A study of learning activity in voluntary and community organisations, (Percy et al., 1988) claimed that whilst professional adult educators would have little difficulty in identifying and accepting the formal learning activities, as being education they would be less likely to recognise the informal learning activities as such. Indeed Percy et al. (1988) concluded that volunteers and members of these organisations did not generally perceive *themselves* to be involved in learning or education, despite the findings that a remarkable amount of intentional, as well as unintentional learning appeared to be taking place. Another study examining learning in voluntary and community organisations (Elsdon, 1995) found learning, whether deliberate or unpremeditated, to be the major feature of experience in voluntary organisations. This supports Brookfield's (1981) study into self-directed learning, in which he concluded that

> These independent adult learners are a sub-merged dimension of educational activity: encounters and exchanges were taking place without accreditation from, or recognition by, professional adult educators. It was as if the town in which most of the subjects lived contained a parallel educational universe alongside the official provision of schools and colleges.
>
> (Brookfield, 1981: 26)

Adult Education and Lifelong Learning

Adult education has close links with the movement of lifelong education. It is after all, the non-compulsory part of education and comprises the vast bulk of lifelong education. Kidd and Titmus (1989) claimed that the lifelong education movement developed largely from the preoccupations of adult education. Stemming from a number of historical and ideological roots, it covers a wide variety of educational activities (Moreland, 1993). However as Percy et al. (1988) have pointed out, not all adult educators will agree on what constitutes adult education. Whilst there is little disagreement about formal adult education, less formal learning activities are often hotly disputed. Lovett (1971) has argued that community action and community development often provide people with opportunities for learning. He claims that community groups in their efforts to solve the problems facing them, are often engaged in learning through doing, picking up practical skills and knowledge. Armstrong and Davies (1977) have also suggested that community action lies at the most informal end of the education spectrum, since it rarely has specific educational aims, but is more concerned with solving community problems. However Belanger (1993) has suggested that it is precisely this linking of problem-solving to lifelong learning which is the fastest growing aspect of the learning society. In their study, Percy et al. (1988) concluded that the learning activity, which takes place in voluntary organisations is not in competition with formal adult education. An Australian study of community-based learning supports this idea, in claiming that formal adult education and community based learning play different, but complementary roles in a learning society (Gloster, 1980). This study suggested that community groups engage in learning which enables them to cope with the problems and issues facing them, in a rapidly changing society.

The following section draws on research into formal, non-formal and informal adult learning opportunities, in order to examine the kinds of learning available to adults in the community. A typology of adult learning opportunities will be presented, in order to discuss the main characteristics of each type.

Belfast - A Learning Society

As the capital city of Northern Ireland, Belfast reflects many of the problems common to urban industrial cities in the West. Whilst the region as a whole has been cited as one of the least prosperous in Europe, Belfast has been described as 'a city in decline' (Simpson, 1983: 20). A number of reports support this view of Northern Ireland (Jenkins, 1989; Rolston and Tomlinson, 1988; Gaffikin and Morrissey, 1990). Whilst the situation of conflict which has existed here for many years has undoubtedly had a number of negative effects on people, several studies have indicated that the main problems which people worry about are lack of money, unemployment, debt, house conditions and health (Birrell et al., 1991; MacNamee and Lovett, 1987; Project Team, 1977). Thus although the 'troubles' have impinged on the social and economic framework of Northern Ireland society, a number of studies suggest that people develop coping mechanisms which enable them to adapt to their situations and treat it as normal (Trew, 1987; Hughes, 1991; Harris, 1972). However, the conflict has also been directly and indirectly partially responsible for strengthening bonds within local communities. Compton and Coward (1989) have claimed that social change has been slower in Northern Ireland than in the rest of the United Kingdom. Despite and perhaps even because of the multiplicity of problems, Belfast is a city with a thriving voluntary and community sector.

Belfast was chosen therefore as an example of a modern industrial city, in which to explore the nature of formal, non-formal and informal adult learning opportunities. The formal sector consisted of all statutory providers whose main aim is education, for example Further Education Colleges, University Extra-Mural and outreach provision, whilst the non-formal sector consisted of those organisations which are non-statutory, whose main aim is education, for example, Workers Education Association, the Ulster People's College. The informal sector comprised community and voluntary organisations and groups, who had already been identified in earlier studies as being engaged in a learning process (Reed and Loughran, 1984; Percy et al., 1988). This sector, was by far the largest, suggesting the vast potential of such learning opportunities. A postal questionnaire was sent out to all providers of adult learning opportunities throughout Belfast. From this, the main characteristics of each sector were drawn up, in order to make comparisons between the sectors.

The survey found that the majority of voluntary and community organisations do perceive themselves to be providing learning activities - 70% of voluntary organisations and 84% of community groups indicated that *learning* was one of the main functions of their group. This supports the findings of other studies in this field, which indicated that these groups are engaged in learning (Reed and Loughran, 1984; Percy et al., 1988, Elsdon, 1995). Findings from the present research however indicated that, contrary to these studies, the majority of community and voluntary organisations also perceive *education* to be the main or an important aspect of their work (63% and 45% respectively). Although the figures are somewhat lower than those indicating involvement in learning they nevertheless suggest an increasing awareness in the informal sector of the role which they can play in a learning society. This represents an important shift in the education paradigm, in that a sizeable proportion of community and voluntary organisations perceive themselves as providers of education! Having established that these providers are engaged in a learning process, the following section examines the characteristics of each sector, in order to assess the nature of learning opportunities, which they provide. These general characteristics are drawn from the results of the questionnaire.

Formal Adult Learning Opportunities

In a range of questions relating to education and learning, respondents in this sector indicated a preference for the term 'education' as opposed to 'community education', 'learning', or 'learning through doing'. The majority of these respondents were involved in professional advancement, outreach and widening access to educational institutions. Whilst focusing largely on individual development, staff and learners sometimes carried out projects which benefited both the individuals and the whole community. With regard to educational practice, all respondents in the formal sector were involved in running courses and very few claimed to encourage others to run courses. Views on the tutor/student relationship were mixed, with just over half indicating that they perceived it as a two-way relationship. On the whole, the student's role in this type of education is passive, with the main activity for learners in using text-books and taking notes. Other features of education in this sector included a structured syllabus, accreditation and professionally recognised tutors. Their main flexibility lay in waiving entry qualifications. Respondents in this sector have a fairly wide catchment area, drawing learners from a number of surrounding communities. Few of these bodies have a management committee, but of those that do, it tends to be appointed, rather than elected. Whilst the main source of funding is from the government, many of these respondents acknowledged the importance of learners' fees as a source of funding. The majority perceived themselves to be accountable to the government only, in terms of funding, methods of practice and success/failure.

Non-Formal Adult Learning Opportunities

These organisations tended not to distinguish between the terms 'education' and 'learning', but perceived themselves to be equally involved in both. The majority felt that education should 'raise awareness of issues and problems'. Respondents in this sector were also likely to indicate that they provided support for local groups, a point further borne out in the responses to questions on the provision of courses. Although the majority of these organisations indicated that they did provide courses (60%), all the groups in this sector indicated that they encouraged others to run courses and focus on those who are excluded from society eg. the poor, unemployed. However they have a wide catchment area, with the majority providing services for people throughout Northern Ireland. In terms of its educational practice, 70% of respondents indicated that the tutor and students are learners together, tutors tended not to have professional qualifications and none of the respondents indicated that courses had entry requirements or that they were accredited. Although, courses tend to have a structured syllabus learners appear to be fairly active in helping to construct courses. Whilst only a minority (30%) responded that learners were involved in teaching courses, this sector was more likely to adopt this technique than any of the other sectors. These groups also tended to carry out projects, related to their aims and activities. The majority were initiated by learners and benefited the organisation, as well as the whole community. The vast majority of these providers have an annually elected management committee, to whom the group is accountable, for methods and success/failure. Funding is obtained from a variety of sources, mainly statutory and trust funds, although these providers perceive themselves to be accountable to statutory authority, in terms of funding.

Informal Adult Learning Opportunities

Well over three-quarters of these respondents indicated that education is an important aspect of their organisation. These groups drew a distinction between the terms 'learning' and 'education', being more likely to indicate that they are involved in learning than education. In an examination of the kinds of education engaged in, these organisations indicated that they are involved in issue-based education, concerned with raising people's awareness of issues and problems. Voluntary organisations were particularly involved in giving advice and information.

Their involvement in providing education is further borne out by the fact that over 70% of respondents in this sector indicated that they ran courses. Whilst the majority of voluntary organisations ran courses and provided staff for courses, community organisations are more likely to provide premises for courses. Three-quarters of respondents indicated that they encourage others to run courses. This sector was least likely to indicate that courses have a structured syllabus and entry qualifications are rarely required, or gained on completion. However over three-quarters suggested that tutors are qualified professionals, although the same figure also maintained that the relationship between tutor and learner is two-way.

Learners in community organisations seem to have a particularly active role, with 60% claiming that learners are involved in constructing courses and half indicating that learners report back on topics to the class. Learning in voluntary organisations does not appear to be as active, with half of these respondents indicating that learners were involved in taking notes. Whilst voluntary organisations have a catchment area of the whole of Northern Ireland, community groups tended to cater for the local community. Other studies (Percy et al., 1988; Elsdon, 1995) have suggested the importance of local branches also in voluntary organisations. This was not a feature of the present research, possible due to the fact that the survey was carried out in Belfast which would be more likely to attract the headquarters of voluntary organisations.

The vast majority of voluntary and community groups have an elected management committee, which is mainly responsible for policy decisions, whilst staff are responsible for strategy decisions. Again, they obtain funding from a whole range of sources and are mainly accountable to statutory authority for funding. Voluntary organisations perceive themselves accountable to the committee for methods and success/failure, whilst community groups view themselves as accountable to statutory authority for success/failure. Community groups also have accountability towards members, as well as the management committee, in terms of methods of practice.

These general characteristics are displayed in the form of a typology, which serves to demonstrate the major differences between the providers of adult learning opportunities. It also highlights some areas of overlap, although on the whole, each sector appears to have marked out an identified territory. Thus providers of formal education tend to cater largely for the unemployed or those at the other end of the scale, wishing to update their professional qualifications, providing structured courses taught in the traditional method. At the informal end of the typology, organisations are more involved in learning than education and offer those marginalised by society opportunities for engaging in issue-based learning. Whilst voluntary organisations serve a wide geographical area, community organisations focus on the local community.

In the middle of the typology, providers of non-formal learning opportunities bridge the two, containing both formal and non-formal elements. Thus they provide structured education, but relate it to the issues and problems facing peoples lives. They have carved out a particular niche in providing support for local groups and whilst they sometimes operate as a stepping stone to more formal education, they are sometimes preferred over their more formal counterparts, for the particular ethos which they have developed.

Discussion

The typology overleaf indicates that a continuum of learning from formal, through non-formal, to informal does exist. In contrast to earlier studies, (Reed and Loughran, 1984; Simkins, 1988) the present research identifies distinctive roles for both non-formal and informal learning. Contrary to other studies (Reed and Loughran, 1984; Percy et al., 1988), these providers do seem to recognise both education and learning as important to their work. Although a smaller percentage of community and voluntary groups indicated that they were involved in providing education, (63% and 45% respectively), this nevertheless represents a sizeable proportion of respondents in this sector. Community groups in particular have given prominence to education as an aspect of their work. It would appear that this is part of a much broader shift in the education paradigm. Such a shift would mean educational institutions no longer hold the monopoly over education and learning, but increasingly outside agencies recognise that they have valuable knowledge, skills and experience which count as a valid educational process. Their preference for the term learning over education may be due to a reticence in using a term normally reserved for formally taught courses. Some support for this idea is found in the latest MORI poll (Campaign for Learning, 1998) which distinguished between *taught* and *non-taught* learning. In this survey, the phrase 'being taught' was most likely to be associated with education, as opposed to learning or training. In a similar vein, findings from this survey revealed that respondents were most likely to have been involved in non-taught learning in the past year and the majority would like to be involved in *non-taught* learning in the

A Typology of Adult Learning Opportunities

Formal	Non-Formal	Informal
Draw learners from neighbouring communities;	Operate on a regional level;	Voluntary organisations operate on a regional level;
Provide education for professional advancement and unemployed;	Provide support for socially excluded groups;	Community organisations operate at community level;
Outreach;	Perceive education to be part of a wider learning process;	More comfortable with learning than education;
Wider access to educational institutions;	Engage in issue-based, problem-solving learning;	Engage in issue-based learning with range of socially excluded groups;
View other providers competitively;	Work in co-operation with other providers;	Concerned with raising awareness of issues and problems;
Tutor as expert in control;	Two-way relationship between tutor and learners;	Work in cooperation with other providers; Professionally qualified tutor;
'Chalk and talk' traditional teaching method;	Non-accredited;	Two-way relationship between tutors and learners;
Structured, accredited courses;	Structured syllabus; Learners active in constructing and teaching on courses;	Courses less structured and non-accredited; Learners in community organisations more active in constructing courses and reporting back topics;
Flexible entry conditions;	Flexible entry conditions;	Flexible entry conditions;
Statutory;	Voluntary;	Voluntary;
Hierarchic, centralised decision-making	More democratic decision-making and accountability;	More democratic decision-making and accountability;
Accountable to statutory authority;		

next year. This suggests that a substantial amount of informal education is taking place.

The MORI survey (Campaign for Learning, 1998) however, in line with Government thinking, was primarily concerned with individuals. The findings of the present research, which focused on adult learning opportunities in the community setting, goes further to suggest that acknowledging the existence of informal education is not simply a recognition of the amount of deliberate learning which adults participate in, but rather of the nature of that learning. The typology above suggests that informal learning in the community is more likely to link in with the issues and problems facing people in their daily lives. Thus it differs qualitatively from formal adult education, which is more concerned about gaining qualifications for increasing job prospects and career advancement. Since this research was carried out, much greater emphasis has been placed on accreditation in the non-formal and informal sectors. In particular, the Open College Network has been responsible for accrediting non-formal and informal education throughout the United Kingdom and this body has now gained UK wide recognition. Change has also come about in part, by greater collaboration between educational institutions and outside agencies, as well as a huge groundswell of demand for recognition of prior learning and prior experiential learning. Initially the demand for accreditation of forms of deliberate learning outside educational institutions had a sense of recognising and valuing such education, in its many shapes and forms. There is a danger however, that this movement could further devalue unaccredited informal education and that the extrinsic goal of gaining qualifications becomes the tantamount reason for engaging in informal education. Despite this shift, it remains true that education is least likely to be accredited in informal settings. Interestingly, respondents in the MORI poll were much more likely to associated 'qualifications' with 'education' as opposed to 'learning' (Campaign for Learning, 1998).

The characteristics of formal adult learning opportunities, as outlined in the typology above, support this view that formal education is concerned with certification. Indeed it has been earlier argued that recent UK government writing on lifelong learning and the learning society adopt an economic approach, whereby lifelong learning is to be valued for its ability to create a workforce suited to the needs of a technological, rapidly changing society. In particular Ainley (1998) has expressed concern in the recent government shift from welfare to workfare, which could he claims further translate into 'learning fare', whereby 'the unemployed are redefined out of existence' (Ainley, 1998: 566). Thus he claims, 'In such a learning society, like actors 'resting' no one would ever be unemployed but only 'learning'. Ainley (1998) further criticises the narrow focus of education and training on outcomes and competencies, which he claims is helping to create a new 'underclass' - those lacking certification or any worthwhile qualifications. These fears echo earlier concerns regarding lifelong learning, expressed by Illich and Verde (1976), where they feared that lifelong learning could become an extension of schooling, further heightening divisions between the classes and causing those marginalised by society to become more and more dependent upon a system which continually recreated the inequalities in society. They stated rather that people have 'the right not to take part in educational processes, that is, the right to satisfy one's own educational needs outside the educational structure' (Illich and Verde, 1976: 19).

The present research suggests that those involved in non-formal and informal learning are doing exactly this and that providers of these adult learning opportunities are responding to a new and very real learning challenge. The key features of these learning opportunities suggest an education which is issue-based, linking problems of everyday life to the educational process and learner-centred. These opportunities value the knowledge and experience of learners and attempt to encourage more active forms of learning, whereby learners become responsible for education themselves.

In terms of Barnett's (1998) four-fold model of the learning society the typology of adult learning opportunities suggests the existence of at least several of these approaches. Whilst the formal sector upholds the economic approach, it also contains the notion of improving individuals quality of life. Likewise, non-formal and informal organisations are concerned with enhancing the quality of individual's lives, although they are also concerned, particularly in community groups, to some extent with collective advancement. However, aspects of the democratic and emancipatory outlooks can be found in their linking of learning with everyday problems and issues, affording people the opportunity both to reflect on these and participate in seeking a solution. The emphasis in non-formal and informal adult learning opportunities, on experiential learning and encouraging learners to take control over the learning process, further suggests a more democratic and emancipatory views of the learning society than are found in the formal sector. These sectors are also more likely to have a more democratic organisational structure, with great accountability towards their members and learners. However, the existence of a management committee does not necessarily constitute a fully participative democracy. Management committee can easily operate as oligarchies and the democratically elected chairperson may well turn out to be a dictator. However, the underlying democratic principles inherent in the structure of non-formal and informal organisations at least presents opportunities for gaining access to decision-making. It would appear therefore, that these alternative versions of the learning society cannot be easily disentangled and indeed it may not be necessary or desirable to do so. Perhaps there is enough space within the learning society to incorporate all these visions and whilst tensions will certainly exist between these visions, this may well offer what Schuller and Field (1998) have alluded to as 'healthy competition' between the sectors. However the differences in the nature of formal, non-formal and informal adult learning opportunities suggest ample room for collaboration.

The need for working in partnerships has been stressed by UK documents on lifelong learning, (DfEE, 1998; DfEE, 1996) and whilst recent changes in funding will no doubt force reluctant institutions into collaboration with others, it is likely that these partnerships in the formal sector will involve schools, further education colleges and universities (HEFCE, 1998). There is a need however, for collaboration *between* rather than simply within the sectors. The typology presented above indicates a willingness on the part of non-formal and informal providers to work in collaboration with others, whilst the formal sector tended to view other providers as competitors. A further issue, related to collaboration is that of widening access to education institutions and increasing participation in formal education, particularly by those who are perceived to be socially excluded (HEFCE, 1998). This would in fact appear to be one of the goals of the UK government strategy for lifelong learning (DfEE, 1998). The typology presented above indicated that widening access to and increasing participation in adult education are concerns of the formal sector. However, given the current emphasis on partnerships, formal adult education providers would do well to note the role of non-formal providers in acting as a bridge between informal and formal adult learning opportunities.

Those involved in promoting formal adult education and training must recognise however, that not all forms of learning, planned or unplanned should be incorporated within the formal system. Promoting lifelong learning and the learning society should not simply be about widening access to and increasing participation in formal educational structures. Rather it ought to truly value the learning, which takes place outside the formal education structure - and not simply by bestowing a number of credits onto it. Perhaps one way of giving recognition to planned learning outside formal education, is to acknowledge that it is part of an educational process, whether one has been taught by self or others!

Conclusion

This chapter had set out to examine the concepts of lifelong learning and the learning society. It is suggested that before adopting strategies aimed at realising these concepts, it is necessary to unpick the definitions of learning and education contained with them. There is also a need to examine the vision of society underlying these concepts and to recognise that they may in fact, include a range of visions, sometimes conflicting. My research highlights the range of learning opportunities currently available to adults in Belfast, suggesting in some loose ad-hoc sense, a learning society. If however, the current UK government is serious about its strategy for lifelong learning, then it needs to adopt a definition of learning much wider than the acquisition of accredited skills and knowledge for increasing employment prospects. If it is serious about encouraging a learning society, where adults play full and active roles as citizens, it must do more than pay lip-service to the many and varied ways in which adults learn.

Resources and funding are needed to ensure the development of informal adult learning opportunities. The research drawn upon for this chapter indicates that this is a very real, thriving and dynamic aspect of the learning society. Its role is often complementary to non-formal and formal adult opportunities and in practice, collaborations and partnerships are becoming more frequent. There is a danger however that formal providers could take control over the 'educational' component of community and voluntary groups activities, thus denying them the right to ownership for their own forms of education. Indeed, it is this very ability to take responsibility for learning which is the desired outlook of the lifelong learner (DfEE, 1998). The present research has suggested that the majority of community and voluntary groups are aware that they are providing opportunities for adults to engage in both planned and unplanned learning. However, as previous adult educators have stated, these activities take place without the need for professional educators or approval from educational institutions (Lovett, 1971; Brookfield, 1981; Hesburg et al., 1974). It is important for community and voluntary groups to remember this, in the stampede for accreditation and not to lose sight of the intrinsic goals of informal education.

References

Ainley, P. (1998) 'Towards a learning or a certified society? Contradictions in the New Labour modernising of lifelong learning', Journal of Education Policy, Vol.13, No.4, pp.559-573.

Armstrong, R. and Davies, C.T. 'Community action, pressure groups and education', *Adult Education*, Vol.50, No.3, 149-154.

Belanger, P. (1993) 'Adult Education: the learning demand and the existing Responses', *Adult Education and Development*, 41. pp.225-238.

Brookfield, S. (1985b) *Self-Directed Learning: from theory to practice*, London, Jossey-Bass.

Brookfield, S. (1985a) 'Self-directed Learning: a conceptual and methodological Exploration', *Studies in Adult Education*, Vol.17, No.1, pp.19-32.

Brookfield, S. (1987) *Developing Critical Thinkers*, Milton Keynes, Open University.

Campaign for Learning (1998) *Attitudes to Learning Survey*, UK, MORI.

Commission of the European Communities (1993) *Guidelines for Community Action in the Field of Education and Training*, Commission Working Paper com (93) 183 Final, Brussels.

Compton, P. and Coward, J. (1989) *Fertility and Family Planning in Northern Ireland*, England, Avebury.

Council for Europe for Cultural Cooperation (1987) *Adult Education and Community Development*, Strasbourg, Council of Europe.

Council for Europe (1992) *Adult Education and Social Change*, Strasbourg, Council of Europe.

Cropley, A.J. (1980) *Towards a System of Lifelong Education*, UK, UNESCO Institute for Education, Hamburg and Pergamon Press.

Darby, J. (1983) *Northern Ireland*, Belfast, Appletree Press.

Department for Education and Employment (1996) *Lifelong Learning: a Policy Framework*, UK, DfEE.

Department for Education and Employment (1998) *The Learning Age: a renaissance for a new Britain*, UK, Stationery Office Ltd.

Elsdon, K.T. (1995) 'Values and Learning in Voluntary Organisations', *International Journal of Lifelong Education*, Vol.4, No.1, pp.75-82.

Fordham, P. (1979) 'The Interaction of Formal and Non-Formal Education, *Studies in Adult Education*, Vol.11, No.1, pp.1-11.

Freire, P. (1974) *Education for Critical Consciousness*, London, Sheed and Ward Ltd.

Gloster, M. (1980) *Non-Formal Education: implications for the recurrent education of teachers*, Paper presented to the Australian Adult Education Association.

Graffikin, F. and Morrissey, M. (1990) *Northern Ireland and the Thatcher Years*, London, Zed.

Harris, R. (1972) *Prejudice and Tolerance in Ulster*, Manchester, Manchester University Press.

Hesburg, T.M., Miller, P.A. and Wharton, C.R. (Jnr) (1974) *Patterns for Lifelong Learning*, London, Jossey-Bass.

Higher Education Funding Council for England (1998) 'Promoting Wider Participation in Higher Education', Workshop paper, HEFCE Annual.

Hughes, E. (ed) (1991) *Culture and Politics in Northern Ireland, 1960-1990 Conference*, London, Open University Press and Anglia Higher Education College.

Illich, I. and Verde, E. (1976) *Imprisoned in the Global Classroom*, London, Writers and Readers Publishing Cooperative.

Ironside, D.J. (1989) *Concepts and Definitions*, in Titmus, C. (ed) (1989) *Lifelong Education for Adults. An International Handbook*, Oxford, Pergamon, pp.22-28.

Jeffs, T. and Smith, M. (1990) *Using Informal Education, an alternative to case-work, teaching and control*, Milton Keynes, Open University.

Lengrand, P. (1989) *Lifelong Education: Growth of the Concept*, in Titmus, C. (ed) (1989) *Lifelong Education for Adults. An International Handbook*, Oxford, Pergamon.

Longworth, N. and Davies, W.K. (1996) *Lifelong Learning*, London, Kogan Page.

Lovett, T. (1971) 'Community Adult Education', *Studies in Adult Education*, Vol.3, np.1, pp.2-14.

MacNamee, P. and Lovett, T. (1987) *Working-Class Community in Northern Ireland*, Belfast, Ulster Peoples College.

Mezirow, J. (1985b) 'A Critical Theory of Self-Directed Learning', in Brookfield, S. (ed) (1985b) *Self-Directed Learning: from theory to practice*, London, Jossey-Bass.

Moreland, R. (1993) *Towards a Learning Society: A Study of Formal, Non-Formal and Informal Adult Learning Opportunities*. DPhil. Thesis, University of Ulster.

National Committee of Inquiry into Higher Education (1997) *Report of the National Committee into Higher Education*, UK, HMS.

NIACE/Gallup (1997) *The Learning Divide*, Leicester, NIACE.

Percy, K., Barnes, B., Graddon, A. and Machell, J. (1988) *Learning in Voluntary Organisations*, Leicester, NIACE.

Project Team (1977) *Belfast Areas of Special Social Need*, Belfast, HMSO.

Reed, H.B. and Loughran, E.L. (1984) *Beyond Schools*, USA, University of Massachusetts.

Rolston, B. and Tomlinson, M. (1988) *Unemployment in West Belfast: The Obair Report*, Belfast, Beyond the Pale.

Schon, D. (1983) *The Reflective Practitioner: how professionals think in action*, New York, Basic Books.

Schon, D. (1987) *Education the Reflective Practitioner*, London, Jossey-Bass.

Schuller, T. and Field, J. (1998) 'Social Capital, Human Capital and the Learning Society', *International Journal of Lifelong Education*, Vol.17, No.4, pp.226-235.

Simkins, T. (1977) *Non-Formal Education and Development Some Critical Issues*, Manchester Monographs II, Manchester, Department of Adult and Higher Education, University of Manchester.

Simpson, J. (1983) *Economic Development: Cause or Effect in the Northern Irish Conflict*, in Darby, J. (ed) (1983) *Northern Ireland*, Belfast, Appletree Press, pp.79-109.

Titmus, C. (ed) (1989) *Lifelong Education for Adults. An International Handbook*, Oxford, Pergamon.

UNESCO (1976) *General Conference, 19th Session Report*, Nairobi, UNESCO.

11 Lifelong Learning: Stretching the Discourse

IAN MARTIN

Abstract

The discourse of lifelong learning has become disconnected from the discourse of social purpose adult education despite the material reality of poverty and the evidence of continuing social polarisation in contemporary British society. The current context of adult education theory, policy and practice exacerbates this problem. The New Labour government in Britain does not seem to herald a new era. Nevertheless, its professed interest in education may offer the opportunity to stretch the discourse of lifelong learning and the learning society so that it begins to reflect some of the key values and purposes of an older tradition in which adult education was an integral part of the struggle for democracy and social justice.

> Yesterday's utopias can become today's reality. Maybe we must first achieve daily utopias that represent a positive dialectic between human realities and human aspirations. (Gelpi, 1997)

Introduction

In this short paper I want to point to the difficulty I have in connecting the radical impulse that lies at the heart of the social purpose tradition in adult and community education - which, it seems to me, was always about catalysing what Gelpi calls 'a positive dialectic between human realities and human aspirations' - with much of the current discussion of lifelong learning and the learning society. In order to do this, having briefly characterised the social purpose tradition, I identify eight particular aspects of the contemporary context of adult education theory, policy and practice (and consequently, of course, research) which impede the reassertion of social purpose. I go on to ask whether New Labour heralds a new era or simply a new version of 'learning to labour' (see Willis, 1977), and to suggest one way in which we can begin to re-make some of the more important connections between lifelong learning and the values and vision of social purpose.

To begin with, however, it is necessary to confront material reality. This shows quite unequivocally that contemporary British society is starkly and systematically unequal and polarised in the most fundamental sense, with the poor getting poorer and the rich richer (eg. see Adonis and Pollard, 1997). As we approach the millennium, it is calculated that a quarter of British children are being brought up in poverty. It is a grim and shameful reality that 'Inequality is perhaps the most salient fact of contemporary British society' (Hutton, 1997). And it is this brute fact that is also, and quite consistently, reflected in the 'learning divide' across society (eg. see Sargant et al., 1997; Barratt Brown, 1998). This is what makes the ludic irony of certain postmodern accounts of adult education seem so privileged, effete and simply out of touch. If the idea of lifelong learning is to be linked with the ideal of active and inclusive citizenship in a democratic society, we must start from Ralph Miliband's uncompromising contention that 'there can be no true citizenship without a rough equality of condition' (Miliband, 1994). We would then be on our guard against some of the worst elisions and evasions wrought by the fashionable euphemisms of 'social exclusion' and the 'underclass'. We would also, perhaps, be less interested in simply celebrating difference and diversity than in reasserting the historical commitment of the radical tradition in adult education to purposeful and partisan engagement with social and economic reality.

This is not, of course, to suggest that the ills of late capitalism are subject to educational solutions. Indeed, we would do well to heed the warning of A.H. Halsey, that insistent advocate of social and educational reform, that we should avoid treating 'education as the waste paper basket of social policy - a repository for dealing with social problems where solutions are uncertain or where there is a disinclination to wrestle with them seriously' (Halsey, 1972). What it does suggest, however, is that it is time, once again, for adult education to take the side of and take its part in the struggles of popular and progressive social movements for the extension of democracy and social justice.

The Loss of Social Purpose

By the radical project in adult education, I mean what Keith Jackson (1995) calls the 'adult education of engagement':

> the view that adults bring something which derives both from their experience of adult life and from their status as citizens to the educational process; that adult education is based on a dialogue rather than a mere transmission of knowledge and skill; that education is not only for personal development and advancement but also for social advancement; that adult education constructs knowledge and does not merely pass it on; that adult education has a dialectical and organic relationship with social movements.

As a way of thinking about and 'doing' education, this tradition can sharpen - and interrogate - the standard vocabulary and rhetoric of adult education because it starts from the collective experience and interests of ordinary people. For example, it stretches and activates the discourse of lifelong learning to the idea of learning for living in order to live a different kind of life, of experiential learning to learning from experience in order to change reality, of social capital and community capacity building to reasserting social purpose and forging solidarity as a common political project. The learner is socially located and recognised as an activist. In engaging with social movements, this kind of adult education seeks to make the educative elements of people's collective experience, ie. what they learn in the struggles of everyday life, more systematically educational. This suggests, incidentally, that educators can often be part of the problem rather than the solution - or, at any rate, that they cannot be part of the solution until they begin to see how they can compound the problem 'Adult educators often overlook the learning dimension that is integral to social life, so intent are they on constructing "education"' (Foley, 1994). In this sense, radical adult education positions itself as the ally of progressive social movements - as distinct from much 'provided education' which is so often used to service, sometimes to suppress, them.

It is in social movements in civil society that people act collectively and dialectically to assert their agency, or their capacity to be free, within the real constraints of structure - often beginning by learning that the first lesson of freedom is to understand the reality of *un*freedom. This is where the struggle of active citizens for a truly democratic learning society must begin, and where the learning society must learn to be a society:

> The history of social movements is a history of people operating in the cracks of superstructures. Of using the energies generated at the margins of systems and organisations. Of exercising considerable imagination, critical thinking, subversion and undutiful behaviour to de-stabilise and de-construct the authority of the inevitable. All of them ways of 'taking back control' based on the inter-relationship between consciousness and courage, between theory and practice. Taking back control and joining with others in collective action to achieve change is at the root of concepts like participation and democracy. It finds its impetus in human agency and can transform people's lives.
>
> (Thompson, 1997)

Historically, this social purpose tradition locates adult education as an integral part of progressive social movements: part of the common cause of liberation, the advancement of collective interests and the political project to create a more just and egalitarian social order. It is at once an educational philosophy, an intellectual commitment and an ideological position. As such, it constitutes, in the words of that great adult educator and lifelong learner Raymond Williams (1983), an important 'resource for a journey of hope':

> The dynamic moment is ... in the difficult business of gaining confidence in our own energies and capacities. It is only in a shared belief and insistence that there are practical alternatives that the balance of forces and chances begins to alter. Once the inevitabilities are challenged, we begin gathering our resources for a journey of hope. If there are no easy answers, there are still available and discoverable hard answers, and it is these we can now learn to make and share.

The problem is that although we live in an increasingly unfair and unequal society (and, indeed, world), the current discourse of lifelong learning and the learning society seldom seems to make any attempt to connect with the material realities of ordinary people's lives. Consequently, it remains at best somewhat abstract and rhetorical; at worst disingenuous and misleading. Moreover, this disjunction occurs within the context of so-called 'postmodernity' in which adult education seems to have become increasingly devoid of any consistent and coherent sense of social purpose. It is only now that we are beginning to see signs of this problem being honestly addressed (see Wildemeersch, Finger and Jansen, 1998; Johnston, 1998).

Consequently, in pursuing the radical project in adult education today, we confront a variety of difficulties, obstacles and contradictions. These inhere in what is increasingly - and, in the context of globalisation, pervasively - expected of us as adult educators (eg. see Walters, 1997). The danger is that as they do their work in us, so we come to discipline ourselves within the terms of an alien and alienating discourse. We become, in short, the agents of our own surveillance and self-censorship.

I would point to *eight particular trends* in current adult education policy, theory and practice which have the effect of de-radicalising our work and divorcing it from popular struggles:

1. We are increasingly exposed - and expected to conform - to the *hegemony of technical rationality* and narrowly conceived and economistic forms of vocationalism and competence.
2. To a greater or lesser extent, we are forced to operate in an *educational market place* in which knowledge becomes commodified and credentialised (often in customised packages of 'continuing education') and educational institutions and agencies exist in relationships of competition rather than co-operation or collaboration with one another.
3. This market place - and, in particular, its workers - are subjected to the rigours of the *new managerialism*, enforcing an accountant's view of the world in which we know the cost of everything and the value of nothing.
4. The construction of the *'self-directed learner'* as consumer or customer puts the emphasis on the non-directive 'facilitation' of individual and individualised learning - as distinct from purposeful educational intervention (and our own agency as educators).
5. There is a growing and seductive tendency to celebrate the authenticity of *personal experience* rather than test its social and educational significance.
6. The *'postmodern turn'* in the current theory of much European and North American adult education seems all too often to cut it off from its historical roots in social purpose, political engagement and the vision of a better world.

7. Rhetorical assertions about the importance of 'active citizenship' and 'social capital' in the *'learning society'* take little or no account of the material realities of context, contingency and differentials of power.
8. Despite its undoubted potential, the growing enthusiasm for *information technology* as the medium of instruction in adult education/learning raises crucial, if widely neglected, questions about the authority of the text, the privatisation of knowledge, the control of learning and the autonomy of the learner.

To sum up in the language of the radical tradition in British adult education, we are in danger of becoming the compliant purveyors of 'merely useful knowledge' (ie. knowledge that is constructed to make people productive, profitable and quiescent workers) as distinct from the active agents of 'really useful knowledge' (ie. knowledge that is calculated to enable people to become critical, autonomous and - if necessary - dissenting citizens) (see Johnson, 1979).

Learning to Labour?

When the Labour government came to power in May 1997 there was real, if cautious, optimism among adult and community educators who identify themselves with the social purpose tradition (eg. see Martin and Shaw, 1997a; 1997b). This waned fairly rapidly as we began to realise that what New Labour meant was, in essence, as little as possible to do with old Labour. We soon learned that New Labour did not herald a new era.

On the other hand, there *was* something new: the government seemed to be prepared to take education seriously - and, in particular, to encourage a policy discourse around the ideas of lifelong learning and the learning society. Perhaps this offered the possibility of harnessing these ideas to a renewed vision of social purpose adult education. The most tangible evidence that this might be the case was the establishment, just one month after the general election, of a National Advisory Group for Continuing Education and Lifelong Learning under the chairmanship of Bob Fryer then Principal of Northern College (quintessentially a repository of the social purpose tradition). The subsequent Fryer Report *Learning for the Twenty-First Century* (Fryer, 1997) is, in some ways, a genuinely expansive and imaginative document, whatever the dilutions and diminutions of it in the subsequent official Green Papers (ie. for England and Wales, and, more recently, Scotland).

The Fryer Report is concerned, among other things, to argue for lifelong learning as, to use R.H. Tawney's Fabian phraseology, a 'strategy of equality' as well as simply a strategy of productivity. It also seeks consistently to link the idea of the learning society to an active, inclusive and, most significantly perhaps, collective notion of democratic citizenship. Neither of these important shifts in the discourse are likely to do more than trickle, incrementally and unevenly, into policy - if they do so at all. The point, however, is that, whatever its deficiencies (eg. in terms of lack of detailed recommendations on funding and implementation) and the widespread disappointment at the government's (lack of) response to it, the report does set a new and unaccustomed tone. This could help to create the conceptual and practical space which we need in order to begin to reassert the social purpose agenda in our work as adult educators. In this sense, there may be the first real opportunity we have had for many years to move from the 'language of critique' to the 'language of possibility' (Giroux, 1992).

For example, the report *does* advocate a universalistic 'culture of lifelong learning for all' which enables people to be autonomous and active citizens:

> This country needs to develop a new learning culture, a culture of lifelong learning for all. It is essential to help the country and all of its people meet the challenges they now face, as they move towards the twenty-first century ... A culture of lifelong learning can act as a resource in the midst of change, helping people to cope with change and in their strivings to shape it to their own devices, as active citizens.

It *does* argue that this vision can only be pursued if we are prepared to confront the reality of growing inequality and material poverty:

> One major and disturbing challenge in recent years has been the widening of social and economic inequality. With it have come increased poverty, social exclusion and reduced life chances for those who have not benefited from economic growth, greater prosperity and new opportunities. These inequalities and divisions range from those of income and wealth to the realms of housing, employment, transport, health, education and training. Many of them are multiple and mutually reinforcing, amounting to compound forms of social

exclusion, on the one hand, and the emergence of a virtual 'super class' of privilege, on the other.

Above all, it *does* make the connection between lifelong learning and social, political and economic change - and thus implicitly seeks to reconnect adult education with the social purpose tradition:

> The personal and social damage inflicted by inequality, social exclusion and restricted opportunity is now widely recognised. Lifelong learning should represent a resource for people, and whole societies, to help them identify such inequalities, probe their origins and begin to challenge them, using skills, information and knowledge to achieve change. Learning alone cannot abolish inequality and social divisions, but it can make a real contribution to combating them, not least by eliminating the ways in which social exclusion is reinforced through the very processes and outcomes of education and training.

In some significant ways, then, this is a distinctive and courageous manifesto - certainly quite unlike anything we have had since the optimistic vision of the Russell and Alexander reports of the early to mid-1970s. Of course, policy, dancing to the Treasury's tune, is a different matter - and there is already evidence that the gnomes of New Labour, armed with their dumbed down politics of the focus group and the sound bite, have done their best to emasculate the more expansive and expensive elements of Fryer's vision of learning and living in the new millennium. But it does set a marker, and it is important that we struggle to use it to reassert our agency as educators and to pursue the social purpose that informs our work.

One way of doing this is to try systematically to stretch the discourse. A discourse, according to Edwards and Usher (1994), 'defines what can be said, which is based on what cannot be said, on what is marginalised, silenced and repressed'. It is essential, therefore, that we try to loosen the discursive blinkers and extend our field of vision. To illustrate the idea of stretching the discourse, I want to take the example of some work I was involved in as a member of the task group on Family, Community and Citizenship Learning, which was one of the four groups assembled to advise the Advisory Group chaired by Bob Fryer (see *Note*). The idea was simply this: to take the acceptable and respectable vocabulary of the current agenda and to stretch its meaning outwards to embrace some of the central concerns of the social purpose tradition. The key words selected for this treatment were: *lifelong learning, citizenship, participation, access, entitlement, partnership* and *capacity building*. The point is that all these words are part and parcel of the lexicon of New Labour, but they are subject to conceptual and ideological stretching. It must be emphasised that this stretching process is also, and essentially, *practical*: potentially, it creates the space local policy makers and workers need to reassert some autonomy and develop radical practice. The result was as follows:

Lifelong learning

Lifelong learning is a continuous social process, encompassing both individual and collective forms of learning. The learning society can only develop out of nurturing a genuine culture of learning in families and communities. Lifelong learning must therefore be rooted in the realities of community life and connect directly and creatively with the interests, aspirations and needs of ordinary people. The concern with community life shifts the focus of interest towards social movements in civil society and away from the institutional structures of the state.

A commitment to lifelong learning in a democratic and pluralist society should be informed by the following key principles, values and purposes:

Learning for citizenship

Citizenship is understood as an active and inclusive category, implying both rights and responsibilities. People learn to become active, informed and critical citizens. In a democratic and pluralist society, lifelong learning must therefore be defined in such a way as to respect the diversity and distinctiveness of communities whilst simultaneously fostering solidarity and a strong civic culture in the wider community.

Democratic participation

All citizens should be both enabled and expected to make an active commitment and contribution to the democratic life of society. The democratic state must be grounded in a democratic way of life. Ultimately, democracy depends upon the health and vitality of families, communities and voluntary associations in civil society. Lifelong learning should therefore be understood to be a key agent of democratic social purpose.

Access to learning

In a democratic learning society everyone has the right to educational opportunities which can help them to develop and thrive in the personal, social and economic aspects of their lives. This implies a concept of access which is understood in terms of access to learning opportunities, including resources for self-directed and autonomous forms of learning, as well as access to educational institutions, progression routes and formal qualifications.

Equity and entitlement

Both social cohesion and shared economic prosperity depend upon social and economic relations which are generally perceived to be fair and just. It is therefore essential that educational opportunities are made available to all citizens in a way that reflects the principles of distributive justice. A commitment to distributive justice in the learning society implies both a recognition that inequality impedes access to educational opportunities and a commitment to dismantle barriers to learning.

Partnership for power sharing

In encouraging partnership arrangements in the provision of opportunities for learning, it is necessary to address the unequal power relations that currently exist between the various 'stakeholders' within the education system as a whole. These relations must be managed in ways that ensure genuine forms of participation, redistribution and 'empowerment', particularly in favour of marginalised and excluded groups. This has significant implications for institutional structures, inter-professional relations, and funding policies and procedures.

Community capacity building

In seeking to develop the capacity of communities, it is essential to avoid an over-simple distinction between education and training, intrinsic value and instrumental objectives, and individual and collective dimensions of learning. In the long run, human capital can serve the economy effectively only if social and cultural capital is systematically developed in communities at local, regional, national and international levels.

Stretching the discourse like this is one way of beginning to construct a 'counter programme of social education' (Barratt Brown, 1998) which can help us to become more strategic about our visions and more visionary about our strategies. In the end, in the words of Jacques Delors (1996) which preface the Fryer Report, lifelong learning in the learning society must be about developing human agency and potential in the most rounded and holistic sense:

> There is a need to rethink and broaden the notion of lifelong education. Not only must it adapt to changes in the nature of work, but it must also constitute a continuous process of forming whole human beings - their knowledge and aptitudes, as well as the critical faculty and ability to act. It should enable people to develop awareness of themselves and their environment and encourage them to play their social role at work and in the community.

This means we must start by understanding and confronting what fundamentally impedes Fryer's vision of a 'culture of lifelong learning for all': the reality of abiding social, educational and material inequality.

Conclusion

It is important to remind New Labour that it stands on the shoulders of a long and worthy tradition in which the 'adult education of engagement' has been an integral part of the historic struggle for social justice and democracy. It is only if we believe this that we can help to make the words of Ettore Gelpi's which I quoted at the beginning of this paper come true: 'Yesterday's utopias can become today's reality'. But what this means is that, first, we must seize and make the opportunity to 'achieve daily utopias' in our work: stretching the discourse is a practical as well as a theoretical challenge. One way of beginning to take on this challenge is to recognise the power of language both to deform and to transform our work - and *our* power to change it. In doing this, we can begin to turn constraints into opportunities because:

Language as a site of contest and struggle raises issues about the possibility or desirability of reclaiming it, exploiting its ambiguity, forcing it to live up to its promise, exposing the shallowness of its application, or rejecting it for an alternative discourse which allows for the possibility of human agency.

(Cook and Shaw, 1996)

Now is the time to renew our commitment to the social purpose tradition. As Richard Taylor (1997) argues, the values 'of social justice and equality, of cooperative and rational systems of economic production, of genuinely democratic participatory practice remain as salient as they ever were'. Ultimately, making the connections between lifelong learning, democratic renewal and inclusive citizenship is an educational task as well as a moral purpose - and it is always and inevitably a political struggle. That struggle continues!

References

Adonis, A. and Pollard, S. (1997) *A Class Act: The Myth of Britain's Classless Society*, London, Hamish Hamilton.

Barratt Brown, M. (1998) *Bugger Bognor!* (Independent Labour Network: Pamphlet No.1), Nottingham, Spokesman.

Cooke, I. and Shaw, M. (eds) (1996) *Radical Community Work: Perspectives from Practice in Scotland*, Edinburgh, Moray House Publications.

Delors, J. (1996) *Learning: The Treasure Within*, Paris, UNESCO.

Edwards, R. and Usher, R. (1994) 'Disciplining the subject: the power of competence', *Studies in the Education of Adults*, 26 (1), pp.1-14.

Foley, G. (1994) 'Adult education and capitalist reorganisation', *Studies in the Education of Adults*, 26 (2), pp.121-143.

Fryer, R.H. (1997) *Learning for the Twenty-First Century* (First report of the National Advisory Group for Continuing Education and Lifelong Learning), London, Department for Education and Employment.

Gelpi, E. (1997) 'Human development as a choice and an action of the people', *Questions de Formation: Issues in the Education of Adults VIII*, (15), pp.71-89.

Giroux, H. (1992) *Border Crossings: Cultural Workers and the Politics of Education*, London, Routledge.

Halsey, A.H. (1972) *Educational Priority: EPA Problems and Policies* (Vol.1), London, HMSO.

Hutton, W. (1997) *The State to Come*, London, Vintage.

Jackson, K. (1995) 'Popular education and the state: a new look at the community debate', in Mayo, M. and Thompson, J. (eds) *Adult Learning, Critical Intelligence and Social Change*, Leicester, NIACE, pp.82-96.

Johnson, R. (1979) '"Really useful knowledge": radical education and working-class culture, 1790-1848', in Clarke, J., Crichter, C. and Johnson, R. (eds) *Working-Class Culture: Studies in History and Theory*, London, Hutchinson, pp.75-102.

Johnston, R. (1998) 'Adult learning for citizenship: shaping a framework for action within civil society'. Paper presented at the 1998 conference of the European Society for Research on the Education of Adults (ESREA): 'Learning to Live in the Learning Society - Challenges and Contradictions in Adults Learning', Brussels.

Martin, I. and Shaw, M. (1997a) 'Sustaining social purpose in the current policy context' in Armstrong, P., Miller, N. and Zukas, M. (eds) *Crossings Borders, Breaking Boundaries: Research in the Education of Adults*. Proceedings of the 27th Annual Conference of the Standing Conference of University Teaching and Research in the Education of Adults (SCUTREA), London, Birkbeck College, University of London, pp.300-304.

Martin, I. and Shaw, M. (1997b) 'Time for social purpose', *Adults Learning*, 9 (3), pp.11-13.

Miliband, R. (1994) *Socialism for a Sceptical Age*, London, Polity Press.

Sargant, N. et al. (1997) *The Learning Divide*, Leicester, NIACE/DfEE.

Taylor, R. (1997) 'The search for a social purpose ethic in adult continuing education in the "New Europe"', *Studies in the Education of Adults*, 29 (1), pp.92-100.

Thompson, J. (1997) *Words in Edgeways: Radical Learning for Social Change*, Leicester, NIACE.

Walters, S. (ed) (1997) *Globalization, Adult Education and Training: Impacts and Issues*, London, Zed Books.

Wildemeersch, D., Finger, M. and Jansen, T. (eds) (1998) *Adult Education and Social Responsibility*, Frankfurt am Main, Peter Lang.

Williams, R. (1983) *Towards 2000*, Harmondsworth, Penguin.

Willis, P. (1977) *Learning to Labour*, Farnborough, Saxon House.

Note

I wish to acknowledge the help I received in this exercise from another member of the task group, Fraser Patrick of Dundee City Council. I must emphasise, however, that the views expressed in this paper are entirely my own.

12 Lifelong Learning for a Sustainable Future

GILLIAN TROREY, CEDRIC CULLINGFORD AND
BARRIE COOPER

Abstract

Environmental education is argued to be the most significant example of lifelong learning, in that it involves issues that affect all, both young and old, and is the most sustained interest for many adults throughout life. Various statements from political agencies about lifelong learning and environmental education are explored and the gaps between them and their delivery into action analysed. It is suggested that the only fundamental answer is to rethink the whole purpose of the school curriculum, with environmental education not as a mere addition to the welter of facts, but as an informing concern both personal and social. In this way both the issues and the natural interests of children and adults will no longer be marginalised.

Introduction

The concept of lifelong learning is not a simple one. It is underpinned by the tension between learning as a personal desire and learning as a response to the demands of society as a whole. Until comparatively recently all arguments about lifelong learning were based on the assumption that this meant nothing more or less than personal growth and the development of individual curiosity. Hoggart (1957) encapsulates the old tradition of literacy and understanding as personal rather than social fulfilment.

More recently such a concept of personal development for its own sake has been replaced by greater instrumentalism; with honing skills for the sake of society. Whilst the individual might be invoked, it is as a product of the skills or adaptability to the demands of new technology and greater global competition.

Nowhere is the distinction between the concerns of the individual and the demands of the state made more ironically apparent than in the great Swedish experiment reported by Marklund (1986). The Swedish government decided that it would invest in the learning of all its employed adult citizens by supporting them in taking University level courses. The assumption was that they would update their skills and knowledge to become more efficient and successful in the workplace. The offer of free courses was very popular. A surprisingly large percentage of the eligible population took up the chance for further study. But what over 95 percent of them chose was to take courses in subjects of their own personal interest, from astronomy to zoology. These had nothing to do with the demands of the workplace or the expectations of the state.

The tension that underlies lifelong learning is rarely fully explored. It needs, however, to be taken seriously since real education that is sustainable must encapsulate both personal desire and social interest.

Environmental Education

A rarely-mentioned component of the concept of lifelong learning is that of the environment. This is both a personal and a social theme. On the one hand there are those examples of curiosity about nature that are real demonstrations of lifelong learning. Millions of people watch nature programmes on UK television. The Royal Society for the Protection of Birds has over one million members, demonstrating a commitment to improving the conditions of the countryside. These are an equally important indication of lifelong learning as those attending vocational and technical courses to improve their skills. The amount of commitment to the personal naturally exceeds any response to externally imposed instrumental demands.

The environment is not only a personal delight and interest but a grave social concern. Issues of pollution, in water and in the air, and what to do about them, concern all in society. The government here can be seen quite rightly to invoke the instrumental, to set targets, to take the kinds of actions that will deal with global warming and the ozone layer, acid rain and all the other threats to the environment. But as the government itself realises, the only actions that will really succeed are those which involve the whole population; everyone who uses water and not only those who drive a car.

The only way in which there can be such widespread action is by understanding and action at the local level. Environmental education therefore combines the necessary ethical and intellectual analysis of the circumstances that face, even threaten, society and the actions that arise from such understanding. Of all lifelong concerns, this is arguably the most important. It is only when all people are involved in the actions that surround sustainability that there will be any real change. This depends on personal understanding and personal commitment - in other words, lifelong education. Unfortunately the personal dimension of understanding on which the state ironically and unknowingly depends is rarely discussed in the official reports on lifelong learning.

It is now generally accepted that environmental education is essential for the future survival of humanity (HMSO, 1991; Smyth, 1995). Only by increasing public environmental awareness and by the creation of a more environmentally-literate workforce can a sustainable future be assured. Over the last two decades there have been a succession of major international reports on the environment, for example the World Commission on the Environment and Development (WCED, 1987) and the United Nations Conference on Environment and Development (UNESCO, 1992), in which the case for environmental education has been made time and again. This has been reflected at the European level (Council of Ministers of the European Community, 1988) and in the United Kingdom:

> Environmental education will need to permeate all levels and aspects of education, beginning with the National Curriculum in schools, continuing in colleges and universities and extending into professional and vocational training. For education, the challenge will never be bigger.
>
> (Chris Patton, Secretary of State for the Environment, 1990-91)

With this level of support, one would expect that the environment would be central to all areas of both formal and informal education. After all, nothing could be more 'lifelong' than such a statement. Yet this is clearly not the case. Learning about the environment must be an ongoing process, involving a debate that is continued and renewed, to ensure a healthy growth of ideas to inform the curriculum.

Lifelong Learning and the Environment

Recent moves towards the new culture of lifelong learning have provided an ideal opportunity for the development of a coherent strategy for environmental education, both within the formal education system and informally through the media. Lifelong learning has been presented as an investment for the future of the economy, the labour market and family and community life, which will have a fundamental effect on the quality of life of people in the UK. The development of a strategy for lifelong learning requires vision, planning and the anticipation of the future needs of people and society. Yet, however effective the lifelong learning strategies, quality of life will not improve if we fail to protect the environment and the life-support systems on which it depends. If lifelong learning is directed solely towards the development of the economy and the labour market, there is a danger that economic growth could be achieved at the expense of the environment. There is an ever greater danger that it will not succeed at all, even in its own narrow terms.

It is therefore vital that all programmes of education, training or skills development introduced as part of the lifelong learning process will also enable participants to develop:

• an understanding of local and global environmental issues
• environmental or 'green' awareness
• an understanding of the notion of sustainability and sustainable development
• a commitment to environmental citizenship
• the skills to implement an environmentally responsible lifestyle
• a personal sense of motivation and curiosity

In their pivotal book on lifelong learning, Longworth and Davies (1996) suggest that the development of environmental awareness must be an important part of any lifelong learning strategy:

> How can lifelong learning provide a framework for the discussion of the contemporary world, national and local problems - environment, the rights of individuals and minorities, employment, demography, using technology wisely, cultural and physical vandalism - and provide potential solutions? Why

are so many people, organisations and governments taking note of a concept expressed in the words of Kuan Tsu in the third century BC?

> 'When planning for a year - sow corn. When planning for a decade - plant trees. When planning for a lifetime - train and educate men'.
> (Longworth and Davies, 1996)

In fact, they go as far as to suggest that the move towards longer-term thinking and the need for holism and completeness in education has been provoked by the debate on the environment and sustainable development. They point out that if the population increases from the current five billion to an estimated eleven billion in the middle of the next century, the strain on global environmental, social, educational and political systems will obstruct the development of a society committed to lifelong learning.

Longworth and Davies trace the development of the concept of lifelong learning from the seminal UNESCO/Club of Rome report *No Limits to Learning* (1979). Since then, major political and social upheavals in both the developed and developing world have resulted in marked changes to the patterns of work, learning and leisure. They identify eight paradigm changes towards a focus on individual learning as a means of realising potential:

- the influence of science and technology
- the restructuring of industry
- global demographics
- the influence of television and other media
- changes in the nature of work
- focus on the individual
- environmental imperatives
- new global power structures

Under 'environmental imperatives' they state that:

> There is a crucial need to educate continually the world's people in environmental matters as a basis for the survival of the species. In this we must remain inventive and innovative about how environmental information is kept constantly in the forefront of popular consciousness. In other words we need a lifelong learning approach to a lifelong survival issue. (Ibid)

All this suggests an international concern that associates lifelong learning with the environment. And yet, when one looks beneath the surface, this message is not really imbibed, or perhaps not genuinely believed in. The UK Government's Green Paper *The Learning Age* (DfEE, 1998) is the most developed approach yet towards the development of a lifelong learning society. Lifelong learning is here defined as the continuous development of the skills, knowledge and understanding that are necessary for employment and fulfilment. Yet, despite some promising comments in the Secretary of State for Education's foreword:

> Investment in Human capital will be the foundation of success in the knowledge-based global economy of the twenty-first century ...
>   ... To achieve stable and sustainable growth, we will need a well-educated, well equipped and adaptable labour force.

There is no specific discussion about the importance of acquiring skills, knowledge and understanding relating to the environment and sustainability issues. The only (passing) reference occurs in the section on learning in the community, which identifies the need to develop a sense of social cohesion, belonging and identify within local communities. It proposes to draw on the experience of community development projects, including those run by environmental organisations, as a means of promoting community learning. Although environmental groups can and do provide a sound basis for local environmental activities, this hardly constitutes a strategy for lifelong environmental understanding.

But more significantly, the language that is used is that of narrow instrumentalism. 'Investment ... in capital' is a clear enough concept even if in human currency. A 'knowledge based ... economy' shifts the commercial necessity from what are seen as old fashioned skills of craftmanship and machine tools to information and technology. For all the invocation of the terms 'sustainable' and 'well educated' the real interest lies in the 'adaptable labour force'.

Similarly, the report *Learning for the Twenty-first Century* (Fryer, 1997) begins with a promising quotation:

> There is a need to rethink and broaden the notion of lifelong education. Not only must it adapt to changes in the nature of work, but it must also constitute a continuous process of forming whole human beings - their knowledge and

aptitudes as well as the critical facility and ability to act. It should enable people to develop awareness of themselves and their environment and encourage them to play their social role at work and in the community.
(Delors (1996), from *Learning: the Treasure within*, cited in Fryer, 1997)

It acknowledges the importance of other human interests than the nature of work. Yet its focus is on the economy and the labour market and the development of new skills for work. The report does propose that more support be given to projects and initiatives which strengthen voluntary organisations and contribute to social and economic regeneration - which could involve local environmental initiatives, although this is not specifically stated. Apart from the opening quote, it is only under the section entitled *Other Challenges and Opportunities* that the environment receives a mention:

In less familiar ways, in such varied realms as transport, the environment, community safety and international relations, we need to be sure that people are equipped through learning, to understand the issues, exercise choices and make the judgements for themselves. These are increasingly essential elements of our changing political culture and lifelong learning should contribute positively to them. (Ibid)

The democratic ideal of understanding social issues is here acknowledged as significant.

We continually witness gestures towards real education before experiencing the 'delivery' of skills. The general and human concerns are constantly undermined by the prerogatives of the government. Some might argue that such a positivist focus on skills is inevitable given the economic dictates of politics. Others would argue that such narrowness is in the long term unsuccessful, indeed as 'unsustainable' as limiting oneself to sowing corn. The instrumental view might be limited but it also undermines all the larger well meaning gestures towards lifelong learning. We find concepts reduced to clichés from 'sustainability' to 'lifelong learning'.

Citizenship and the Environment

The most recent token word to emerge from this undercurrent of debate is 'citizenship'. The initial report of the Advisory group, *Education for citizenship and the teaching of democracy in schools* (QCA, 1998) describes citizenship education as composed of three parts:

- social and moral responsibility
- community involvement
- political literacy

'Responsibility' is considered to be both a political and moral virtue, as it implies care for others, premeditation and calculation about what effect actions are likely to have on others, and understanding and care for the consequences. Volunteering and community involvement are considered to be necessary conditions of civil society and democracy. The report also points out that citizenship education can both inform and draw upon other subjects and aspects of the curriculum.

The problem with adding citizenship to the curriculum is that it becomes yet another token gesture. The National Curriculum itself, with its heavy emphasis on literacy and numeracy, marginalises sustained debate on ethical issues just as it suppresses critical thinking with its emphasis on fact (Quinn, 1997). Attempts to introduce concepts of personal social responsibility, including enacting the tenets of democracy, are well meant but even when seriously introduced, fail to make a fundamental impact on the usual ethos of schools or of society. In one study of schools which had produced a series of policies and policy documents which celebrated the participation of their pupils in all decision making - in order to teach them citizenship - the actual reaction of the self same pupils was a consistent 'what participation?' and 'they don't listen to us' (Greenfield, 1996).

Despite the good intentions of the final report (Crick, 1998), cynics might argue that what is really intended is greater political awareness rather than a reconceptualisation of the purposes of the curriculum. Nevertheless, citizenship, including the duties of sustaining the environment, is a clear example of lifelong learning.

The Fryer Report (1997) does emphasise that lifelong learning has a clear role to play in the creation of contemporary citizenship and community development:

> Through learning, competing values can be reviewed, their relevance for society today and tomorrow can be assessed, and newly emerging values can be transmitted. These are all features of the creation of contemporary

citizenship in our country and the enrichment of contemporary 'civil society'. Such a citizenship involves a greater emphasis on self-activity, initiative and pluralism, and is pursued in a variety of spheres and forms, through many different sorts of agency and process... In facing this challenge, lifelong learning, with its opportunities for critical reflection and creative initiative, can strengthen democracy and community development, enlarging the place of individuals and groups in them both.

Concern for the environment is frequently included in discussions of the spiritual and moral dimensions of education. The Dearing *Review of Qualifications for 16-19 year olds* (SCAA, 1996) considers that spiritual and moral development should include:

care for and appreciation of the natural world, the wish to know and understand, a sense of awe and wonder, sometimes at the simplest everyday things.

He recommends that all providers of education, including regulatory and awarding bodies, should take account of spiritual and moral issues during the design, approval and delivery of programmes for young people.

However, in other quarters there is much discussion about whether environmental ethics can and should be taught; although it is recognised that young people should have access to appropriate and relevant information to enable them to develop and put into practice their own environmental values, there are concerns about possible 'indoctrination with radical green agendas' (Royal Geographical Society, 1998).

Support for Environmental Education

During the last thirty years there has been a growing recognition of the importance of environmental education. The term 'environmental education' was probably first introduced at the 1965 Keele Conference, where education specialists and conservationists were brought together for the first time (Sterling, 1992). The importance of environmental education was acknowledged and it was recommended that local education authorities should provide in-service training for teachers in a 'broad environmental approach which would help break down out-dated barriers between many school subjects' (Nature Conservancy Council, 1965). This led to the formation of the Council for Environmental Education (CEE), which was established to provide a focal point for co-ordinating and disseminating advice on environmental education. The scope of environmental education was considerably broadened by the introduction of the *Belgrade Charter* (UNESCO-UNEP, 1976) where emphasis was placed on values and attitudes as well as skills and understanding - calling for a 'global ethic' that will require individuals to demonstrate a 'commitment to the improvement of the quality of the environment and of life for the world's people'. The following year, the Tbilisi Conference (UNESCO-UNEP, 1977), established, with considerable international acceptance, five categories for environmental education - awareness, knowledge, attitudes, skills and participation. The World Conservation Strategy (IUCN, 1980) also advocated participation as a strategy for achieving the purposes of environmental education and transforming the behaviour of societies. Within Europe, the Council of Ministers of the European Community adopted a resolution on environmental education requiring each member state to:

> promote the introduction of environmental education in all sectors of education, including vocational training and adult education.
>
> (Council of Ministers of the European Community, 1988)

In 1990 the Regional Conference of Ministers, in its report *Action for a Common Future*, pointed out that sustainable development would only be possible through education:

> ... adapting school curricula and educational material on sustainable development and by designing education and training programmes that enable students, workers, businessmen and decision-makers to appreciate the connection between their specialisms and environmental issues.
>
> (WCED, 1990)

The 1992 Earth Summit was, of course, an important landmark in the history of environmental education. Chapter 36 of *Agenda 21*, entitled *Promoting Public Awareness, Education and Training* (UNCED, 1992) produced yet more official endorsement of the importance of the role of environmental education in the development of sustainable societies. One of the frequently quoted statements from this document is:

Education is critical for achieving environmental and ethical awareness, values and attitudes, skills and behaviour consistent with sustainable development and for effective participation in decision making. (UNCED, 1992)

Within the UK, environmental education has been slowly evolving since the 1960s. With its roots in biology and geography, environmental education was formally introduced into the English and Welsh National Curriculum in 1990 as one of five 'cross curricular themes'. Curriculum Guidance 7: Environmental Education (NCC, 1990) described the aims of environmental education as being to:

- provide opportunities to acquire the knowledge, values and attitudes, commitment and skills to protect and improve the environment
- encourage pupils to examine and interpret the environment from a variety of perspectives
- arouse pupils' awareness and curiosity about the environment and encourage active participation in resolving environmental problems.

(NCC, 1990)

Lakin (1996) describe the complexity of attempting to implement this cross-curricular theme, where contributions may be required from English, Mathematics, Science, Geography, History, Technology, Art, Music and even PE. Since the 1995 National Curriculum revisions, the management of the cross-curricular themes has been largely left to individual schools. In many, environmental education has become a low priority, and is frequently left to individual teachers who have an interest in the area, in schools where such individuals exist.

Support for environmental education from UK local government has also been inconsistent. However, some local authorities have been particularly active in attempting to raise awareness of the importance of environmental understanding and conservation, by for example, opening field studies centres for use by local schools, creating country parks which host a range of events and activities, providing grants to develop school grounds and employing specialist advisors to work with schools.

The advent of Local Agenda 21 has been the most important initiative in developing a programme of lifelong learning which encompasses environmental and sustainability education at the local level. Agenda 21, one of the four major agreements to be signed at the 1992 Earth Summit, sets out what needs to be done to achieve sustainable development in the

21st century. A key principle is that global problems need to be tackled at the local level. Local Agenda 21 promotes the development of local action plans (or LA 21s) that aim to protect and improve the quality of the local environment, and thus the quality of life for local people. They recognise that all members of the community need to become involved for sustainable development to become a reality. The Local Government Management Board has been actively encouraging and supporting local authorities in the development of their LA 21s and has published *Education for a Sustainable Local Authority* (LGMB, 1994), which emphasises the role of education within the sustainability process.

Support for environmental education has clearly been evident at local, national and international levels, and many strategies and initiatives have been instigated. Yet many, including Gayford (1996a) question why it has not had a more profound impact on all aspects and levels of education. He suggests that this may be due in part to the way that environmental education has grown organically in recent years, resulting in a change of perspectives and priorities even among experienced practitioners. Certain aspects are unavoidably political, or suffer from no real consensus of views. Many teachers feel that environmental education is largely 'issues based' and that the issues, such as tropical rain forest destruction, nuclear power and pollution are broad and complex and have no straightforward answers.

Education for Sustainability

There has been a move in recent years from environmental education towards 'education for sustainability' or 'sustainable development'. Education for sustainability has been defined as:

> ... a lifelong learning process that leads to an informed and involved citizenry having the creative problem-solving skills, scientific and social literacy, and commitment to engage in responsible individual and cooperative actions. These actions will help ensure an environmentally sound and economically prosperous future. Education for Sustainability has the potential to serve as a tool for building stronger bridges between the classroom and business, and between schools and communities.
>
> (President's Council on Sustainable Development, 1994)

Education for sustainability, according to Firth and Plant (1996) requires a reconceptualisation of environmental education and some of the assumptions upon which it has been based:

> How people see themselves in terms of their community and environment is at the core of the issue of identity and of our educational programmes. Making sense of the world and our place in it is not achieved through abstract, rational thought and ideas, but by reflecting on the realm of everyday experiences and how it constructs our sense of ourselves ... If environmental education is to develop an environmental citizenship as a status endowed with social and ecological entitlements which people can legitimately claim, then to be a citizen is to regard these entitlements as one's own ...   (Firth and Plant, 1996)

This approach reinforces the notion that environmental or sustainability education is not just an addition to the curriculum but something far more central. This is not only because of the importance, but also the unavoidability of the issue.

Cullingford (1998) considers that children cannot avoid issues of ethics and the environment, as they are encountered long before formal schooling begins. He suggests that they observe their environment closely from the earliest years and understand far more about the issues involved than is generally expected. Bonnet and Williams (1998) also show that children at the primary stage are acutely aware of issues about nature and the environment. Cullingford (1998) identifies a second phase 'of moral absolutes and certainties without ambiguity or irony' (usually around the ages of eight to thirteen) where there is a strong connection between ethics and political correctness, for example in the strong feelings engendered by animal rights, such as fox hunting, or dying sea birds after oil spills, in response to images in the media. He observes that children are more likely to discuss environmental issues outside the classroom than in formal issues. Stanisstreet and Boyes (1996) feel that children of secondary school age also have a natural enthusiasm and concern for the environment. The question is what use can be made of these concerns.

Dearling and Armstrong (1997) point out that young people (aged fourteen and over) feel increasingly angry at the way they see the natural and the human environment being treated. Many see involvement in environmental projects, such as local conservation and clean-up schemes, as a way of doing something 'real' which can actually lead to change as well as 'celebrate cultural and environmental diversity'.

However, Gayford (1996a) showed that although 85% of primary teachers and 69% of secondary teachers involved in environmental education felt that participation in the maintenance or improvement of the local environment was important, only 47% of primary teachers and 53% of secondary actually became involved or encouraged their pupils to do so.

A study by Palmer (1992) into the formative experiences of those now involved as environmental educators, found that 90% of those surveyed cited memorable experiences outdoors as a child (being brought up in the countryside, going on holiday, outdoor activities) and 59% cited parents, close relatives or friends as having a marked influence on their present day concern for the environment. School or higher education influenced 58% of respondents, and organisations such as scouts and guides, natural history clubs and 'green' political and campaigning bodies 36%. TV and the media accounted for 23%.

Clearly, all the above have a role to play, but the message seems to be that concern for, and learning about, the environment must begin when children are young, and should involve active, local participation in field work or other conservation activities. A considerable amount is already being done. Local conservation groups abound, but their work, although locally effective, is patchy, may not involve schools or young people, and lacks regional coordination. Much relies on the enthusiasm of just a few volunteers. School grounds are often an excellent starting point for local conservation projects, and support and information is available nationally from organisations such as *Learning Through Landscapes*, the *Council for Environmental Education* (CEE) and the *Royal Society for the Protection of Birds* (RSPB). The CEE/RSPB publications, *Develop an environmental policy: a call to action for schools* (CEE/RSPB, 1995) and *Our World, Our Responsibility* (CEE/RSPB, 1996) provide a framework for pupil's learning about the environment, the development of positive attitudes to the environment and the opportunity to participate locally in resolving environmental problems.

Support for environmental education teaching, mainly in the form of resources, is liberally provided from non-governmental organisations such as the RSPB, Friends of the Earth, the World Wide Fund for Nature, the National Association for Environmental Education and the CEE, and commercial and industrial organisations. They are too numerous to list here. According to Gayford (1996b):

> ... there are many examples of materials and projects directed towards the perceived needs of schools. The overall situation has therefore become one in which there is no lack of resources and materials, but a deficiency of evaluation or other mechanisms to make them easier for hard-pressed teachers or non-formal educators to use them.

A lack of resources is not, therefore, the problem. This lies much more in the nature of personal commitment, and belief in its importance. There is a huge capital and personal investment in the lifelong concerns of environmental education. In the case of the young, the personal investment on behalf of children, rather than the capital, is lacking. Those who are most committed and enthusiastic about environmental issues have a personal interest, almost for its own sake. Children have a natural and even passionate concern. The two are too rarely brought together. Inadequate coordination within institutions and between organisations has also characterised the support that is being offered.

A number of specific texts (e.g. Palmer and Neil, 1994 for primary and secondary schools, and Dearling and Armstrong, 1997 for youth workers) provide support for 'hard-pressed teachers or non-formal eductors' in the organisation and delivery of environmental education and/or awareness. It has long been recognised, however, that the delivery of environmental or sustainability education within geography or science, or a named higher education course is not sufficient. It needs to be integrated into all subjects at all levels (Palmer and Neal, 1994). Further and higher education (FHE) has been supported in this respect by the Toyne Report (DfEE 1993), which identified a role for FHE in the development of environmental awareness in the student body as a whole, not just for those on specific 'environmental' courses. Yet a review (Ali Khan, 1996) of the implementation of the Toyne recommendations showed that very little progress has been made, with only 114 out of 750 institutions stating that they had, or were developing, an environmental policy. It is unlikely that the inclusion of environmental education into the curriculum can be made to work without colleges themselves complying with environmentally sound principles. Even more disappointing was that only seventeen institutions were identifying a common learning agenda of sustainability themes for all their students.

More recently, Ali Khan (1998) has surveyed University teacher education faculties in an attempt to assess the extent to which education for sustainability and sustainable development themes are included in the curriculum. Just 5% of respondents claimed to be systematically integrating most of the themes. Many teacher educators suggested that such themes might be more appropriately covered in subject degree programmes.

Yet degree programme subjects are themselves contentious. A degree in environmental science can range in content from ecology and field work to the politics of globalisation. Neither will enable students to progress to a one year PGCE, as environmental science is not a National Curriculum subject. Are we missing the opportunity for individual 'experts' in environmental science to deliver interesting and relevant environmental education in our schools, and relying on science and geography graduates who may have a marginal interest or understanding? Where are the real 'naturalists' who can enthusiastically lead children on a nature trip and point out all the trees, plants and animal tracks? Certainly not in a recent environmental science graduate, interviewed for our PGCE in post-compulsory education, who, when asked how he would plan a woodland ecology trip with six formers, notably remarked:

> Oh, I can't name individual trees. I know why they should not be cut down, but I can't identify them.

Should we go back to the fieldwork and conservation approach to environmental education of the 1970s - at least for primary school pupils and teachers? Who will be left to influence and enthuse future generations? Or is the problem deeper? Is it a lack of clarity in the purpose of the whole curriculum, especially when looked at from the point of view of lifelong learning?

The Government set up a Sustainable Development Education Panel in February 1998, with a view to improving understanding of the social, economic, environmental and technological dimensions of its policies. The formation of the Regional Development Agencies during 1999 will offer a real opportunity, via the development of Regional Sustainability Plans, to promote both lifelong learning and sustainability education at all levels, in a form appropriate to each region. Each will need to develop a carefully planned strategy, which clearly sets out its vision and the principles by which it intends to develop strategy and change practice. The strategy must be developed in close collaboration with the many other bodies which will be responsible for implementation. A clear strategic framework, with an accompanying set of targets, must be set out, so that progress toward them can be monitored and reviewed. Ideally, the Regional Development Agencies will also provide a lead in the coordination of local initiatives. All the good work done so successfully by individuals within the community deserves more support and coordination.

But this must have an impact on the school curriculum if it is to be sustainable, and there is now a real opportunity for this to take place, within the Qualifications and Curriculum Authority's (QCA) review of the curriculum. The Sustainable Development Education Panel has produced recommendations for learning outcomes at each Key Stage, and QCA is looking at how education for sustainability, citizenship, spiritual and moral education and personal and social education can be introduced into a revised curriculum. To become effective, education for sustainability must become more than a 'cross curricular theme'. We know that the teaching and learning resources are there, and enthusiasm for the environment at the local level. What is needed now is a thorough evaluation of these resources, effective pre- and in-service teacher training and the bringing together of schools and local environmental organisations.

Although we expressed initial disappointment at the lack of reference to sustainability education in the Fryer Report, Fryer (1998) recently cited many examples of where understanding the environment could play a part in lifelong learning. It seems appropriate then, to end this chapter with some of those examples:

> One of the main aims of lifelong learning is to enable individuals to make sense of what is going on, to make sense of change. We need to be able to make informed choices about world climate, about the environment and beef on the bone. We need to be able to adapt to change; through learning we become part of that change and take a share in the direction of that change - a deeply democratic promise that goes to the very heart of being a citizen. Lifelong learning is far too important to be left to educational institutions - it means community groups, environmental groups and social services. Community organisation is increasingly important - to protect the countryside, to campaign for opening up a pathway, to protest against a local development. It is about linking up with other like-minded people - a meaningful form of practical participation.

Here we have the essential theme encapsulated. Lifelong learning is about bringing together two things: personal enthusiasm and social understanding. Such education is not a choice but a necessity. Everyone goes on learning and reacting to the environment and to other people in one way or another. The question is whether this reaction is positive or negative. Only by involving people at the earliest opportunities can the lifelong learning questions be answered.

References

Ali Khan, S. (1996) *Environmental responsibility: a review of the 1993 Toyne Report*, London, HMSO.

Ali Khan, S. (1998) *Forum for the Future Higher Education 21 Project: Teacher Education Curriculum Audit*, Survey Report, London, Forum for the Future.

Bonnet, M. and Williams, T. (1998) 'Environmental Education and Primary Children's Attitudes towards Nature and the Environment', *Cambridge Journal of Education*, 28 (2) pp.159-174.

CEE/RSPB (1995) *Develop an environmental policy: a call to action for schools*, Council for Environmental Education/Royal Society for the Protection of Birds.

CEE/RSPB (1996) *Our World, Our Responsibility*, Council for Environmental Education/Royal Society for the Protection of Birds.

Council of Ministers of the European Community (1988) 'Resolution on Environmental Education', *Official Journal of the European Communities*. No.C177/8.

Crick, B. (1998) *Education for Citizenship and the teaching of Democracy in Schools*, London, HMSO.

Cullingford, C. (1999) 'Personal ethics and the real environment', *Ethics, Place and Environment*, 2 (1) pp.96-99.

Dearling, A. and Armstrong, H. (1997) *Youth Action and the Environment*, Lyme Regis, Russell House Publishing.

DfEE (1993) *Environmental Responsibility: an Agenda for Further and Higher Education*, The Toyne Report, London, HMSO.

DfEE (1998) *The Learning Age: a renaissance for a new Britain*, Green paper, London, HMSO.

Firth, R. and Plant, M. (1996) 'Education for the Environment: from rhetoric to realisation', in Harris, G. and Blackwell, C. (eds) *Environmental Issues in Education*, Aldershot, Ashgate.

Fryer, R. (1997) *Learning for the Twenty-first Century: First Report of the National Advisory Group for Continuing Education and Lifelong Learning.*

Fryer, R. (1998) *Lifelong Learning*, Speech at the Annual Meeting of Huddersfield Technical College, December 1998.

Gayford, C. (1996a) 'The nature and purposes of environmental education', in Harris, G. and Blackwell, C. (eds) *Environmental Issues in Education*, Aldershot, Ashgate.

Gayford, C. (1996b) 'Support systems in environmental education', in Harris, G. and Blackwell, C. (eds) *Environmental Issues in Education*, Aldershot, Ashgate.

Greenfield, C. (1996) *The Teaching and Learning of Citizenship in an English Comprehensive School*, Bristol, Doctoral Dissertation.

HMSO (1991) *Our Common Inheritance: Britain's Environmental Strategy*, Cm 1200, London, HMSO.

Hoggart, R. (1957) *The Uses of Literacy*, London, Chatto and Windus.

IUCN (1980) *World Conservation Strategy*, Gland, International Union for the Conservation of Nature.

Lakin, L. (1996) 'Environmental Education, the National Curriculum and the way ahead', in Harris, G. and Blackwell, C. (eds) *Environmental Issues in Education*, Aldershot, Ashgate.

LGMB (1994) *Education for a sustainable local authority*, Luton, Local Government Management Board.

Longworth, N. and Davies, W.K. (1996) *Lifelong Learning: New vision, new implications, new roles for people, organisations and communities in the Twenty-first century*, London, Kogan Page.

Marklund, S. (1986) *Integration of School and World of Work*, London, Department of International and Comparative Education.

Nature Conservancy Council (1965) *The Countryside in 1970. Second Conference*, Proceedings of the Conference on Education, University of Keele, March 1995.

NCC (1990) *Curriculum Guidance 7: Environmental Education*, York, National Curriculum Council.

Palmer, J. (1992) 'Life experiences of environmental educators: first report on autobiographical research data', *Environmental Education* 41, Wolverhampton, National Association for Environmental Education.

Palmer, J. and Neal, P. (1994) *The Handbook of Environmental Education*, London, Routledge.

QCA (1998) *Education for citizenship and the teaching of democracy in schools*, Advisory group initial report, London, Qualifications and Curriculum Authority.

Quinn, V. (1997) *Critical Thinking in Young Minds*, London, David Fulton.

Royal Geographical Society (1998) Environmental Education, Ethics and Citizenship: a discussion forum, 20 May 1998, London, The Royal Geographical Society.

SCAA (1996) *Review of Qualifications for 16-19 year olds (the Dearing Report)*, London, SCAA publications.

Smyth, J.C. (1995) 'Environment and Education; a view of a changing scene', *Environment Education Research* 1 (1) pp.3-20.

Stanisstreet, M. and Boyes, E. (1996) 'Young people's ideas about global environmental issues', in Harris, G. and Blackwell, C. (eds) *Environmental Issues in Education*, Aldershot, Ashgate.

Sterling, S. (1992) *Coming of Age: a short history of Environmental Education to 1989*, Wolverhampton, National Association for Environmental Education.

UNCED (1992) *Promoting Education and Public Awareness and Training*, Conches, Agenda 21 Conference on Environment and Development.

UNESCO-UNEP (1976) *International Environmental Workshop: a global framework for environmental education* (The Belgrade Charter) Connect 1 pp.1-3.

UNESCO-UNEP (1978) *Intergovernmental Conference on Environmental Education*, Tbilisi, USSR. Final Report, Paris, UNESCO.

UNESCO/Club of Rome (1979) *No Limits to Learning*, Paris, UNESCO.

United Nations (1992) *UN Conference on Environment and Development: Agenda 21 Rio Declaration*, Paris, UNESCO.

WCED (1987) *Our Common Future* (The Bruntland Report), World Commission on Environment and Development, Oxford, Oxford University Press.

WCED (1990) *Action for a Common Future*, World Commission on Environment and Development, Oxford, Oxford University Press.

13 Employer Involvement in Lifelong Learning

JILL MANNION BRUNT

Abstract

Employers have always had a degree of involvement in adult and continuing education, but as the lifelong learning agenda gathers momentum, it is becoming increasingly clear that the involvement which proliferated in the 1980s is set to continue. The paper sets out to document some of this involvement and the possible reasons for such a proliferation during the Conservative administration of the 80s. The UK still has a long way to go in developing a truly inclusive learning society and although Government may wish employers to be at the heart of such a development, the following arguments are put forward in an attempt to question the wisdom of such a strategy.

Introduction

Employer involvement in adult education is not a new phenomena, but it may be argued that the contemporary situation shows an involvement that pervades almost every aspect of adult provision, from policy formation through to institutional and community delivery. It is essential that we examine the development of this involvement and consider the current context in which adult education is now operating.

During the last thirty years, several documents have been produced by Government or Government appointed bodies, which have explored adult education and made recommendations for the future funding and delivery of the service. Policy frameworks produced during the Conservative administration 1978-97, were concentrated in the realm of training and perhaps did more to strengthen the vocational/non-vocational divide than in any other previous administration. In many ways this was a great shame since the advent and proliferation of the term 'Lifelong Learning' gave us an ideal opportunity to bridge the divide between vocational and non-

215

vocational and simply consider education and training opportunities as 'learning' opportunities. Unfortunately, an ideological dye had been cast and during this period it was only possible to see adult learning in terms of skills development and economic prosperity.

In 1996 the Government produced a document - Lifetime Learning: a Policy Framework, setting out what they considered to be the main priority areas for funding and support (DfEE, 1996). The Framework built upon the tide of employer involvement that had been so prevalent in the 1980s. The introduction set out a now familiar agenda:

> Lifetime learning is not a Government programme, or the property of one institution. It is a shared goal relating to the attitudes and behaviour of many employers, individuals and organisations.   (DfEE, 1996)

The document went on to set out eleven key areas which were seen to be important factors in lifetime learning; the first seven had a direct relationship to economic prosperity, business development, labour market changes, new technology, employer needs and higher wages.

There is no disputing the fact that there is generally a collective good in a nation's economic prosperity and indeed that most people in the UK value economic prosperity. The difficulty lies in the assumption by Governments that an economic, employer-led educational agenda will solve the nation's ills. The employer-led movement created in the 1980s and now permeating the 1990s and a new political administration, has systematically failed to solve the intermediate skills crisis, or the enormous gap between those who have qualifications and those who have none. Sargent et al set out some of the key concerns:

> Social class continues to be the key discriminator in understanding participation in learning. Over half of all upper and middle class (AB respondents are current or recent learners, compared with one third of the skilled working class (C2) and one quarter of unskilled working class people and people on limited incomes (DE).   (Sargent, 1997)

> Despite new programmes of funding, including European initiatives and Single Regeneration Budgets, the learning participation rate in the social classes C2 and DE fell between 1990 and 1996.   (Sargent, 1997)

The National Education and Training Targets were first proposed to Government by the Confederation of British Industry in 1989 and agreed in 1991. The targets were later re-named as Training and Education Targets, to give more prominence to training rather than education. The targets have never been achieved and indeed were amended in 1995 in an attempt to make them more achievable. Although considerable time, resources and energy have been put into the development of National Vocational Qualifications, the take up rate has been slow:

> There is however, a relatively low level of take up of courses leading to NVQ's, SVQ's, GNVQ's or GSVQ's (12%).   (Sargent, 1997)

The constant push during this period, towards vocational qualifications, failed to recognise the starting point of many individuals. There are a myriad of ways in which adults return to education for the first time and many of these are leisure related or linked to community activity. Education and training need to co-exist in order to maximise the contribution each may have:

> Attempts to increase access to vocational education are being undermined by lack of a grounding of general cultural education on which to build training needs.   (Oglesby, 1991)

In the early 1990s the Government released funding to support workplace learning programmes for organisations that recognised the importance of wider learning opportunities for their staff. Much of this was linked to the Investors in People strategy and will be discussed later in more detail.

Previous comments have outlined, albeit briefly, Government preoccupation with employer involvement in lifelong learning and the subsequent failure to develop an inclusive society. Despite prevailing skill shortages and groups of adults who remain without any formal qualifications at all, employers and employer representatives have still remained at the forefront of Government lifelong initiatives.

Shifting Traditions

In 1973 and 1998 two papers were produced which set out to radically alter the United Kingdom's position vis-à-vis adult learning:

> The Russell Report - Adult Education: A Plan for Development and the Fryer Report - Learning for the 21st Century.   (HMSO, 1973 and Fryer, 1997)

Many practitioners in the field of Adult Education had awaited both reports with great anticipation. The Russell Report, though not as revolutionary as some would have wanted, set out three basic educational needs:

1. The promotion of equality of educational opportunity, including second chance education and 'education about education'.

2. Individual personal development, including creative, physical and social activity.

3. Education for active citizenship; assisting individuals to play a full and active part in society.

It is notable that there is no mention within these broad categories, o employer involvement or economic good. Historical context is all and given the educational agenda over the last twenty years, the Russell Report now looks markedly revolutionary.

The Fryer Report reiterates much of Russell and more, although linguistic remnants of the previous political administration are alarmingly present. The Report explores the barriers to participation and has a clea view about the future of those who have been disadvantaged by previou educational policies and funding regimes. There is however no attempt i the report to challenge the structures set up by the previous administration despite the fact that many of these structures and organisations were and continue to be, responsible for creating many of the barriers to learning Training and Enterprise Councils (TECs) continue to dominate the lifelon learning agenda, particularly in terms of community regeneration and man groups and educational institutions struggle to find support from the TEC for their 'broader' learning initiatives.

The Fryer Report does present a glimmer of hope for lifelong learning but it lost a great deal in the translation from advisory report, to Government Green Paper. Funding streams which have now been set up to support lifelong learning, are still based on the previous administration's notions of 'individual commitment', employer led initiatives and a very competitive bidding process; a funding stream for Trade Union led educational initiatives is however a welcome addition to the Government's programme. The following recent case study highlights the difficulties people continue to have if they fall outside the traditional learner categories.

A female registered nurse, working in a District General Hospital setting with mentally ill patients was hoping to top up her nurse qualification to degree level. After seeking financial support from her employer - refused on the grounds that she was already qualified and a degree was not a necessity, she sought advice from the Learning Direct Service. This is a new national phone line service which offers advice and information to would-be learners. She had already tried her local authority who informed her that although they would like to, they were unable to support part-time degree courses; she was unable to study full-time as she had a young family and could not afford a career break. The nurse had also attempted to gain some tax relief for learning, but was told this was not possible because the degree course was not vocational. The only avenue open to this person, was a career development loan - an unacceptable solution to someone already tied in to a mortgage and other on-going commitments.

The above case study neatly demonstrates the divide between the rhetoric and the reality of lifelong learning.

Successive Governments have yet to deliver a funding strategy to support adults who wish to pursue higher education on a part-time basis and many adults from working class backgrounds have questioned entry to higher education because of the new fee structures. As such, much of the Fryer vision for disadvantaged adults, remains an admirable aspiration.

Much has been written about the demise of the liberal tradition in adult education, but upon close examination it is not altogether clear how deeply imbedded such a tradition was in the UK, nor how well supported by practitioners, local authorities, politicians and students themselves. There has never been a groundswell of public opposition to adult education cuts, no matter how severe some of these cuts may have been. On reflection, it is possible to see how this might have occurred given the disparate nature o: adult education per se. There was no clarity about the adult educatior profession or about who indeed was an adult educationalist. People whc worked in adult education were drawn from many different areas; Extra Mural Departments in Universities, the Workers Education Association Trade Union Studies Tutors - in Universities and the Trade Unior movement, the Adult, Long Term Residential Colleges, history tutors literature tutors, economics tutors. Some of the practitioners held meetings seminars and conferences to discuss different aspects of adult educatior and some wrote regularly in a journal called the Industrial Tutor. A basic skills tutor working in a community education setting would conside: her/himself an adult educator, but would have little in common witl someone who for instance regularly contributed to the Industrial Tutor You don't have to be a marketing guru to see that this is not the greates basis for building a united front against government opposition to traditional forms of adult learning.

The Conservative Government made it easier for the employers and employer-led bodies to peddle their views, but they did not appear out o thin air. This was a reaction to a cleft within the current debates and practices in adult education, which paved the way for such an employe onslaught.

Within this shifting and complex agenda therefore, it is wortl examining the role of adult education practitioners and commentator alongside that of employers and policy makers. Alan Tuckett suggests tha practitioners had difficulty arguing for the adult education services durin; this period, because the analysis of take up rates suggested that the middl classes and those who already had qualifications were dominating the provision. Analysis also suggested that black and working class adults were anxious to obtain nationally recognised qualifications from their studies This was not a strong position from which to argue the merits of traditiona working class adult education (Tuckett, in Westwood and Thomas, 1991) There was a distinct failure during this period to recognise the diversitie and complexities of adult education. Whilst traditional adult educatior practitioners stood back, new movements took centre stage. Probably the most dynamic of these was the access movement and this was helpe enormously by the Further Education Funding Council and the new fundin; strategies which favoured 'positive outcomes' in the form of recognise qualifications. Further Education Colleges and new Universities too centre stage in terms of bringing working class people into education, whilst the adult education traditionalists lamented a past long gone.

The Struggle for Position

To be fair, adult education felt the full force of Conservative education policy in the 1980s and as previously discussed, there is little remission forthcoming from the new political administration, despite a more liberal approach taken by the Fryer Report. The emphasis remains upon education for economic prosperity and as such, employers have retained their positions in many of the bodies that determine policy and set guidelines for the funding and delivery of adult provision. Although there is much talk of partnership and consultation, the struggle for adult education hegemony continues, as education practitioners remain deferential within an employer-led agenda.

It is however a simplistic argument to suggest that employers have such a high profile in this area because the prevailing political conditions are sympathetic to their needs and that a functional approach to adult education meets the needs of the employment market. The historical conjuncture in the 1980s requires close examination if we are to be clear about the demise of the adult education tradition. The debates around the tradition and radical adult education are not conclusive, neither are they particularly transparent to anyone but a small group of deeply immersed practitioners and academics. It is perhaps the case that there has never been an uncontested, transparent set of beliefs, values and practices in adult education which could form the basis of a defence against the assaults of the 1980s.

In this sense adult education is not alone and a comparable debate about the broader political context emerged in the 1980s. Stuart Hall argues that during the 1980s the political Right re-established its monopoly over good ideas and this was only possible because the Left were in such disarray (Hall and Jacques, 1983). The shift to the right, which he explores in detail, was only possible because the left was so weak, or certainly weak in terms of developing ideas that had populist appeal amongst a fragmented electorate. Social and economic formations are all important in the examination of employer involvement in adult education. A distinct parallel can be drawn from Hall's argument:

> The radical right therefore does not appear out of thin air. It has to b
> understood in direct relation to alternative political formations attempting t
> occupy and command the same space.   (Hall and Jacques, 1983

In the same way, employers were able to put forward a seemingly radica
agenda for workplace education, whilst practitioners and academics argue
about vocational, non-vocational and liberal adult education.

Arguments such as these are not new. Functional approaches to adul
education have been emerging since the nineteenth century and usually i
response to economic and industrial decline. In the early nineteenth centur
it was recognised by employers and Government alike that different skill
were required of the workforce than had previously been the case in pre
industrial society. Educating the workforce and hence the industria
working class, was a much debated topic during this period.

In response to Samuel Whitbread's Parochial Schools' Bill, put befor
the House of Commons in 1807, Daniel Giddy commented that educatio
for the labouring poor would be 'prejudicial to their morals and happiness
(Fieldhouse, 1996). It would certainly have enabled them to read seditiou
pamphlets. Despite government concerns employers felt inclined to educat
their employees at least so that they would be able to read the instruction
on new machinery. Given the growing competition from other countrie
and Britain's wavering position as a leading industrial nation (1860s
employers felt the need to take a firm hold of adult education and not leav
it entirely in the hands of the self-help movements which had develope
during the industrial era. It was felt important to improve Britain'
international economic competitiveness, through education and in th
1880s the first Technical Education Committees were set up (Fieldhous
1996).

Organisations set up to educate the working class, such as Mechanic
Institutes and the Society for the Diffusion of Useful Knowledge wer
spurned by the more radical movements of the nineteenth century. 'Reall
Useful Knowledge' - a parody on the previously mentioned societ
consisted of social science, political knowledge and economics. Th
radicalism of this period demanded a political base for education an
rejected the skills and technical base that was being forwarded by th
Mechanics Institutes. Working class people were later to reject th
curriculum offered by the Institutes in demand of a more liberal an

creative one. These arguments have of course been revisited time and again.

New Management Initiatives

The contemporary employer agenda is a revisionist one and has been an integral component of the new Human Resource Management strategies invading the UK, particularly within the larger manufacturing industries. It can be argued that the new management ideology was only possible because the Trade Union and adult education worlds were undergoing rapid changes, many of which were being imposed upon them through legislation or changing markets. Phil Bassett outlined the new pragmatism amongst some Trade Unions in the 1890s, as they increasingly signed up to single union deals with no strike agreements and pendulum arbitration. Bassett describes the context:

> Strikes during the winter of discontent made a vital contribution to the Conservative victory in the 1979 General Election, and reforming the trade unions was placed at the centre of the Government's whole ideological, economic and social strategy. But this was not an isolated policy: it both drew from and contributed to decisive and perhaps permanent changes not just in industrial relations, but in the economy, in industry, in employment more generally. All these changes are inextricably interwoven.   (Bassett, 1987)

The changing relationship between employers and trade unions, the new human resource management initiatives and the demise of trade union education all contributed to the creation of a new context within the workplace. Influences from the pacific rim and the USA contributed greatly to this new context and the UK began to witness significant changes in attitude towards education and training in the workplace. This was particularly so in the larger UK workplaces such as car manufacturing plants. In the USA, joint training programmes had been particularly successful in the 1980s and were an example of collaboration between the company, the union and educational institutions. Set up to counteract the severe global competition facing USA companies, the joint training programmes also boasted more altruistic objectives:

> The UAW - GM PEL programme represents a promising model for company
> union and educational institutions seeking to work together to increase
> business viability while improving the quality of life for American workers
> (UAW - GM PEL - Union of Automative Workers - General Motors Paid
> Educational Leave)   (Ferman et al., 1991

The USA was facing similar economic and social circumstances as the UK
notably technological change, increased competition, industria
restructuring and qualification levels of the employees. Joint Training
Programmes clearly operate a mixed motive approach where, in thei
terms, there are no losers - only winners. The programmes operate on a
number of different fronts:

> It is our conviction that joint training initiatives represent a unique opportunit
> to address simultaneously management concerns with competitiveness and
> flexibility, labor concerns with employment security and career opportunities
> and government concerns with human resource capabilities.
>   (Ferman et al., 1991

UK management were also well aware of some of the human resourc
strategies employed by successful Japanese manufacturers, wher
managers valued both the intellectual and physical input of the employees
Their objectives include the facilitation of educationally, well developed
responsible and empowered workers in order to 'mobilise every ounce o
intelligence'.

Many UK companies, in an attempt to transform their organisation
and produce high quality goods, took note not only of the educationa
initiatives going on in the USA and Japan, but also of the positions bein
put forward by the so-called management and quality gurus. Developin
employees' potential was seen as the key to transformational success an
education was a vital component of this approach. Out of this desire fc
transformation came an acceptance that traditional industrial approaches t
education and training were no longer viable and that the models bein
espoused in the USA were worthy of consideration. One such model wa
the Ford EDAP scheme, (Employee Development and Assistanc
Programme). This had been successfully pioneered in the USA an
transported to sister car plants in Halewood and Dagenham. The scheme i
organised around an agreement between management and unions, whereb
a proportion of the total company budget is invested in an educationa

programme that is open to all sections of the workforce. Employees may choose from a range of learning activities, many of which are provided on site and around shift patterns. Employees follow the programmes in their own time and the company pays the bill. There is a financial limit to adhere to but in general, employees can take part in any learning activity of their choice. This liberal attitude towards the curriculum content of learning is welcomed by some employers but scorned by others. EDAP has been hugely successful, with many employees now gaining nationally recognised qualifications in further and higher education. Other employers have followed the example set by Ford and set up their own schemes, although many have set clear parameters for what can and cannot be studied. In the early 1990s Employment Department released funding for organisations who wished to pursue employee development schemes and subsequently TECs also supported similar initiatives within their localities.

Having worked on employee development schemes in the early nineties, it is possible to give some insight into initial reactions from employers and educationalists alike. When employee development schemes first came on stream, there were some fairly entrenched positions taken by colleagues in adult education. These included complete opposition to any scheme organised by management, deep suspicion around management intentions, reluctance to work around shift patterns in industry and opposition to any workplace learning that wasn't orchestrated by trade unions. Again, diversity and complexity were not taken into account when these positions were assumed and nor was there any recognition that this kind of scheme might actually embrace some of the groups which had been sadly absent in trade union classes - black workers, part-time and temporary workers and women.

There were some difficult discussions during this period and many suspicions existed between employers and education providers. Employers saw educationalists as inflexible, unable to customise provision and elitist; educationalists felt employers saw education as a possible vehicle for personal economic prosperity and not a community good. What was difficult to ignore was the take up rate by the workforces involved in employee development. In one small to medium enterprise, 95% of the workforce had taken up a learning opportunity as part of the company scheme (Mannion Brunt, 1994). No matter what motivation the managers may have had, the figures were staggering and as far as some educational practitioners were concerned, more adults who had not previously been involved in education, were now engaged in a learning activity. Although some mutual understanding between educationalists and employers did develop during this period, on the whole relations remained poor. On many occasions, in-company employee development schemes looked to the private sector to meet their educational needs as they appeared to be more flexible and competitively priced. They were also able to provide customised courses, whilst Colleges often talked of in-filling existing courses with employees from the schemes.

It was a great shame that employers and educationalists were not able to pool their experience and enthusiasm within this learning arena and create real and meaningful partnerships. Some Colleges were able to sustain employee development relationships with local employers, but these were the few and not the many. As employee development schemes proliferated across the UK, employers were yet again able to monopolise the lifelong learning agenda, with educational practitioners being seen as service providers and not partners.

In 1993 a National Employers Forum was set up consisting of employers who had successfully developed employee development schemes in their companies. In the initial stages of the Forum, educationalists were invited to participate if they were actively involved in supporting employee development schemes. Within a few months this invitation was no longer extended to educationalists as it was felt they were changing the tenor of the meetings.

Successful schemes did however create a space in which employers could reflect upon adult learning generally:

> There is a thought that perhaps in the past there has been too much push rathei than developmental pull. Perhaps we are too professional with learning provision and even more could be done with those who are willing, rather than those whom it is their profession to organise learning for others. Perhaps we need to bring back all the local community Mechanics Institutes who were supported by the people in the community, for the people, in providing vocational education and learning.   (Hearson, 1996, UK Glass Industry)

Well, yes maybe we should but perhaps we should also recognise that Local Authorities were providing community education on a grand scale until central Government funding methodologies changed and they were no longer able to do so. It is also interesting to note in the above comment that despite the shift from the Taylorist control model of management, to a human resources model, even enlightened managers still speak of employees as things which can be pushed or pulled. Adults can and do take control of their own learning when the opportunities are offered and when confidence and self-esteem allow. The success rate of the scheme in his own organisation is testament to this - over 40 companies and 2,000 learners have been involved in the scheme.

Although employee development schemes now exist in a number of diverse organisations, the national learning workforce picture is not a rosy one. There are beacons of good practice, usually in the larger companies and often in organisations that have been able to access central government funding to support their developments. It is debatable as to whether some well-known organisations would have been quite so radical had they not had support from central government. In the early 1990s a large supermarket chain received substantial funding from the Government's Gateways to Learning Scheme and were able to develop an in-house guidance scheme for their employees. Similarly a large UK manufacturing company received a substantial amount of money from the Department of Employment to set up it's own employee development scheme. Where external funding is not forthcoming, there is often less will to engage in these kinds of activity. Forrester, Payne and Ward cite various statistical reports to highlight the problems and found that 29% of companies in Britain had no training plan, 34% no training budget at all and that many firms spend less than 0.5% of turnover on training (Forrester et al., 1995).

There is also a degree of cynicism amongst managers themselves about the relevance and success rates of new management initiatives. Total Quality Management, Business Process Re-engineering and Business Transformations are all open to criticism in terms of their success rates. Peter Wickens, author of the Ascendant Organisation, speaks of managerial 'fad surfers':

> We ride the wave of the latest business fad until it is beached and then paddle out again, seeking the next big wave and the exhilarating sense that we can solve anything.   (Wickens, 1995)

Professor John Kotter also charts the failures:

Over the past decade I have watched more than 100 companies try to remake themselves into significantly better competitors ... These efforts have gone under many banners: total quality management, re-engineering, rightsizing, restructuring, cultural change and turnaround. But in almost every case the basic goal has been the same: to make fundamental changes in how business is conducted in order to help cope with a new, more challenging market environment. A few of these corporate change efforts have been very successful. A few have been utter failures. Most fall somewhere in between, with a distinct tilt towards the lower end of the scale.   (Kotter, 1995)

Working Forward

So, what of the future? Employers have had a fair hearing in terms of lifelong learning and they have been an intrinsic part of policy formation and implementation for the last 20 years. From previous discussion it can be seen that with the exception of a few radical and enlightened employers, their track record is not a good one. Meanwhile, arguments around functional versus liberal, vocational versus non-vocational adult education continue. The intervention of a populist version of lifelong learning under the new political administration offers a small glimmer of opportunity should adequate funding be forthcoming.

What is clear is that a consensus has to be reached between Government, employers, adult students and practitioners, if we are to make any headway in lifelong learning. Entrenched positions in the market place or in the Liberal Tradition can no longer be maintained and neither can it be assumed that lifelong learning is the property of employers or practitioners. There are now thousands of adult returners in the system, either as new entrants or students making their way through the further and higher education system. Their experience and insight is invaluable and we should now be asking them some really pertinent questions about their learning experiences and future aspirations. It is more than likely they will have some 'really useful knowledge' about the realities of lifelong learning.

Adult learning is too precious to leave to the whims and fads of managerial fad surfers; it is too precious to be left vacillating between educational practitioners with differing ideological stances; it is too precious to leave to the political point scoring of successive administrations and it is much too precious to leave to the mercy of the market.

Perhaps we should let the students speak for themselves.

References

Bassett, P. (1987) *Strike Free*, MacMillan, p.14.

Ferman, L., Hoyman, M., Cutcher-Gershenfeld, J. and Savoie, E.J. (1991) *Joint Training Programs*, New York, ILR Press.

Fieldhouse, R. and Associates (1996) *A History of Modern British Adult Education*, NIACE, p.2-4

Forrester, K., Payne, J. and Ward, K. (1995) *Workplace Learning*, Aldershot, Avebury, p.37-39.

Fryer, R.H. (1997) *Learning for the 21st Century, First Report of the National Advisory Group for Continuing Education and Lifelong Learning*.

Hall, S. and Jacques, M. (eds) (1983) *The Politics of Thatcherism*, Lawrence and Wisehart, p.25.

Hearson, A. (1996) Final Report on the UK Glass Industry Employee Development Scheme, October.

HMSO (1973) *Adult Education: a Plan for Development* (cited as Russell Report).

Kotter, J.P. (1995) 'Leading Change: Why Transformations Fail', in *Harvard Business Review*, March-April.

Mannion Brunt, J. 'Derbyshire Employee Development Initiative', in *NIACE Workplace Learning: Case Studies and Good Practice from Around the UK*, Leicester, NIACE.

Sargent, N. and Associates (1997) *The Learning Divide*, Leicester, NIACE, p.11-17.

Tuckett, A. (1991) in Westwood, S. and Thomas, J.E. *The Politics of Adult Education*, NIACE, p.26-29.

Wickens, P. (1995) 'Getting the most out of your Employees', *People Management*, March.

14 On Parenting and Being a Child: Lifelong or Short-Term Learning?

CEDRIC CULLINGFORD AND MARY MORRISON

Abstract

This chapter explores the issue of parenting, which is both a personal matter and one that has become part of the government's lifelong learning agenda. It is based on a study of parenting classes and how they affect the children and their performance in schools. It analyses the learning issues for all involved.

Introduction

In the past the combination of the terms 'learning' and 'lifelong' would have seemed absurd. How could they be separated or define anything different from the obvious? For Socrates and his ideals the whole point of life is learning, for the constant improvement, through understanding, of the individual and of society. For those with no such ideals there was a less self-conscious inevitability about maturity, the gradual accumulation of wisdom through experience and observation that would also lead to the same Confucian end. If living is about learning what is the meaning of a political, if not philosophical, edict about 'lifelong learning'?

Government initiatives, invoking the term, highlight unawares some of the ambiguities about the process of education. Can it be imposed from outside, or is it a natural innate curiosity? Is learning for the sake of the individual, or is it a duty for society? Or, to follow the deepest question, do people have a natural tendency to learn, which is so emphatically removed from them by their experience of the formal social system, or do they depend upon the support, the 'scaffolding' of others to sustain and develop their understanding?

231

Each of these questions begs a book in answer and there are enough clues in the questions themselves to suggest all those avenues of response that have already been followed. It is sufficient here to remind ourselves of the context of the question. The tensions in the concept of 'lifelong learning', the growth of the economy or the well-being of the individual are clear. The fact that human activities are increasingly abstracted from their traditional sites like family and neighbourhood, makes the tensions the more pointed (Strain, 1998). The obvious technological changes like information technology and globalization raise a whole host of what learning means both to the individual and society.

The ambiguities between the personal ideal of learning and the political desire to utilize the skills of individuals are never as clear as when there are interventions into what seem the most private of spheres. Nothing could highlight so well the theoretical and practical dilemmas we face than the notion of parenting.

In the Platonic notion of the maturity of learning, each individual goes through a succession of phases, not tied to years or regimented Piagetian development, but dependent on personal and idiosyncratic insight (Egan, 1997). This implies that all essential learning is rooted in the critical faculties and intellectual insights of the individual. This is 'learning', rather than being taught. Against this is set the notion of outside intervention. That a State education system should wish to elicit skills from its citizens is understandable. The constant urge to be more competitive, more flexible, more able to learn how to deal with new demands is the driving force behind lifelong learning. But the way it is presented is through the language of *personal* response. Just as 'Investors in People' is about organizational efficiency whilst being couched in the language of personal development, so the government's concern with lifelong learning to an extent counters the notions of the National Curriculum with designs on the individual's personal capacity to change and adapt. It suggests a cast of mind, a critical capacity rather than the imposition of new or different competencies.

There is one aspect of personal behaviour, linked to learning, which has now become the target of official concern. Parents, or rather the failure of parents, have been singled out for particular criticism. At first it was single parents, taken to mean single mothers, who were held accountable. Then there were attempts made to make parents responsible for the actions of their children, most notably in fining them when their children are persistent offenders (Blacktop and Blyth, 1999). But, as the Parenting Orders and Child Safety Orders make clear, there is a growing will to intervene in areas that were once seen as essentially private and personal (Home Office, 1998).

It is possible to understand why a government would wish to take a close interest in parenting. The old Jesuit dictum about the importance of the early years is continually corroborated by research evidence, sometimes summarised by official reports and constantly accumulating in many research studies (Pugh, 1997). If the early years are so important and in particular parents have such a central part to play to what extent should there be intervention in what has traditionally been seen as private and personal? If the attitude and approach of parents makes such a difference to pupils' performance in schools, can the State dare not intervene? If there is a connection between the early years of home and subsequent criminality, has society not a duty to intervene? (Cullingford, 1999).

As yet there is no clear policy framework about parenting, but there are many signs of the fact that it is receiving growing attention (Grimshaw and Macguire, 1998). National initiatives such as Sure Start, the establishment of a National Institute for the Family and Parenting, let alone 'parenting orders' are all indications of this. The question remains what all these amount to. Will there be parenting programmes, voluntary or imposed? Can, indeed, parenting be learned or do we take it as the most naturally learned activity of all, relying on instinct and the accumulated wisdom of the past. Clearly parents are willing to learn, from midwives about feeding, from Dr Spock about relying on themselves, from Boulby and others about maternal love. But is there anything more to parenting than the natural emotional attachment and the physical support? Has not learning been traditionally left to the school?

In one way the State has already intervened, through formal educational channels, in the early lives of children. Whilst other countries resolutely leave formal schooling until later, they have nevertheless had extended social systems of support for early learning, from the 'crèche' to the kindergarten. Here it is done differently, and the emphasis is unusual. The underlying assumption is to draw young children ever earlier into the education system. The encouragement of different kinds of programmes, from play schemes to nurseries, the entitlement to placement from the age of four, and the imposition of baseline assessments are all signs of early official intervention. One might argue that this supersedes the need for parenting programmes. But one could equally argue that these orders actually draw parents more into school.

The relationships between parents and the education system are, of course, complex; and need not be rehearsed here (Cullingford, 1996). But they are also ubiquitous and potentially of vital importance. The idea of parental involvement, as assistants in school, as supporters and partners of schools, of schools as community centres, are all a central tenet of primary school philosophy. Whilst there is an irony in the fact that the government initiatives to give parents more direct influence and control has had the opposite effect, there is still a strong feeling amongst both teachers and parents, particularly in the early years, that they need to be partners, that the more one knows about what the other is doing, the better.

The involvement of parents in the education of their children has a long history. There are many instances of home-school collaboration, particularly in the teaching of reading (Hewison, 1985). What we are exploring here, however, is somewhat different. Parenting classes are concerned with a range of issues that directly involve adults in thinking about their own learning, and their own role as informal teachers. They go beyond ante-natal classes or even 'parent-craft' classes. They are designed to present some kind of formality of understanding linked to better practice. They demand new knowledge and awareness. Their success or failure depends on whether parents learn new or extended skills - if they needed to.

The Research

This study looks at examples of parenting programmes. As part of a larger programme which explored all kinds of community involvement in school, and which gave the extra resources that made this possible, a number of home-school liaison workers were appointed specifically to act as leaders of parenting classes, and to encourage the parents themselves to extend their own learning. This programme took place in an area that felt itself to have been deprived for several generations, a deprivation to which new minority ethnic groups had been added. The official motivation of the programme was to find ways of improving children's school performance, but an underlying one was the feeling that the whole community should be involved in lifelong learning, that mothers, in particular, should be given the opportunity to learn new skills and explore new interests.

One of the essential skills, allied to learning, was deemed to be parenting. Even if only for the sake of their children, the parents needed to be encouraged to take part. This was in itself a delicate act. Difficulties of attendance, because of lack of childcare, shyness and lack of confidence and the fear of being labelled a 'bad' parent were all impediments, as well as the time of the social workers. Nevertheless, some parenting programmes were set up and evaluated.

The evaluation took a number of forms. Reviews of the documentation included the field notes and reports that had been gathered. All the personnel involved were interviewed, including teachers and headteachers. There were a number of focus group meetings followed by transcription and analysis of the taped materials. Children and parents were observed. The material that is reported here comes essentially from the experience and observations made by the home-school liaison teachers who worked with parents both on an individual basis, and more particularly, on the parenting classes. The total number of parents involved was 70. Some classes were quite small, involving four parents; others grew to accommodate as many as 12. All the illuminative quotations bar the first are from the home-school liaison teachers.

The professionals involved, the agencies and the parents believed in the potential of parenting classes. They felt that there was an obvious need for some kind of mutual support group. There were very few parents who eschewed the principle of parental classes even if a significant number found it impossible to attend - for practical or personal reasons. From the professionals' point of view the positive benefits lay in the support for their more traditional roles, for health and education.

> There should be more parental involvement, for reinforcement of what we actually do. (Teacher)

But the parents also thought that there were tangible benefits from the classes. The way they expressed these was significant. They did not begin with the premise that they had anything new to learn, but valued the benefits of support, from groups of people in a similar circumstance, and from the feeling that they were extending their network of potential friends.

The starting point of concern for parents and professionals was therefore different. The parents wanted help and support for what they were doing. The professionals believed the parents needed help and required support in order to improve. For the parents it was a relief to find others sharing experiences. For the professionals the example of others, and how they dealt with this experience, was crucial. But if the starting point was different there soon grew to be a mutual understanding of the significance of the outcomes. What they all talked about soon turned to better relationships with the children and a greater knowledge of child development.

Research into the effects of parenting, positive and negative, demonstrates what needs to be done from the point of view of the parent. Usually this is summarised as a balancing act between the two extremes of harshness and indifference (Bettelheim, 1987). The pathological extremes of poor parenting are commonly depicted as either the 'laissez-faire' or the 'authoritarian'. One shows complete indifference to the behaviour and experience of their children. It is easier to ignore than confront. The other is the kind of control that is not only indifferent to the child's needs or point of view, but asserts complete control, often brutally. One of the prime concerns for the professionals is the prevention of poor parenting through the instillation of new insights and understandings.

The motivation for parenting classes is not just a general one of assuming it would be a 'good thing' but reinforced by experience. This can emerge either from conversation or observation. The parents who enter the school, and who exchange information with the teachers often reveal their approach to difficulties at home, and invest much of their hope in the prowess and authority of teachers. They reveal that their expectation of the teacher is to take on responsibility for social relationships and moral behaviour. And they also reveal why this is so.

> Went to one parent and said 'your child's not doing any reading at home' and she was saying 'I've tried to encourage him but every time I try he just starts banging his head and goes mad so if you can have a word with the head and tell him to smack him' ...

There are countless experiences of teachers being asked by parents to discipline their child. At home the child knows exactly what to do to prevent something he does not like. The conclusion of the parent is that only by the imposition of greater authority, and a 'good smack' will the child be forced to behave.

Even in the days of the banning of physical punishment and the contemplation of the criminalization of parental physical discipline, there are many examples of parents' belief in the moral or legal authority of the State, and its officers, over their own. They reveal how difficult they find it to handle their intractable children. Such revelations abound. The immediate reaction is to question what is going on in the home. Is the sense that 'I can't handle him, at all' or 'she has a will of her own' a sign not only of failure but future difficulty? Can such a pattern of behaviour, or a series of attitudes, be changed? If the parent thinks that any difficulty is too great for one or two people, is that an abrogation of responsibility to the State? Given that governments are inclined to blame parents, is there a middle-ground of learning? Can parents learn the art or craft of what has never been consciously learned?

When parents both inadvertently confess their failures, or pointedly reveal the limits of their own capacities, is that an invitation for some kind of professional intervention? At one level it seems it should be welcomed, but at another it is not. What these parents seek is intervention with their child, not with them. They are passing on responsibility rather than seeking help with taking it on. For there are two sides to this approach to, or belief in, the professionals. On the one hand it reveals a belief in someone else's greater power. On the other it is a sign of lack of self-confidence, a submission not only to the authority of outsiders but to the intractability of the problem. The urgency of '*you* deal with it' is just the sign of all that can go wrong.

One of the greatest inhibitions to the attendance at parenting classes is just this awe of the professionals. Against teachers, social workers and other representatives of the State, parents feel a lack of confidence. When they feel they do not know what they are doing they reveal such a low self-esteem that even opportunities for growth, or learning, are eschewed. In order to make any intervention programme successful, this problem needs to be understood. Just as greater formal powers prevent parents being involved in schools, so the 'system', presented as an outside, self-confident force, has an alienating effect. The barriers to confidence are widespread, certainly amongst the population who most need help.

> You've got about 1% of the complete parental population who feel confident about actually doing that [coming into school].

Parents might learn from experience but they do not like the idea of being told what to do. They want a sense of their own personal autonomy in learning. They remember their own experience of school, and evoke the memories of their parents. They cannot simply acquire a sudden self-assertion of their rights and abilities. They therefore prefer the obscurity of muddle rather than the assertion of outsider advice. The answer to this is to approach parents with great delicacy. Those who are least in need of support are those most likely to come for it. The question is how to encourage the most needy to recognise their need.

The home school liaison teachers all learned the importance of the sensitive, delicate touch.

> It's not a case of a professional walking in and saying 'This is going on, come and join us, it's good for you, we know what's best for you'.

Whilst there is much to be learned about parenting, people do not like being told. It is after all an atavistic axiom that parents know best. It is a private sphere and even advice, if not sought, is intrusive. Not only the symbolism of State institutions but the approach of the 'professionals' can be off-putting. The desire for help has to come from the parent. The main assumption is that help is not imposed. The very idea of needing help is a slight. Support and advice can be useful, especially in the guise of shared experiences. But the more the parent is singled out as needing help the greater sense of failure.

One of the most crucial conditions for parenting programmes is that they involve *all* parents. Once there is a stigma attached, when only the failures attend - those who most need the intervention - then the programmes fail. This is why the tone of the government's orders are so unhelpful. They sound like blame and drive away those very parents who could most benefit. But when we say 'most' benefit, a distinction must be drawn between those most obvious targets who do not know how to handle their children and all the others who can still benefit. All learn by sharing the load and by simple observation. Parenting programmes are not a punishment. If all kinds of parents are involved then there are the possibilities of learning. Once their attendance is linked to failure then they will not voluntarily come again; and as yet there are no orders that compel parents to do so.

Because I can't single out one parent and say 'You need to learn how to be a proper parent, you need to learn how to be with your children'.

The right conditions for parenting programmes are crucial. Mutual respect and support rather than the culture of blame and accusation are essential. If learning is to be a natural part of life it needs to be sought rather than imposed. Nevertheless learning, even of parenting, is not a spontaneous growth, in isolation. The example of others is vital. Information is vital. The question, for lifelong learning, is whether it is sought. And the question then is, if it is sought, is it effective? Can something as intimate and personal as parenting be learned? Can something essentially private be elaborated, extended into shared insights and understandings?

One difficulty in establishing the success or failure of parenting programmes is the question of measurement. Do we detect differences, or marked improvement? How can we isolate variables that might define the impact of the parenting programmes? To understand the views of parents, and their perceptions of their own experiences is comparatively easy. Those parents who took part were, on the whole, satisfied. Half tended to rate the advice received as helpful. The question is what impact it made on their own relationships with their children.

The most interesting findings from this survey derive from the observation of the professionals involved. Whatever the parents might think, the proof was held to be in their behaviour. Naturally there is a lot of belief in the efficacy of such programmes, as well as the need for them. There is agreement about the necessary conditions. But can success be demonstrated? In the experience of those involved there were signs that it could be.

We see children progress from just coming in and racing around, and going bananas and the parents just practically ignoring them and sitting in groups chatting. From there we now see, sometimes you'll see parents sitting with a child, quietly in a corner on their own, sharing a book or doing a puzzle or something.

Parenting classes are often associated with parents being told what to do, in isolation from their children. What this programme demonstrated was the usefulness of actual contact, of examples, of taking it in turns to talk and listen and to act. A parenting class is not the equivalent of a book read out loud. It is the personal demonstration of skills, the sharing of insights and the observation of actions. Those parents who do not know how to 'handle' their children begin to be involved in a different kind of interaction and dialogue. The purely physical is joined by the intellectual. There are then opportunities to share a book or a puzzle, a process of learning that is far more ancient than any system.

Parents learn from the programmes that the approach that professionals take is far less didactic than they had imagined. Knowledge is not imposed. The learning needs of each individual is taken into account. The interaction between teacher and learner is seen to be far more complex than that envisaged. This has an impact on the parent that allows him or her to take on a similar role.

> A lot of them come with the attitude of, initially, I'm going to come here, the kids can run riot and you're going to look after them ... some start like that and then they sort of copy. You're rôle modelling and they start to copy. And they might even start to copy the way they speak, you know instead of saying 'get here now' you know to their kids, they might start to speak to them a bit more pleasantly.

The first relief for some parent is the possibility that someone else can take on the responsibility of control. It's not that they want their children to 'run riot' but that they want to have some relief from the demands of authority. But observation of other people has two effects. They see that the techniques of professionals do not depend on some kind of given authority. Their children, unlike them, are not in awe of status. And they also realise that the subtle art of discipline depends on dialogue as well as power, on disinterested concern for others as well as personal confidence.

Conclusion

Parenting programmes are seen as necessary and are generally welcomed. When they succeed, however, they do so because they work in a subtle way. Progress is measured in behaviour, in changed relationships, in different styles of dialogue. How can one measure changes in attitudes? These are subtle matters, but changes are clearly observed.

> If we can get these parents and children to operate in one room, that they can help their children to learn basic skills that they will need in a nursery, that the children can operate as a social group ...

Parents do not wish to learn theoretically about parenting. They want to learn how to do it. If parenting programmes are presented as packages to make up for deficiencies they have no chance of success. But if they are a natural event for all parents, a coming together of mutual support and understanding, then all kinds of effects take place. 'Operating' together, and teaching their own children 'basic skills' puts parents far more close to being teachers themselves. That is the ultimate goal, both to a lifelong learning system and to the best relationships parents can have with their children. Instead of 'in loco parentis' we have 'in loco magister'. At best the two become a partnership in which each side is allowed to enter into the understanding of the other.

Parenting is traditionally the most private and personal of activities involving just two or three people. It is the most ancient and deepest domain of learning, from all points of view. Lifelong, parents make a difference. But does that mean that there is nothing to be learned, nothing to be presented from the outside?

There is a natural antipathy to outside interference. The Home Office measures, the targets and the blame might be well intentioned but could be counter-productive. The desire of all parents is at a subconscious level for understanding; and at a conscious level for help. To what extent therefore is intervention feasible? We know that parenting programmes depend on parents sharing experiences, on feeling included, on all having access to them, on giving a sense of empowerment, and on paying attention to children's perceptions.

We also know about the delicate balance between need and intervention. Parenting has traditionally been private. But in the past it was never isolated. Parents used to have a network in the immediate and extended community. The advice of grandparents and others was like a natural learning circle that embraced and cajoled, that offered advice, wanted and unwanted, that provided consolation, needed and unneeded. It was a body of accumulated wisdom and knowledge.

If parenting programmes embody the principles of lifelong learning, in the old sense, then they could transform the way that society operates. The fact that these networks are formal rather than informal is a real challenge. Perhaps the concept of community is getting larger. We have the oldest learning curve of lifelong learning, being a growing human being, from child to parent and grandparent, juxtaposed against the newest impositions on learning - the intervention of the State. Perhaps the future depends on both learning together.

References

Bettelheim, B. (1987) *A Good Enough Parent*, London, Thames & Hudson.

Blacktop, J. and Blyth, E. (1999) 'School attendance and the role of law in England and Wales', in Blyth, E. and Milner, J. (eds) *Improving School Attendance*, London, Routledge.

Cullingford, C. (1996) *Parents, Education and the State*, Aldershot, Ashgate.

Cullingford, C. (1999) *The Causes of Exclusion*, London, Kogan Page.

Egan, E. (1997) *The Educated Mind: How Cognitive Tools Shape Our Understanding*, University of Chicago Press.

Grimshaw, R. and Macguire, C. (1998) *Evaluating Parenting Programmes: A Study of Stakeholders' Views*, London, National Childrens Bureau.

Hewison, J. (1985) 'The evidence of case studies of parents' involvement in schools', in Cullingford, C., *Parents, Teachers and Schools*, London, Royce.

Home Office (1998) *Guidance for Parenting Orders and Child Safety Orders*, London, Juvenile Offenders Unit.

Pugh, G. (1997) 'Early childhood education finds its voice: but is anyone listening?', in Cullingford, C. (ed) *The Politics of Primary Education*, Buckingham, Open University Press.

Strain, M. (1998) 'Towards an economy of Lifelong Learning: reconceptualising relations between learning and life', *British Journal of Educational Studies*, Vol.46, No.3, pp.264-277.